Lecture Notes in Computer Science 16349

Founding Editors

Gerhard Goos
Juris Hartmanis

Series Editors

Elisa Bertino , *Purdue University, West Lafayette, IN, USA*
Wen Gao, *Peking University, Beijing, China*
Bernhard Steffen, *TU Dortmund University, Dortmund, Germany*
Moti Yung, *Columbia University, New York, NY, USA*

The series Lecture Notes in Computer Science (LNCS), including its subseries Lecture Notes in Artificial Intelligence (LNAI) and Lecture Notes in Bioinformatics (LNBI), has established itself as a medium for the publication of new developments in computer science and information technology research, teaching, and education.

LNCS enjoys close cooperation with the computer science R & D community, the series counts many renowned academics among its volume editors and paper authors, and collaborates with prestigious societies. Its mission is to serve this international community by providing an invaluable service, mainly focused on the publication of conference and workshop proceedings and postproceedings. LNCS commenced publication in 1973.

Domenico Garlisi · Dimitris Chatzopoulos
Editors

Algorithmic Aspects of Cloud Computing

10th International Symposium, ALGOCLOUD 2025
Warsaw, Poland, September 15–16, 2025
Revised Selected Papers

 Springer

Editors
Domenico Garlisi
University of Palermo
Palermo, Italy

Dimitris Chatzopoulos
University College Dublin
Dublin, Ireland

ISSN 0302-9743   ISSN 1611-3349 (electronic)
Lecture Notes in Computer Science
ISBN 978-3-032-13743-2   ISBN 978-3-032-13744-9 (eBook)
https://doi.org/10.1007/978-3-032-13744-9

This Springer imprint is published by the registered company Springer Nature Switzerland AG
The registered company address is: Gewerbestrasse 11, 6330 Cham, Switzerland

If disposing of this product, please recycle the paper.

Preface

The International Symposium on Algorithmic Aspects of Cloud Computing (ALGO-CLOUD) is an annual event aiming to tackle the diverse new topics in the emerging area of algorithmic aspects of computing and data management within modern cloud-based environments. Its scope is interpreted broadly so as to encompass edge and fog computing, cloudlets, microservices, virtualization platforms, decentralized systems, and dynamic networks.

ALGOCLOUD aims to bring together researchers, students, and practitioners to present research activities and results on topics related to theoretical, design, and implementation aspects of modern cloud-based systems. It specifically encourages novel algorithms related to cloud and edge computing, cloud architectures, and the cloud-edge continuum. Experimental work evaluating contemporary cloud-edge approaches and relevant applications is of particular interest. In addition, ALGOCLOUD welcomes demonstration manuscripts that highlight successful system developments, as well as articles that discuss experiences, use cases, and high-quality survey papers.

ALGOCLOUD 2025 took place on September 15-16, 2025, in Warsaw, Poland. It was collocated with and was part of ALGO 2025 (September 15–19, 2025), the major annual congress that combines the premier algorithmic conference "European Symposium on Algorithms" (ESA) and a number of other specialized symposiums and workshops, all related to algorithms and their applications, making ALGO the major European event for researchers, students, and practitioners in algorithms.

There was a positive response to the ALGOCLOUD 2025 call for papers. The diverse nature of the 15 papers submitted demonstrated the vitality of algorithmic aspects of cloud computing. All submissions went through a rigorous single-blind peer review process and were reviewed by at least three members of the Program Committee (PC). The submissions were evaluated on the basis of their quality, originality, and relevance to the symposium. Following the recommendations of the reviewers, the PC accepted ten original research papers, covering a variety of topics, and these were presented at the symposium. We would like to thank all PC members for their significant contribution to the review process.

The selected papers cover three major areas. One area focuses on the use of machine learning in distributed environments, including approaches such as federated learning applied to streaming data collected across decentralized systems. Another key topic is task orchestration within distributed infrastructures. Security also plays a central role, with contributions exploring blockchain-based management of distributed cyber-physical systems. Finally, the remaining papers address the analysis and the configuration of distributed infrastructures, particularly those based on containerization technologies.

Apart from the contributed talks, ALGOCLOUD 2025 included an invited keynote presentation by Eiko Yoneki from the University of Cambridge, UK, titled "Optimising Computer Systems in High Dimensional and Complex Parameter Space".

We wish to thank all authors who submitted their research to this conference, contributing to the high-quality program, the PC for their scholarly effort, and all referees who assisted the PC in the evaluation process. We also thank the steering committee of ALGOCLOUD 2025 for its continuous support. We thank Springer for sponsoring the best paper and best student paper awards taking into account the reviews and selection process followed by the PC. The best paper award was given to Pierluigi Locatelli, Tiziana Cattai, Pietro Spadaccino and Francesca Cuomo for the paper "Secure Management of a Water Distribution Network in Multi-tenant Scenarios". The best student paper award was given to Mahtab Masoori, Lata Narayanan and Denis Pankratov for their work titled "Renting Servers in the Cloud: Empirical Study on Real-World Data".

We hope that these proceedings will help researchers, students, and practitioners understand and be aware of state-of-the-art algorithmic aspects of cloud computing, and that they will stimulate further research in the domain of algorithmic approaches in cloud computing in general.

October 2025

Domenico Garlisi
Dimitris Chatzopoulos

Organization

Steering Committee

Spyros Sioutas	Ionian University, Greece
Peter Triantafillou	University of Warwick, UK
Christos D. Zaroliagis	University of Patras, Greece – Chair

Symposium Chairs

Domenico Garlisi	Università degli Studi di Palermo, Italy
Dimitris Chatzopoulos	University College Dublin, Ireland

Program Committee

Ioannis Chatzigiannakis	Sapienza University of Rome, Italy
Santaromita Giuseppe	IMDEA, Spain
John Byabazaire	University College Dublin, Ireland
Tiziana Cattai	University of Rome "La Sapienza", Italy
Dimitrios Amaxilatis	Spark Works Ltd, Ireland
Giuseppe Piro	Politecnico di Bari, Italy
Antonio Skarmeta Gomez	Universidad de Murcia, Spain
Symeon Papavassiliou	National Technical University of Athens, Greece
Christos Kotselidis	University of Manchester, UK
Aris Leivadeas	ÉTS Montréal, Canada
Giacomo Verticale	Politecnico di Milano, Italy
Ngo Trung Kien	Posts and Telecommunications Institute of Technology, Vietnam
Francesco Gringoli	University of Brescia, Italy
Katerina Doka	National Technical University of Athens, Greece
Raffaele Gravina	University of Calabria, Italy
Spyros Lalis	University of Thessaly, Greece
Christoforos Ntantogian	Ionian University, Greece
Ioannis Karydis	Ionian University, Greece
Krzysztof Grochla	Institute of Theoretical and Applied Informatics, Poland

Contents

A Federated Learning Approach for Predicting Marine Heat Waves 1
Vincenzo Taormina, Sergio Dimarca, Silvia Schilleci,
Maria Del Mar Bosch-Belmar, Francesco Paolo Mancuso,
Ilenia Tinnirello, Gianluca Sarà, and Domenico Garlisi

Cooper: A Lightweight Event Recording and Visualization Framework
for Data Center Simulations 16
Mark Doyle, Theodoros Aslanidis, and Dimitris Chatzopoulos

Policy Agents for Zero-Trust Kubernetes: A Comprehensive Survey 31
Sonika Arora, Prashanth Josyula, Anant Kumar,
and Gangadharayya Hiremath

Constrained Adaptive Partial Training for Federated Learning
on Heterogeneous Clients 43
Mohan Xu and Lena Wiese

Split Learning Based GAN Training for Non-IID Federated Learning 58
Joana Tirana, Andreas Chouliaras, Theodoros Aslanidis,
John Byabazaire, Spyridon Mastorakis, and Dimitris Chatzopoulos

Task Orchestration in the Cloud Continuum via Multi-objective
Evolutionary Algorithms 73
Konstantinos Karathanasis, Spyros Kontogiannis, and Christos Zaroliagis

Duplication-Based Workflow Scheduling with Communication Awareness
for Heterogeneous Cloud Computing Environments 94
Yani Ping and Rizos Sakellariou

Secure Management of a Water Distribution Network in Multi-tenant
Scenarios 108
Pierluigi Locatelli, Tiziana Cattai, Pietro Spadaccino,
and Francesca Cuomo

A Comparative Study of Local Community Detection Algorithms in Static
Graphs 122
Konstantinos Christopoulos, Georgios Tsiamis,
and Konstantinos Tsichlas

Renting Servers in the Cloud: Empirical Study on Real-World Data 138
  Mahtab Masoori, Lata Narayanan, and Denis Pankratov

Author Index 159

A Federated Learning Approach for Predicting Marine Heat Waves

Vincenzo Taormina[1], Sergio Dimarca[1], Silvia Schilleci[1,2], Maria Del Mar Bosch-Belmar[1], Francesco Paolo Mancuso[1], Ilenia Tinnirello[1,2,3], Gianluca Sarà[1], and Domenico Garlisi[1,2,3,4(✉)]

[1] University of Palermo, Palermo, Italy
{vincenzo.taormina,silvia.schilleci,mariadelmar.boschbelmar,
francesco.mancuso,ilenia.tinnirello,gianluca.sara}@unipa.it,
sergio.dimarca@you.unipa.it
[2] CNIT, Parma, Italy
domenico.garlisi@unipa.it
[3] Center of Sustainability and Ecological Transition, University of Palermo, Palermo, Italy
[4] Istituto Nazionale di Alta Matematica "Francesco Severi" (INDAM), Roma, Italy

Abstract. Marine Heat Waves (MHWs) are extreme ocean temperature anomalies that can disrupt marine ecosystems, fisheries and coastal economies. Early and accurate prediction of MHWs is critical to support environmental monitoring and effective mitigation strategies. In this paper, we propose a novel federated learning framework for distributed prediction of MHWs using Sea Surface Temperature (SST) data collected from in situ sensors located along the Italian coastline. Our approach leverages the decentralized nature of marine monitoring infrastructures, allowing each coastal station to train local models in site-specific SST time series without sharing raw data, thus preserving data privacy and compliance with data sovereignty regulations. The system employs two LSTM architectures, used with FedAvg and personalized federated learning strategies to collaboratively aggregate local models. The collaborative federated learning paradigm improves the predictions of SST and MHW by effectively capturing distributed regional dynamics. Experimental results show that the proposed federated learning approach outperforms local on-site training (average RMSE over 1 to 7 day forecasts: $0.89\,^{\circ}\mathrm{C}$ vs $1.11\,^{\circ}\mathrm{C}$) and almost matches the accuracy of centralized training, which assumes access to all raw data from every site ($0.82\,^{\circ}\mathrm{C}$). Our work lays the foundation for a scalable and privacy-aware digital infrastructure for climate resilience in marine environments.

Keywords: Federated Learning · Marine Heat Waves · Environmental monitoring · Time-Series Forecasting · Privacy-Preserving Analytics · LSTM · Wireless Sensor Networks · Edge Computing · LoRaWAN · LPWAN

D. Garlisi and D. Chatzopoulos (Eds.): ALGOCLOUD 2025, LNCS 16349, pp. 1–15, 2026.
https://doi.org/10.1007/978-3-032-13744-9_1

1 Introduction

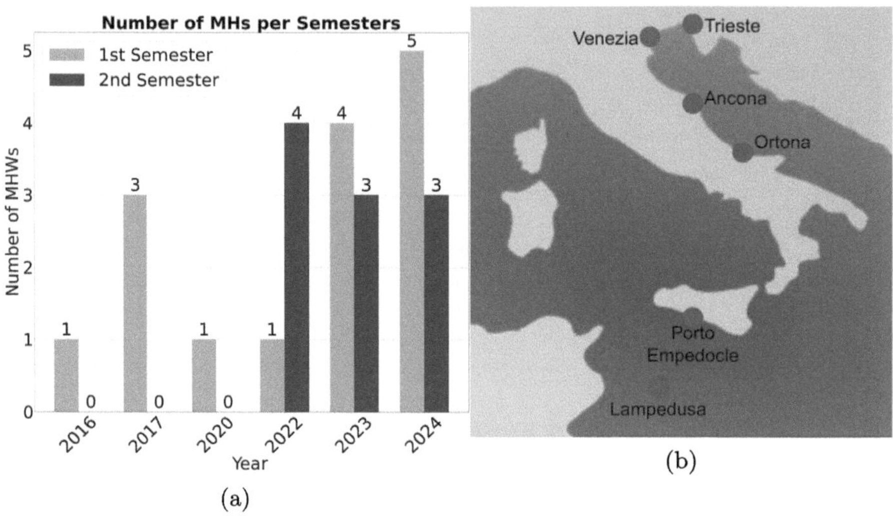

Fig. 1. (**a**) Annual count of MHW events broken down by semester from 2010 to 2024, showing an increasing trend. (**b**) Map of the six analyzed coastal stations in this paper.

Marine Heat Waves (MHWs) are prolonged periods of anomalously high Sea Surface Temperatures (SST), characterized by intensity, duration, frequency, and spatial coverage [2]. According to [3], MHWs are quantified as SSTs greater than the 90th percentile over five or more consecutive days, calculated using a 30-year climatology with an 11-day running window. Although their severity and occurrence have been present historically, climate change has significantly increased their frequency and intensity, prompting increased scientific and public attention [11].

These phenomena pose serious threats to marine biodiversity, the functioning of coastal ecosystems, and key economic sectors such as tourism and fishing. Within the Mediterranean Sea, the Italian coast stands out as a climate change hotspot and frequently experiences MHWs [4,7].

Precise forecasts of the MHWs extremes are crucial for various sectors of contemporary society. Consequently, MHW forecasting can help in numerous adaptive and management strategies for Mediterranean marine ecosystems and stakeholders. Moreover, early detection and prediction are critical, yet data heterogeneity, data privacy, and sparse sensing coverage in distributed marine sensors interfere with standard centralized machine learning methods. The data in the ocean are often sparse, noisy, and locally perturbed, which interferes with modeling generalization.

In this work, we consider data sourced from the National Mareographic Network [8], provided by the Italian Institute for Environmental Protection and

Research (ISPRA), coming from 36 coastal measurement stations, most of which are located in port regions along the Italian coast. These incorporate meteorological and oceanographic data via in-situ sensors. A first analysis of this dataset, reported in Fig. 1a, indicates that the phenomena have become more frequent over the last 10 years. In fact, the figure shows the annual number of MHW events, split by semester, revealing an increased frequency of these extreme temperature events in both portions of recent years.

In recent years, there has been growing interest in Machine Learning (ML) approaches for ocean forecasting. SST prediction is typically framed as a time-series regression problem, which can be based either on measurements at specific locations or on spatially averaged data over larger regions. This study explores decentralized data learning through Federated Learning (FL) to predict SST and MHWs from distributed coastal sensors, highlighting its benefits in computational efficiency, precision, data flow reduction, and privacy. We also compare the FL approach with local on-site training and centralized training, where all data are available. To the best of our knowledge, just a few studies have used Long-Short-Term Memory Networks (LSTM) models to predict sea surface temperature, and there is no work applying FL to the prediction of SST.

Reference Scenario and Challenges in Marine Monitoring. In coastal marine environments, diverse stakeholders, such as aquaculture operators, underwater archeology teams, and ecological monitoring agencies, carry out specialized activities that depend on sensor-based data collection. These locally deployed sensors monitor variables ranging from site-specific environmental variables, farmed organisms health indicators to underwater biodiversity conservation status. However, data from individual sites are often sparse, fragmented, and insufficient to train high-performance predictive models. Aggregating data from various sites significantly improves model precision and environmental understanding. Our research involves environmental sensing data from six Italian sites, evenly spread from north to south. However, the process of training predictive models for MHWs is hampered by two main challenges: i) many remote locations rely on low-bandwidth networks, such as Low-Power Wide-Area Networks (LPWANs), LoRaWAN is the focus of this study [6], which are unable to support continuous transmission of a large volume of data; and ii) stakeholders are often unwilling to share raw data due to commercial, competitive, or regulatory issues.

Federated Learning as a Solution for MHW Prediction. Among emerging technologies such as distributed ML, privacy-preserving analytics, and edge intelligence, all of which are revolutionizing environmental monitoring by enabling efficient, decentralized analysis of large-scale and heterogeneous datasets, FL stands out as a particularly promising solution. FL addresses directly the challenges of fragmented marine data, bandwidth limitations, and stakeholder data privacy. As an emerging ML paradigm, FL enables collaborative model training across multiple decentralized data sources without requiring the exchange of raw data. This is crucial in the context of MHWs, where accurate predictions require integrating data from distributed and often commercially sensitive sources. FL allows models to be trained collaboratively across multiple nodes, with raw data remaining local and only model updates being shared. This paradigm ensures data confidentiality, reduces communication overhead, and supports regulatory compliance [10].

To maximize the potential of FL in this domain, we propose a predictive tool designed to operate collaboratively on distributed data sources. Our specific contribution is an FL-based framework for the prediction of distributed MHWs. In this framework, each participating node, such as coastal observatories, buoys, or marine research centers, trains a local model on its SST time-series data. Only model weights are shared with a central aggregator, which combines them into a global model using techniques such as Federated Averaging (FedAvg).

This design preserves data privacy and sovereignty, while significantly reducing bandwidth consumption and meeting local operational constraints. Our approach is based on recent advances in FL time series [9], applying them to the marine domain with an LSTM-based architecture to capture temporal patterns in SST data. The system is designed to be robust to heterogeneity of data and asynchronous participation and is evaluated across data extracted from multiple nodes in the Mediterranean Sea, particularly around Italy, to predict the onset, duration and severity of MHW. The key contributions of this paper are as follows:

- We design and implement an FL framework for SST and MHW prediction using SST and other data collected from in situ sensors of the Italian National Mareographic Network operated by ISPRA.
- We propose a time-series LSTM architecture suitable for FL across heterogeneous coastal stations.
- We evaluate the ability of the system to predict SST and MHW with lead times ranging from 1 to 7 days at various deployed sites, highlighting performance differences between local on-site models, our federated approach, and centralized training.

The remainder of this paper is structured as follows. Section 2 reviews related work, while Sect. 3 details our proposed approach to predict MHWs and SST. Section 4 summarizes the results of this work and, finally, Sect. 5 draws conclusions.

2   Related Work

This section, aligned with our contribution, is divided into two main parts. The first part reviews ML applications in the literature for predicting SST and MHW, underscoring the growing significance of data-driven ocean forecasting, which, however, still relies heavily on centralized models and datasets. The second part examines FL in environmental and geophysical settings. Although FL is a powerful approach for decentralized model training that preserves privacy and data ownership, our study uniquely applies FL to the prediction of extreme MHWs, enabling site-specific and privacy-aware forecasts.

ML Approaches for Marine Heatwave Prediction. Recent years have witnessed a growing adoption of ML techniques to forecast SST and extreme oceanic events such as MHW, in response to their increasing frequency and significant ecological and socioeconomic impacts. Bonino et al. [1] present a significant application of ML models, including Random Forest (RF), LSTM, and Convolutional Neural Networks (CNN), to forecast SST and MHWs in 16 macroregions of the Mediterranean Sea. Their models leverage satellite-derived SST and atmospheric reanalysis data to predict MHW occurrences up to seven days in advance. Despite its effectiveness, their approach is based on spatially aggregated data and a centralized training paradigm, which limits the ability to capture fine-grained, site-specific oceanographic dynamics.

Hobday et al. [3] provide a framework for the detection and categorization of MHWs, introducing a standardized classification based on intensity relative to climatological thresholds. Although not predictive, their scheme is widely used to define MHW events and evaluate ML-based forecasts.

LSTM networks effectively address time-series challenges in oceanography and climatology by mitigating the vanishing gradient problem typical of standard RNNs [12]. LSTMs have been widely applied to SST forecasting, capturing complex temporal patterns and improving prediction of MHWs and other oceanic phenomena [5].

Our work extends these centralized approaches by introducing FL into the domain of MHW forecasting. In our system, each monitoring node, equipped with in-situ temperature sensors deployed along the Italian coast, trains a localized LSTM model using its own SST time series.

Federated Learning for Privacy-Aware MHW Prediction. The application of FL has attracted growing interest in various fields, including environmental and geophysical monitoring, due to its ability to handle distributed data while preserving privacy. For example, in disaster forecasting, FL has been successfully applied to develop earthquake early-warning systems. The system proposed in [9] uses FL to integrate multiple data sources into a global model, applying time series regression to predict earthquakes. Our study combines site-specific SST data, LSTM, and deep training to support localized, privacy-aware predictions of extreme MHW. This new approach addresses the limitations of centralized methods, enabling the privacy-preserving analysis of highly localized oceanographic data.

3   Methodology

This section outlines the methodology employed in this study, including data collection, preprocessing, and the design of the FL framework. It is organized into two main parts, the first describes the measurement stations, observed parameters, and preprocessing for daily time series and MHW events. While the second details the FL framework, including the LSTM-based model, personalized training, privacy-preserving aggregation and fine-tuning techniques to enhance prediction accuracy across all locations.

3.1 Data Collection and Preprocessing

The data used in this study are sourced from the National Mareographic Network [8], provided by ISPRA. The dataset comprises observations from 36 coastal measurement stations, most of which are situated in port regions along the Italian coastline[1]. These stations record both meteorological and oceanographic data via in-situ sensors.

Each station utilizes systems for data acquisition, storage, and transmission, typically via LPWAN, cellular networks and occasionally via IRIDIUM satellite technology, to monitor key marine and coastal environmental variables. Measured data include sea temperature (°C), air temperature (°C), relative humidity (%), atmospheric pressure (hPa), wind direction (degrees), and wind speed (m/s).

We enrich the dataset by computing the day of the year for each observation. Subsequently, MHWs are identified as periods when daily sea temperatures exceed the local 90th percentile threshold for at least five consecutive days, following the definition in [2]. A binary label vector is generated to denote MHW presence (1) or absence (0) each day. The 90th percentile threshold was also included as an additional feature. A correlation analysis is conducted to determine the features most associated with the MHW labels.

For our analysis, we focus on six stations: Ancona, Lampedusa, Porto Empedocle, Trieste, Ortona, and Venice (refer to Fig. 1b), using daily records from January 1, 2010, to November 29, 2024. These sites are selected to ensure a representative geographic coverage from north to south and to capture diverse coastal environments, ranging from enclosed lagoon areas such as Venice to open-sea locations like Lampedusa.

3.2 Federated Learning Scheme and LSTM Architectures

In this study, we first develop a model for MHW classification and subsequently extend it to a temperature regression model. These two aspects are strongly correlated, as reliable temperature regression facilitates accurate extraction and analysis of MHW events. This section details the architecture and training strategy of the proposed FL system, which addresses local data processing to achieve robust global predictions while minimizing communication overhead. Figure 2 illustrates the architecture of our FL scheme. At the core of the system is a centralized server that hosts a global LSTM model, structurally identical to the local LSTM models deployed across the edge devices in multiple private IoT networks. The global model itself is not directly trained; instead, it stores the averaged weights received from all participating clients during each training round. Training is performed exclusively on the client side, using local site-specific data. After each local training epoch at time i, client k transmits its updated model weights $W_{(i+1)}^{k}$ to the server. The server then computes the weighted average

---

[1] ISPRA Dataset - Istituto Superiore per la Protezione e la Ricerca Ambientale. Retrieved from https://w3id.org/italia/env/ld/rmn/dataset.

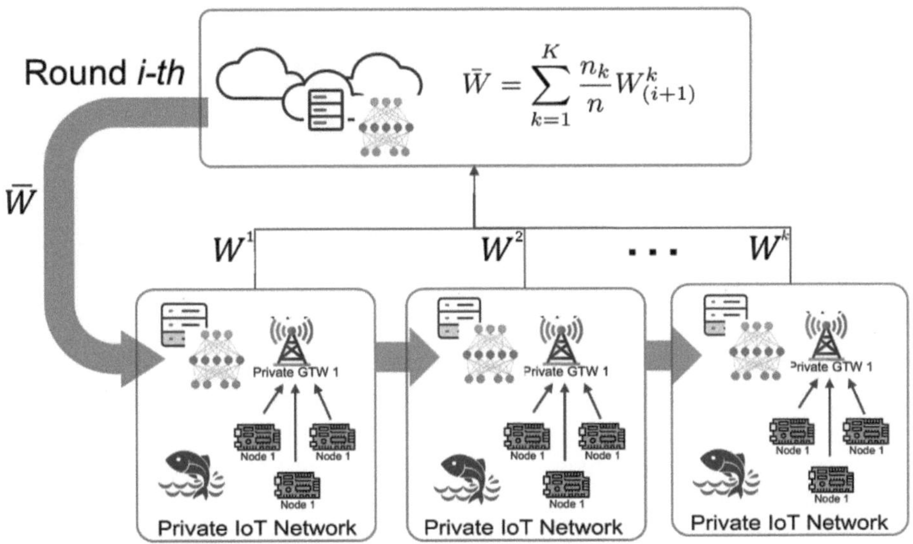

Fig. 2. Federated Learning architecture for distributed LSTM training in IoT networks for MHWs prediction.

of the received weights based on the number of samples n_k processed by each client. This operation follows the FedAvg strategy:

$$\bar{W} = \sum_{k=1}^{K} \frac{n_k}{n} W_{(i+1)}^{k} \tag{1}$$

where $n = \sum_{k=1}^{K} n_k$ is the total number of samples across all devices. The resulting averaged weights $\bar{W}$ are then redistributed to the clients, replacing their prior local model parameters. These updated weights serve as the initialization for the next local training round.

This process is repeated over multiple communication rounds, allowing the global model to evolve through client-side training without centralizing any local features. The entire scheme supports privacy-preserving learning and enables scalable, energy-efficient communication by using LoRaWAN-based gateways within each IoT subnetwork.

In this study, we explore two LSTM architectures to evaluate the trade-off between predictive accuracy and communication overhead, defining two FL variants: FL-strong and FL-soft. FL-strong is based on a deeper architecture with an LSTM layer of 64 units followed by dropout (20%), a second LSTM layer of 32 units with dropout (20%) and a dense output layer with sigmoid activation. FL-soft uses a lighter architecture with an LSTM layer of 32 units with dropout (30%), a second LSTM layer of 16 units with dropout (30%), an intermediate dense layer of 8 units with ReLU, and a final dense sigmoid layer. The higher capacity of FL-strong allows richer temporal feature extraction at the cost of exchanging larger model weight updates during federated rounds, while FL-soft reduces communication load and computational complexity at the expense of representational power.

Each LSTM cell computes its internal states according to:

$$
\begin{aligned}
i_t &= \sigma(W_i x_t + U_i h_{t-1} + b_i), & f_t &= \sigma(W_f x_t + U_f h_{t-1} + b_f), \\
o_t &= \sigma(W_o x_t + U_o h_{t-1} + b_o), & \tilde{c}_t &= \tanh(W_c x_t + U_c h_{t-1} + b_c), \\
c_t &= f_t \odot c_{t-1} + i_t \odot \tilde{c}_t, & h_t &= o_t \odot \tanh(c_t).
\end{aligned}
$$

where $\sigma(\cdot)$ denotes the sigmoid activation, $\odot$ denotes element-wise multiplication, and:

- i_t is the **input gate**, which controls how much new information from $\tilde{c}_t$ enters the cell state;
- f_t is the **forget gate**, which modulates what information from the previous cell state c_{t-1} is retained;
- o_t is the **output gate**, which governs how much of the updated cell state c_t is exposed to the output h_t;
- $\tilde{c}_t$ is the **candidate cell state**, representing new content that can be added to the cell;
- c_t is the updated **cell state**, capturing long-term dependencies across time;
- h_t is the **hidden state** output at time t, used either for predictions at each time step or as input to the next LSTM cell.

Both FL-strong and FL-soft architectures are trained on sequential data for either regression or binary classification tasks. All models are trained for 50 epochs using the Adam optimizer with an initial learning rate of 0.001, a batch size of 32, and early stopping with a patience of 10 epochs, monitoring the validation loss. 20% of the training data is used for validation. For regression tasks, models are compiled with Mean Squared Error (MSE) loss, while for classification tasks, binary cross-entropy loss is used. In the latter case, to mitigate class imbalance, we applied class weighting during training, assigning higher weights to underrepresented classes to balance their contribution to the loss function. The model output $\hat{y}$ is defined as:

$$
\hat{y} = \begin{cases} W_y h_T + b_y, & \text{for regression,} \\ \sigma(W_y h_T + b_y), & \text{for binary classification,} \end{cases}
$$

where W_y and b_y are trainable parameters of the output layer, and h_T is the last hidden state of the LSTM.

For each forecasting task, both binary MHW prediction and SST regression, model's performance is evaluated across different forecast horizons, from 1 to 7 days ahead. Different input time sequences are constructed with sliding windows of varying lengths, defined by $L \in 3, 5, 7, 9, 11, 13, 15$. For each architecture, for each of the seven forecast horizons, and for each sequence length, the dataset is partitioned using a 10-fold time series cross-validation strategy.

The features are standardized using Z-score normalization with parameters computed only on the training set of each cross-validation split, then applied to the corresponding test set to avoid data leakage. Model outputs are denormalized only for regression tasks to recover predictions on the original scale before computing evaluation metrics.

In addition to the standard FedAvg strategy, we also implement Personalized Federated Learning (PFL). The initial process for PFL is identical to the FedAvg approach: the central server aggregates the weighted model updates from all participating clients, to compute the averaged weights $\bar{W}$. These averaged weights are then redistributed to the clients. However, in PFL, before evaluating the global model, each client performs a local fine-tuning step. This involves additional training epochs on their own private, site-specific data, using the global weights received as an initialization point. For this personalized fine-tuning, we used a reduced number of training epochs (five) and the same modalities and hyperparameters described earlier. Typically, a few epochs are sufficient to fit the global model to local data distributions without overfitting or disrupting global knowledge. This fine-tuning allows each client to personalize the global model, adapting it to the unique characteristics and distributions of their local datasets.

4 Experimental Evaluation

To evaluate the effectiveness of the proposed distributed learning framework, we considered multiple approaches, including centralized learning, FedAvg with two variants (FL-strong and FL-soft), and local learning (on-site training). These methods are applied to address both classification and regression tasks. This section is organized into two subsections: the first focuses on MHW classification experiments, while the second analyzes regression. All experiments were performed in a high-performance computational environment featuring an Intel Xeon w7-3455 CPU (2.5 GHz, 24 cores) and 187 GB of RAM.

4.1 MHW Classification

To assess the ability of our system to correctly identify heat wave events before performing any temperature forecasting, we conduct a preliminary binary classification step using the LSTM-based architecture introduced in Sect. 3.2, here referred to as FL-strong. Given the imbalanced nature of the dataset, which contains significantly fewer days with heatwave events compared to non-heatwave days, a well-established performance metric for binary classification problems under class imbalance is the BAlanced Accuracy (BAC), that is defined as:

$$BAC = \frac{TPR + TNR}{2} \tag{2}$$

where $TPR = \frac{TP}{TP+FN}$ is the true positive rate (sensitivity), and $TNR = \frac{TN}{TN+FP}$ is the true negative rate (specificity), with TP, TN, FP, and FN denoting the numbers of true positives (correctly predicted heatwave events), true negatives (correctly predicted non-heatwave events), false positives (non-heatwave events incorrectly predicted as heatwaves), and false negatives (missed heatwave events), respectively. Table 1 reports the average BAC scores computed across all 6 sites for forecast horizons from 1 to 7 days. The results confirm that the FL-strong classifier maintains good performance over time, achieving BAC values close to 0.80 for short-term forecasts and remaining robust even as the forecast horizon extends to 7 days. This preliminary step ensures reliable identification of MHW.

Table 1. BAC of the daily MHW classification averaged over the sites considered.

BAC values						
Day 1	Day 2	Day 3	Day 4	Day 5	Day 6	Day 7
0.795	0.780	0.766	0.758	0.759	0.756	0.743

4.2   MHW Regression

In this study, we treat SST prediction as a multistep regression task, aiming to forecast temperature variations over multiple days. Our goal is to approximate the time development of the temperature to numerical precision. To this end, we employ the Root Mean Square Error (RMSE) as a measure for the comparison of models. RMSE is a commonly applied metric in the SST forecast domain, allowing a direct quantitative assessment of predictive skill. RMSE is defined as:

$$\text{RMSE} = \sqrt{\frac{1}{N} \sum_{i=1}^{N} (T_i - F_i)^2} \tag{3}$$

where T_i is the observed SST value from the dataset, F_i is the predicted SST value for the corresponding time index, and N is the number of samples in the test set.

The RMSE provides a straightforward estimate of the deviation between observed and predicted time series and is widely used in the literature as a reference metric for temperature forecasting problems [1]. Furthermore, for each FL result shown, we report the best RMSE obtained by selecting the lower error between two FL strategies: the standard FedAvg and the PFL approach. This allows us to present the most accurate performance achievable within our federated framework.

Analysis of FL Across Training Rounds. Our initial analysis to demonstrate the efficacy of the FL method in obtaining accurate predictions involves examining the trend of RMSE (°C) as the number of training rounds increases. As shown in Fig. 3, it is evident that the RMSE prediction consistently decreases for each site as the number of training rounds increases. RMSE decreases sharply during initial rounds before stabilizing, indicating convergence. Although the final error values vary between sites, with Trieste showing the highest RMSE and sites such as Ortona and Venezia achieving lower errors, all participating nodes demonstrate an improvement in predictive accuracy with continued training. This consistent reduction in RMSE at all sites serves as a strong indicator of the effectiveness and suitability of FL to accurately predict MHWs, demonstrating its ability to improve model performance through collaborative learning. Unless otherwise specified, all subsequent results in the paper refer to the models obtained in round 5, which represents a good balance between training stability and predictive performance.

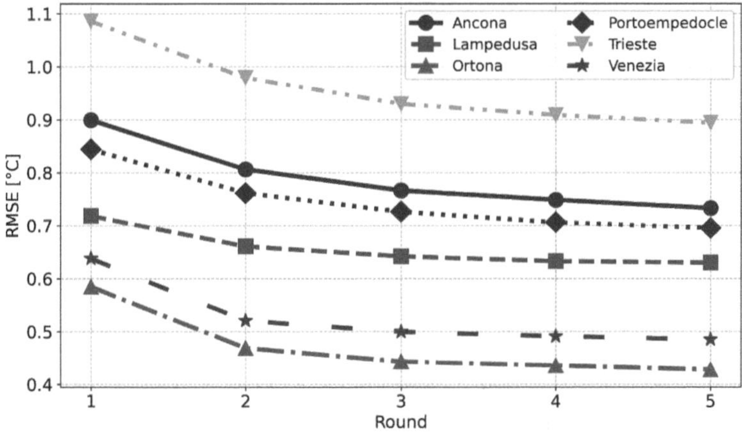

Fig. 3. RMSE trend among sites as the number of training rounds changes

Comparative Evaluation of Predictive Methods Using RMSE. To compare the predictive capacity of each training method, we calculate the RMSE and compare the average errors over the 7-day forecast horizon for all methods examined for each site. Table 2 shows the results for: On-site training, centralized method, and FL. In the on-site (Local Learning) approach, each model is trained using only its own local data, whereas in centralized learning, a single global model is trained on the complete dataset, combining data from all six sites.

Table 2 summarizes the predictive performance of the three training methods. Independent "On-site" training performs poorly due to isolated data processing. In contrast, the "Centralized" and "Federated Learning" methods yield decreased RMSE values by leveraging shared data to improve generalization. The average RMSE displayed in the table final column indicates that centralized and federated models outperform on-site implementations. Despite low RMSE, centralized models require full data access, increasing communication costs and

Table 2. Comparative Assessment of Prediction Techniques: Average 1-to-7 Day RMSE Regression

SITES	RMSE (°C)		
	On-site	Centralized	Federated Learning
Ancona	1.346	1.069	0.969
Lampedusa	0.802	0.657	0.781
Ortona	0.920	0.867	0.642
Portoempedocle	1.143	0.558	1.025
Trieste	1.420	0.872	1.150
Venezia	1.047	0.872	0.746
Error AVG	1.113	0.816	0.886

raising privacy issues. FL offers a comparable RMSE, maintaining data privacy and scalability. These findings confirm that our federated approach, which integrates FedAvg and PFL, serves as an effective balance of prediction accuracy, efficiency, and privacy. The trend is shown in the Table 2 is further visualized in Fig. 4, which shows the daily RMSE averaged at all sites for each method over the 7-day forecast horizon. The graph shows that the on-site approach consistently yields the highest RMSE values, indicating its less effective predictive capacity when data are processed in isolation.

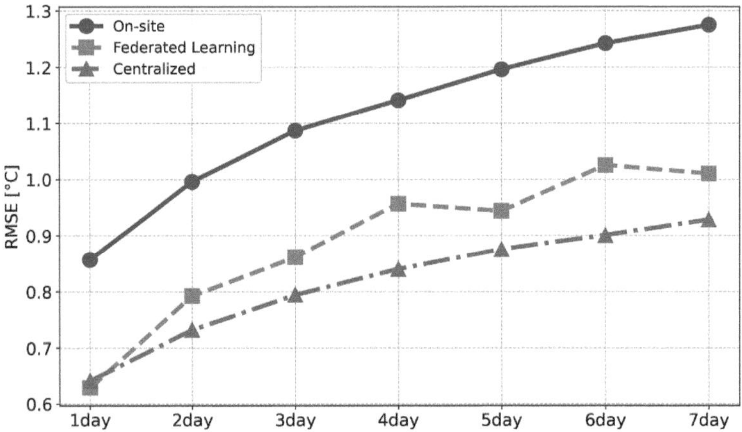

Fig. 4. Average RMSE (°C) per day across considered sites for On-site, FL, and Centralized training methods.

In contrast, the centralized approach achieves the lowest RMSE, benefiting from a comprehensive view of all data, albeit with associated privacy and communication overheads.

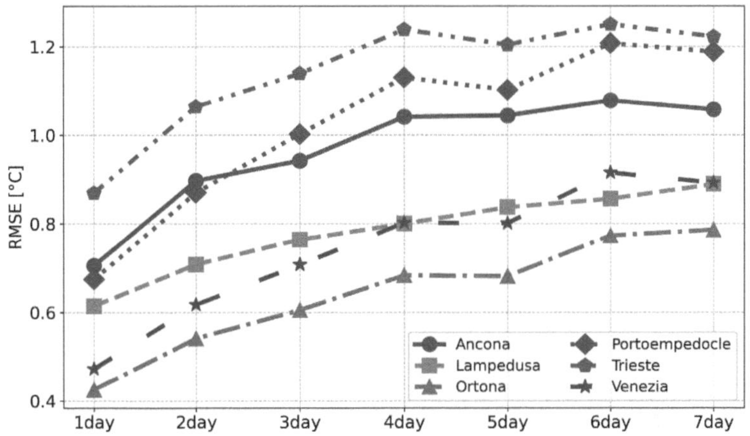

Fig. 5. Evolution of RMSE (°C) from FL at various locations for each forecast day.

To further illustrate the forecast character of the FL setting, Fig. 5 shows the trend of the RMSE (°C) predicted by the FL for each site and for each time horizon from 1 to 7 days. It is evident how the error remains small overall even as the forecast period increases. Moreover, comparing the different curves shows good stability among the analyzed sites: differences in performance among stations are minimal, and RMSE values increase only marginally in the transition from 1 to 7 days.

4.3 Efficiency in Data Transmission

Finally, we evaluate the effectiveness of the different methods by measuring the daily data transmission required during model training, considering both the centralized approach and the two FL architectures (FL-strong and FL-soft), as detailed in Table 3. In the centralized system, raw sensor data from edge devices are sent to the central server for training, which requires 197 kB of data per day per site. This value can be explained as follows: each site includes 30 sensors, and each sensor generates 240 readings per day. Every reading consists of 7 features, and each feature is represented using 4 bytes. In contrast, FL trains models locally, sending only updated weights to the server. As previously introduced, the FL scheme employs two LSTM architectures, FL-strong and FL-soft, that balance predictive capacity and communication cost. Specifically, FL-strong transmits the full set of weight (31,100 model parameters) per training round, corresponding to 121 kB per day (represented using 4 bytes), while FL-soft, with its lighter architecture, sends 8,500 parameters, totaling only 33 kB per day (represented using 4 bytes). Efficiency is measured as the percentage reduction in daily transmitted data compared to the centralized method. These findings highlight the advantage of FL in resource-constrained IoT systems, optimizing bandwidth and securing data privacy by limiting raw data transfer. The FL approach demonstrates balanced performance, consistently positioning its RMSE values between those of on-site and centralized methods by reducing transmitted data to 83%.

Table 3. Data [kB] Transmitted per Day

	Centralized	FL-strong	FL-soft
Model weight	–	121 kB	33 kB
Sensors Data	197kB	–	–
Reduction	0%	**38%**	**83%**

5   Conclusion

In conclusion, this paper presents an FL framework to predict MHWs using SST data from coastal sensors in the Mediterranean, with a particular focus on the Italian coast. The framework addresses decentralized marine monitoring to train models on local time-series data. This design avoids sharing raw data, ensuring privacy and compliance with data sovereignty. Two LSTM architectures are utilized, in which localized LSTM models are aggregated through a central server using the FedAvg algorithm. This enables accurate predictions of the onset and severity of MHW while addressing regional thermal dynamics. Experimental results with real SST datasets and measured MHW events show that the method effectively predicts short-term thermal anomalies, offering a scalable and privacy-conscious solution to improve climate resilience. Personalized federated models consistently outperform site-specific models in predictive accuracy, achieving stable and low RMSE values during training. Future work will extend the analysis to additional coastal sites and refine the feature selection process. We also plan to explore advanced techniques, such as clustered federated learning, to further enhance model personalization and performance.

Acknowledgment. This work is partially supported by the Project SERICS (PE00000014 - CUP D33C22001300002) under the PNRRP MUR program funded by the EU-NGEU, and by the project RESTART (PE00000001 - CUP E83C22004640001) under the NRRP MUR program funded by the EU-NGEU, under the focus project SPRINT.

References

1. Bonino, G., Galimberti, G., Masina, S., McAdam, R., Clementi, E.: Machine learning methods to predict sea surface temperature and marine heatwave occurrence: a case study of the mediterranean sea. Ocean Sci. **20**(2), 417–432 (2024). https://doi.org/10.5194/os-20-417-2024. https://os.copernicus.org/articles/20/417/2024/
2. Hobday, A.J., et al.: A hierarchical approach to defining marine heatwaves. Prog. Oceanogr. **141**, 227–238 (2016). https://doi.org/10.1016/j.pocean.2015.12.014. https://www.sciencedirect.com/science/article/pii/S0079661116000057
3. Hobday, A.J., et al.: Categorizing and naming marine heatwaves. Oceanography **issue_volume** (2018). https://doi.org/10.5670/oceanog.2018.205
4. Jones, T., et al.: Massive mortality of a planktivorous seabird in response to a marine heatwave. Geophys. Res. Lett. **45**(7), 3193–3202 (2018)
5. Liu, L., Lu, Y., An, L., Liang, H., Zhou, C., Zhang, Z.: Time-EAPCR: a deep learning-based novel approach for anomaly detection applied to the environmental field. arXiv preprint arXiv:2503.09200 (2025)
6. Musonda, S.K., Ndiaye, M., Libati, H.M., Abu-Mahfouz, A.M.: Reliability of loRaWAN communications in mining environments: a survey on challenges and design requirements. J. Sens. Actuator Netw. **13**(1), 16 (2024)
7. Oliver, E.C., et al.: Longer and more frequent marine heatwaves over the past century. Nat. Commun. **9**(1), 1324 (2018)
8. Picone, M., Orasi, A., Nardone, G.: Sea surface temperature monitoring in Italian seas: analysis of long-term trends and short-term dynamics. Measurement **129**, 260–267 (2018)
9. Tehseen, R., Farooq, M.S., Abid, A.: EPS: an earthquake prediction system using federated learning. In: 2021 International Conference on Innovative Computing (ICIC), pp. 1–8. IEEE (2021)
10. Victor, N., et al.: Federated learning for IoUT: concepts, applications, challenges and opportunities. arXiv preprint arXiv:2207.13976 (2022)
11. Zhang, D.D., Brecke, P., Lee, H.F., He, Y.Q., Zhang, J.: Global climate change, war, and population decline in recent human history. Proc. Natl. Acad. Sci. **104**(49), 19214–19219 (2007). https://doi.org/10.1073/pnas.0703073104. https://www.pnas.org/doi/abs/10.1073/pnas.0703073104
12. Zhang, Q., Wang, H., Dong, J., Zhong, G., Sun, X.: Prediction of sea surface temperature using long short-term memory. IEEE Geosci. Remote Sens. Lett. **14**(10), 1745–1749 (2017)

Cooper: A Lightweight Event Recording and Visualization Framework for Data Center Simulations

Mark Doyle, Theodoros Aslanidis$^{(\boxtimes)}$, and Dimitris Chatzopoulos

School of Computer Science, University College Dublin, Dublin, Ireland
{mark.doyle6, theodoros.aslanidis}@ucdconnect.ie,
dimitris.chatzopoulos@ucd.ie

Abstract. Cloud simulation tools are essential for modeling and evaluating complex cloud computing infrastructures, enabling researchers to study resource allocation strategies, scheduling algorithms, and overall system performance. CloudSim Plus is a widely used Java framework for building such simulations. However, despite its rich feature set, it offers only limited support for post-simulation analysis, providing primarily static ASCII tables that summarize final resource states. As simulation complexity grows, this output format becomes insufficient, highlighting the need for more interactive and insightful analysis tools.

In this work, we present Cooper, a lightweight and modular visualization framework that extends CloudSim Plus with standardized event collection and timeline-based visualization. Cooper enables detailed temporal analysis of simulation runs, helping users understand dynamic system behavior, resource utilization patterns, and the effects of scheduling decisions. The event logging library runs entirely in memory, introduces minimal runtime overhead, and does not require external database or server infrastructure. Its design reduces integration effort and promotes reproducibility by decoupling simulation from visualization.

Keywords: Cloud Computing · Simulation Visualization · CloudSim · Resource Management · Data Center Simulation

1 Introduction

Cloud simulation frameworks are essential tools for researchers and practitioners, enabling cost-effective modeling of large-scale cloud infrastructures without physical deployment. Among them, CloudSim [8] has become the de facto standard for simulating cloud environments at scale [3]. These frameworks allow systematic exploration of resource management strategies, such as virtual machine (VM) scheduling, cloudlet placement, and energy-aware policies, through configurable experiments under controlled conditions.

Building on CloudSim's foundation, CloudSim Plus emerged as a modern, extensible Java-based simulator [30]. It offers advanced features including

© The Author(s), under exclusive license to Springer Nature Switzerland AG 2026
D. Garlisi and D. Chatzopoulos (Eds.): ALGOCLOUD 2025, LNCS 16349, pp. 16–30, 2026.
https://doi.org/10.1007/978-3-032-13744-9_2

multi-cloud environments, VM scaling, energy- and network-awareness, and fine-grained control over simulation logic. Its modular, object-oriented architecture supports customization and has been widely adopted in academic research [3]. Extensions like iFogSim [13] further adapt it for fog and IoT environments.

However, all these tools lack support for temporal introspection and post-simulation analysis. For example, CloudSim Plus provides static ASCII summaries that obfuscate critical behaviors such as workload spikes or scheduling inefficiencies [25]. Users often rely on ad hoc workflows, manual logs, custom scripts, or external tools (e.g., Python, Excel, Matplotlib) that are time-consuming and hinder reproducibility. Hunt et al. [16] emphasize that such fragmented practices limit collaboration and the ability to replicate findings.

This reflects a broader gap; although simulators like CloudSim Plus internally track rich event timelines, they lack standard infrastructure to capture and visualize them. In real cloud systems and simulations alike, resource metrics (e.g., CPU, memory, I/O, network) naturally form multivariate time series essential for both automated control and human analysis. Interactive visual analytics are crucial for interpreting these patterns and validating behavior [25].

Despite advancements such as EdgeCloudSim (mobility), ContainerCloudSim (containers), CloudSimSC (serverless) [22], and iQuantum (quantum resources) [26], these tools still rely on static logs and manual analysis. Surveys confirm this limitation [16,30], calling for FAIR (findable, accessible, interoperable, reusable) workflows and visual analytics. At the same time, as cloud resource management techniques become more complex—spanning reinforcement learning approaches for dynamic cloud environments [4], transferable frameworks for the cloud-edge continuum [5], hybrid learning-based optimization [38], and intelligent IoT-edge integrations [7]—understanding workload dynamics makes visualizing temporal simulation data critical. Without visual introspection, the evaluation and improvement of such techniques within simulators becomes cumbersome, as static logs obscure the evolution of scheduling decisions, resource contention, and overall system behavior over time.

To address this, we introduce Cooper, a lightweight, open-source extension for CloudSim Plus that adds temporal introspection and interactive visualization. It includes *(i)* a Java-based event recorder that logs cloudlet lifecycles, VM states, and host metrics into structured JSON, and *(ii)* a Vite [41], React [23], TypeScript [39] web frontend that renders zoomable, filterable timelines for dynamic exploration of simulation behavior. By providing standardized visual insights into simulation dynamics, Cooper simplifies analysis, enhances reproducibility, and enables a deeper understanding of complex cloud scenarios.

Contributions. This work makes the following key contributions to the cloud simulation research community.

- We survey and contextualize the current state and state-of-the-art in visualization techniques for cloud infrastructures, covering both industrial and academic efforts, in both real and simulated environments.
- We design an efficient and lightweight recording process that captures key simulation events entirely in-memory without relying on external databases,

avoiding disk I/O overhead, and simplifying deployment while maintaining high performance.

- We develop and open-source a standalone, minimal-intrusion Java library named *Cooper*, which is compatible with CloudSim Plus, offering a straight-forward API to record simulation events and export them in a structured, human- and machine-readable JSON format.
- We build a static, client-side visualization tool: a web application that runs entirely in the browser (requiring no backend server or database) and enables intuitive exploration of cloudlet scheduling, VM allocation, and host utilization over time. The tool is fully self-contained and can be easily self-hosted or used locally by simply opening the HTML page in any modern browser.
- We evaluate the performance impact of our recording mechanism and measure the CPU, memory, and execution time overhead during simulation.

The remainder of the paper is organized as follows. Section 2 presents the related work. Section 3 discusses our methodology. Section 4 evaluates the Cooper framework's event recording mechanism, measures its overhead, and provides an estimate of Cooper's log file size. Finally, Sect. 5 presents our conclusions and outlines possible directions for future work.

2 Related Work

Cloud simulation frameworks such as CloudSim [8] and CloudSim Plus [10] have long served as critical testbeds for research on infrastructure scheduling, resource allocation, and energy efficiency. Although simulation engines have advanced in functionality and extensibility, their supporting analysis and visualization tools have not kept pace.

Tools such as CloudAnalyst [42] introduced graphical components for CloudSim, focusing on the geographic visualization of user bases and datacenter locations. Although CloudAnalyst allowed limited visual exploration, it lacked support for temporal metrics and is incompatible with newer frameworks like CloudSim Plus. In particular, the tool has not been updated for more than a decade.

CloudSim Plus emphasizes extensibility and object-oriented design, but does not offer built-in visualization capabilities. As a result, researchers often resort to manual log inspection or develop custom plotting scripts, which is time-consuming and discourages detailed temporal analysis.

Modern cloud providers, including Amazon Web Services (AWS), Google Cloud, and Microsoft Azure [24], offer rich performance monitoring and visualization tools. For example, AWS CloudWatch [2] provides scalable time-series visualizations with support for event annotations, anomaly detection, and interactive dashboards [31]. These platforms achieve low monitoring overhead—often below 2% CPU—through efficient data aggregation techniques [20].

Such commercial systems demonstrate best practices in aggregation, interactivity, and user experience that are conspicuously absent from most cloud simulation tools. Key features include: *(i)* interactive time-series charts, *(ii)* event overlays (e.g., instance lifecycle or threshold violations), and *(iii)* minimalist, intuitive user interface (UI) designs.

DigitalOcean's dashboard, known for its clarity and responsiveness [1], further supports the case for simple, research-friendly post-simulation visualization.

A core requirement for effective simulation monitoring is non-intrusive instrumentation with minimal performance overhead. For example, CloudProcMon achieves monitoring with less than 2% CPU impact [36]. Timestamped lifecycle events facilitate replay and dynamic analysis of simulations [6], while hierarchical telemetry models support efficient aggregation and drill-down at the datacenter, host, VM and cloudlet levels [9,11].

Structured formats such as nested JSON and HDF5 [15] are well-suited for encoding simulation data in ways that preserve hierarchy and support scalable ingestion and visualization. Adaptive-resolution dashboards balance high-frequency data collection with overhead and latency concerns [36].

In contrast, cloud simulation workflows remain largely static and fragmented. Researchers often rely on tools like Excel or Matplotlib, which lack interactivity, semantic integration, or temporal navigation. This contrasts to commercial monitoring platforms, which provide hierarchical visualizations, real-time filtering, and dynamic granularity adjustment across thousands of resources [31].

Several efforts have attempted to address this gap through graphical UI (GUI) extensions to CloudSim. More concretely, CloudSimSDN [33] extends CloudSim with support for SDN-aware simulation and includes a GUI for editing and visualizing topologies (hosts, switches, VMs, and links). Its focus is primarily on pre-simulation configuration, with limited post-simulation insight. CloudSim 7G [3] introduces a redesigned CloudSim architecture with modular interfaces and integrated post-simulation visualization for comparing VM scheduling algorithms. CloudReports [37] offers an open-source GUI aimed at energy-aware experiments, providing graphs of host CPU usage and energy metrics over time. TeachCloud [18] and CloudExp [19] are educational and experimental GUIs built on CloudSim. They allow users to configure infrastructure, define workloads, and view simulation results visually. Although useful for learning and basic scenarios, they are not designed for fine-grained temporal exploration. DARTCSim [21] simplifies simulation workflows with a GUI that hides the low-level configuration and presents results through static charts. It focuses on ease of use rather than detailed telemetry. VMAgent [32] focuses on reinforcement learning for VM scheduling using real Huawei Cloud traces. It includes a visualization module, SchedVis, which can display metrics such as VM CPU load, memory usage, and migration events over time. The authors in [14] developed a GUI-based extension to simulate sensor-cloud environments. Users can interactively configure sensor and cloudlet scheduling policies and visualize performance outcomes.

Despite these efforts, most tools lack features such as interactive zoomable timelines, event-based overlays, and integrated UI elements to analyze large-scale simulations. In many cases, visualization is either limited to static graphs or tightly coupled to specific simulation types.

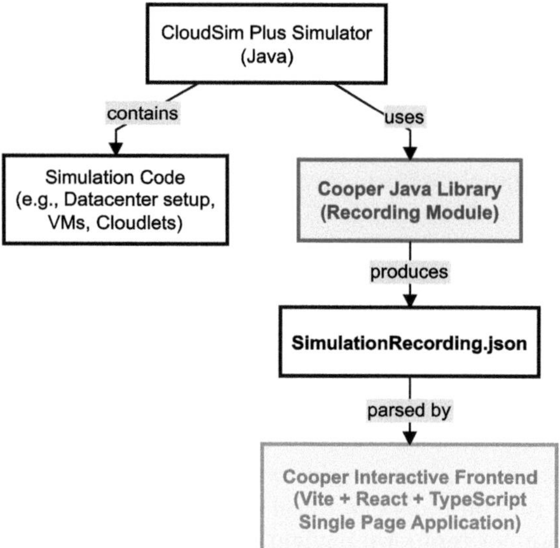

Fig. 1. Cooper's architecture diagram.

There is a clear need for a modern visualization layer that bridges this gap—providing interactive, hierarchical, and temporally-aware dashboards over CloudSim Plus simulation logs. Such tools would enable more insightful exploration, facilitate debugging, and make simulation research more reproducible and transparent.

3   Methodology

The Cooper framework is composed of two distinct components, reflecting an architectural decision that cleanly separates the simulation and post-simulation phases. The first component is responsible for recording simulation events and generating a structured JSON log that captures the full execution trace. The second component is a frontend UI that parses this JSON file and visualizes the recorded events in an interactive, easy-to-navigate interface. This separation promotes modularity and allows Cooper to seamlessly integrate into existing CloudSim Plus workflows. The frontend enables users to analyze simulation behavior through intuitive timelines, resource views, and event overlays. Figure 1 illustrates the architecture and the relationships between Cooper's components.

3.1   Data Collection Layer

Cooper contains a standalone Java library designed for seamless integration with CloudSim Plus simulations, requiring minimal code changes. Entities (hosts, VMs, and cloudlets) are tracked by their unique IDs, and the output is structured as hierarchical JSON compatible with the web-based visualization tool.

```
1  import org.cooper.simulation.SimulationRecording;
2  // necessary Java imports
3  // necessary CloudSim Plus imports
4
5  // simulation code for setting up the experiment
6
7  var recording = new SimulationRecording("SimRec", dc);
8
9  simulation.start();
10
11 String out = recording.end();
12
13 // save the recording
14 // exception handling omitted for brevity
15 Files.writeString(Path.of("SimRec.json"), out);
```

Listing 1.1. Minimal Cooper example using CloudSim Plus in asynchronous mode.

```
1  import org.cooper.simulation.SimulationRecording;
2  // necessary Java imports
3  // necessary CloudSim Plus imports
4
5  // simulation code for setting up the experiment
6
7  var recording = new SimulationRecording("SimRec", dc);
8
9  simulation.startSync();
10
11 while (simulation.isRunning()) {
12    simulation.runFor(1);
13 }
14
15 String out = recording.end();
16
17 // save the recording
18 // exception handling omitted for brevity
19 Files.writeString(Path.of("SimRec.json"), out);
```

Listing 1.2. Minimal Cooper example using CloudSim Plus in synchronous mode.

To use Cooper, users instantiate a `SimulationRecording` object and invoke `end()` after the simulation has ended. The library produces a JSON document that captures the complete simulation state, including both metadata and a hierarchical view of cloud resources. At the top level, it records simulation-wide details such as the ID, name, start time, and total duration. Each host entry includes its active time span and the VMs it hosted. VMs log their lifecycle events and contain the cloudlets they executed, while each cloudlet records its execution status, progress, and completion timestamps. This structured JSON file can be saved to disk or passed to downstream tools.

Fig. 2. Cooper's panel for viewing past simulations and uploading new ones.

Listing 1.1 shows a minimal example of using Cooper with CloudSim Plus in asynchronous mode. Cooper can also be used seamlessly when the simulation runs in synchronous mode, as shown in Listing 1.2.

The publishing of the Java library is fully automated through GitHub Actions CI/CD [12]. Upon tagging a new release, the workflow authenticates with Sonatype [35] and publishes the package to Maven Central Repository [34].

Cooper includes regression tests that compare JSON outputs between versions. These tests run known simulation scenarios and validate that the generated outputs remain consistent with reference files. This protects against unintended changes to the recording logic or the JSON structure, ensuring backward compatibility with the visualization tool.

The recording of simulation events is performed entirely in memory, without relying on any external database systems. This design choice eliminates the overhead associated with disk I/O operations and avoids dependence on external services, resulting in a lightweight and highly efficient data capture process. By maintaining all event data in memory during simulation runtime, the system achieves fast performance and simplified deployment, making it ideal for handling moderately large datasets without introducing the complexity or latency often associated with database interactions.

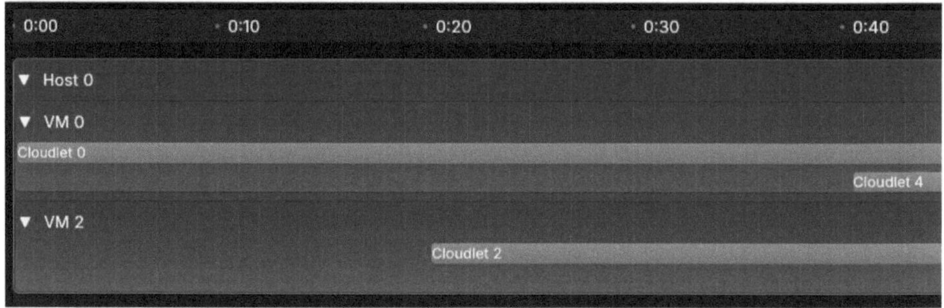

Fig. 3. Cooper's simulation timeline view.

3.2   Visualization Interface

Cooper's visualization interface is designed to provide an intuitive and interactive way to explore the simulation results of CloudSim Plus, structured around the relationships between hosts, VMs, and cloudlets.

On the left side of the interface, a sidebar component allows users to upload JSON files containing simulation data and select which simulation to view (Fig. 2). Uploaded files are saved in the browser's local storage, allowing users to access previously loaded simulations between sessions without reuploading.

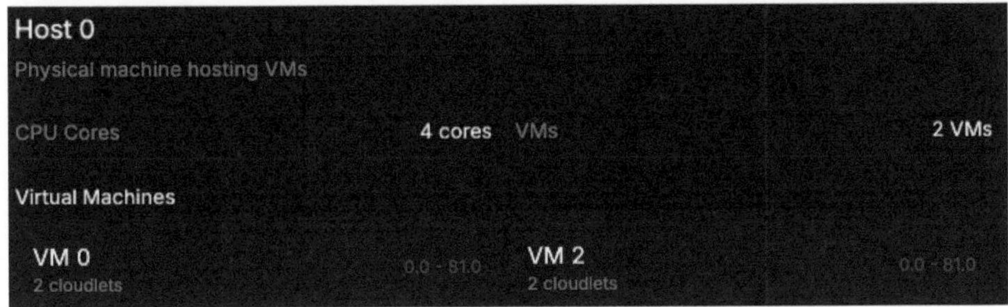

Fig. 4. Cooper's host information view.

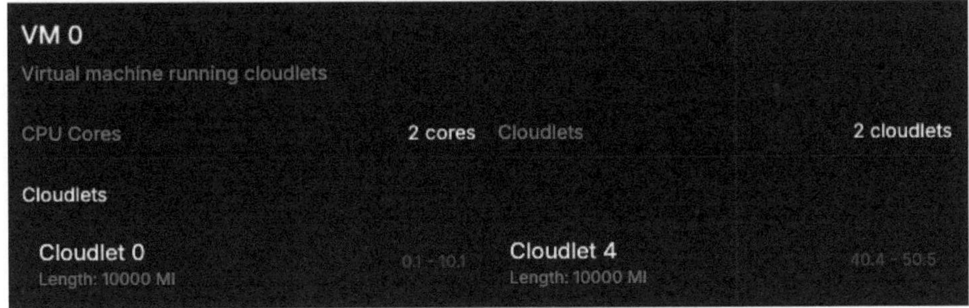

Fig. 5. Cooper's VM information view.

The central element of the visualization interface is the scrubber component, which provides a hierarchical, time-based view of the simulation (Fig. 3). It represents structural relationships between hosts, VMs, and cloudlets in a nested layout: each host is visualized as a container holding its VMs, which in turn contain the cloudlets they execute. The horizontal axis encodes simulation time with regularly spaced markers, enabling intuitive identification of scheduling patterns, idle periods, and overlapping executions. Color coding is used to distinguish resource types, improve clarity, and facilitate rapid interpretation of

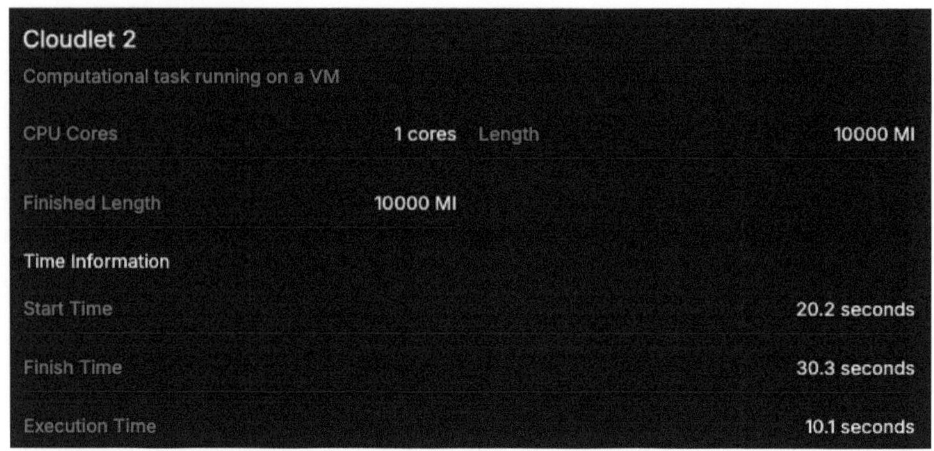

Fig. 6. Cooper's cloudlet information view.

the timeline. The entities in the simulation timeline are clickable: selecting a host displays its information on the top panel (Fig. 4), selecting a VM shows its details (Fig. 5), and selecting a cloudlet reveals its attributes (Fig. 6). This timeline view enables users to examine simulation events, such as cloudlet execution and VM allocation—across the duration of the simulation.

Navigation is seamlessly integrated with the browser's native history system. The current view (including the selected simulation and resource) is encoded as URL query parameters. This allows users to navigate with standard browser controls, bookmark specific views, and share direct links to particular simulation states. This approach efficiently manages the navigation state without relying on external routing libraries or server-side infrastructure.

Together, these components form a cohesive interface that supports detailed and temporal exploration of complex cloud resource activity, making it easier to analyze utilization patterns, resource allocation, and scheduling behavior.

To ensure responsiveness, the interface employs efficient state management (i.e., React hooks [29]) and hardware-accelerated animations. The use of memoization and CSS transforms guaranties smooth interactions, even for simulations with extended timelines.

3.3   Framework Distribution and Accessibility

Cooper is distributed as a Maven package, simplifying integration into CloudSim Plus projects. The visualization tool is hosted as a static web application using Vercel [40] at https://cloudsim.mdoyle.sh. Researchers can also run the web interface locally for offline use. The source code, along with the build instructions for Cooper and self-hosting the web application using pnpm and Node.js, is available on GitHub at https://github.com/doylemark/cooper.

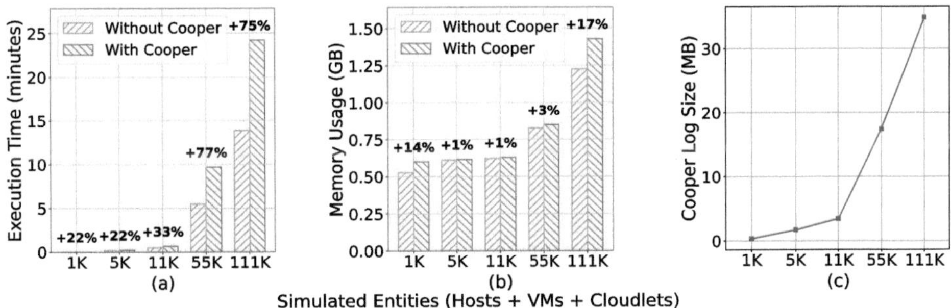

Fig. 7. Overhead analysis of Cooper showing *(a)* execution time, *(b)* memory usage and *(c)* log size, versus total simulated entities (hosts + VMs + cloudlets).

3.4   Limitations

Although the proposed toolkit significantly enhances the analysis capabilities of CloudSim Plus simulations, several limitations warrant consideration. First, the visualization interface, although effective for moderately sized experiments, is not optimized for very large-scale simulations involving thousands of hosts, VMs, or cloudlets. As the scale of the simulated environment grows, the timeline representation may become increasingly cluttered, potentially impairing usability and interpretability. Current features such as collapsibility mitigate this issue to some extent; however, more work is necessary to ensure scalability and maintain clarity in more complex scenarios.

Despite these limitations, the modular and extensible architecture of the toolkit provides a solid foundation for future enhancements. Addressing scalability concerns and broadening compatibility with diverse simulation execution models represent promising directions for future research and development.

4   Experiments

In this section, we present the overhead analysis of Cooper's event recording mechanism. Specifically, we evaluate Cooper's overhead in terms of total execution time, memory usage, and CPU time. We also measure the total log size (in MB) and provide a precise equation for its calculation.

4.1   Evaluation of Cooper's Java Library Overhead

To evaluate the overhead introduced by Cooper's recording mechanism, we conducted a series of experiments with varying numbers of hosts to assess how performance scales with simulation size. In each experiment, every host runs 10 VMs, and each VM runs 10 cloudlets. Thus, the total number of entities simulated, denoted by T, is:

$$T = H + V + C = 110H \tag{1}$$

We evaluated Cooper's runtime, memory, and logging overhead across simulations ranging from 1,000 to 100,000 simulated entities (hosts, VMs, and cloudlets). The results are summarized in Fig. 7.

As shown in Fig. 7a, the execution time increases moderately with the simulation scale. Cooper introduces an average wall-clock time overhead of approximately 22% for small- to medium-scale simulations (up to 10,000 entities) and up to 77% for the larger configurations (50,000 − 100,000 entities). These overhead levels are comparable to those reported for well-known instrumentation tools such as OpenTelemetry [28] and Jaeger [17], where detailed event tracing can cause slowdowns of 20−80% [27], and specialized profilers, which in extreme cases can cause $2 \times -10\times$ slowdowns [43]. This trade-off is widely accepted for the richer post-execution insights these tools provide.

Figure 7b reports memory consumption, which remains stable across all scales. The additional heap usage introduced by Cooper ranges between +1% and +17%, indicating that the event recording process incurs only a small, predictable memory footprint even in large-scale simulations.

The resulting log file sizes, shown in Fig. 7c, grow linearly with the number of entities and recorded events, from 0.34 MB at 1,000 entities to 34.9 MB at 100,000. This linear trend confirms that Cooper's data output scales predictably, enabling fine-grained introspection without excessive storage demands.

Overall, these results demonstrate that Cooper introduces moderate but acceptable overhead, consistent with expectations for event-capturing systems. The observed costs are outweighed by the analytical benefits of post-simulation visualization and introspection. In addition, Cooper's event-driven design, built on CloudSim Plus's listener interface, ensures that events are recorded only when triggered, avoiding busy-waiting or redundant polling. This passive architecture minimizes runtime interference and keeps CPU and memory overheads under control, even as the simulation size increases.

4.2   Log File Size Estimation

Let e_h be the recorded events per host, e_v the recorded events per VM, e_c the recorded events per cloudlet, e_s the fixed simulation-wide recorded events, α the average log size per event (in MB/event), and β the fixed log overhead (in MB).

Then, the total number of recorded events is:

$$E = e_h \cdot H + e_v \cdot V + e_c \cdot C + e_s \tag{2}$$

The estimated log file size L (in megabytes) is given by:

$$L = \alpha \cdot E + \beta \tag{3}$$

In our experiments, the values used are as follows:

$$e_h = 4,\ e_v = 4,\ e_c = 8,\ e_s = 4,\ \alpha \approx 4.019 \times 10^{-5},\ \beta \approx -2.124 \times 10^{-3} \tag{4}$$

Thus, the equation becomes:

$$L = \alpha \cdot (4H + 4V + 8C + 4) + \beta \tag{5}$$

If we assume fixed relationships between entities (i.e., $V = 10H$ and $C = 100H$), and also fixed numbers of recorded events per entity type (i.e., $e_h = 4$, $e_v = 4$, $e_c = 8$), then the expression simplifies to:

$$L = \alpha \cdot (864H + 4) + \beta \tag{6}$$

The size of the log increases linearly with the number of simulated entities and with the number of recorded metrics.

5   Conclusions and Future Work

In this work, we addressed a key limitation of CloudSim Plus by replacing its static tabular output with an interactive workflow that visualizes the complete simulation lifecycle. The resulting toolchain, Cooper, comprises two components: *(i)* a lightweight Java library that records host, VM, and cloudlet states as structured JSON, and *(ii)* a React-based web application that visualizes these data as an interactive timeline. Designed for minimal intrusion, Cooper adds reasonable runtime overhead while shifting analysis from log scraping to visual exploration. This enables researchers to identify temporal patterns, such as overlapping cloudlets or idle periods, to analyze scheduling behavior that is difficult to infer from textual logs. Moreover, simulations can be shared as a single JSON file and inspected on any device with a browser.

Future work will focus on improving scalability and extending event coverage. Although the interface supports hierarchical collapsibility, it is not yet optimized for large-scale simulations. Planned enhancements—including hierarchical aggregation, adaptive level of detail, and incremental rendering—will improve performance and navigation in large experiments, similar to how interactive maps reveal details upon zooming. Further extensions will add new metrics (e.g., cost, power, network, failures, VM migrations, and multi-datacenter support) and allow users to subscribe to specific events. These developments will make Cooper more flexible and suitable for diverse cloud simulation scenarios.

Acknowledgments. This work has been supported by the Horizon Europe research and innovation program of the European Union, under grant agreement no. 101092912, project MLSysOps.

References

1. Ahmad, M.A.: User experience in cloud computing: a comparative evaluation of AWS and UpCloud management consoles. Master's thesis, Haaga-Helia University of Applied Sciences (2024)
2. Amazon Web Services, Inc.: Amazon cloudwatch. https://aws.amazon.com/cloudwatch/. Accessed 08 Oct 2025

3. Andreoli, R., Zhao, J., Cucinotta, T., Buyya, R.: Cloudsim 7G: an integrated toolkit for modeling and simulation of future generation cloud computing environments. Pract. Exper. Softw. (2025)
4. Aslanidis, T., Chouliaras, A., Chatzopoulos, D.: Reinforcement learning techniques for optimizing system configuration on the cloud: a taxonomy and open problems. In: Proceedings of the 2023 International Conference on Embedded Wireless Systems and Networks, EWSN, pp. 25–27 (2023)
5. Aslanidis, T., Kosta, S., Lalis, S., Chatzopoulos, D.: Cross-domain DRL agents for efficient job placement in the cloud-edge continuum. In: Proceedings of the 5th Workshop on Machine Learning and Systems, pp. 276–285 (2025)
6. Bauer, A.C., et al.: In situ methods, infrastructures, and applications on high performance computing platforms. Comput. Graph. Forum **35**(3), 577–597 (2016). https://doi.org/10.1111/cgf.12930
7. Byabazaire, J., et al.: Deep learning and the internet of things: applications, challenges, and opportunities. Internet of Things A to Z: Technologies and Applications, pp. 193–228 (2025)
8. Calheiros, R.N., Ranjan, R., De Rose, C.A., Buyya, R.: CloudSim: a novel framework for modeling and simulation of cloud computing infrastructures and services. arXiv preprint arXiv:0903.2525 (2009)
9. da Cunha Rodrigues, G., et al.: Monitoring of cloud computing environments: concepts, solutions, trends, and future directions. In: Proceedings of the 31st Annual ACM Symposium on Applied Computing, pp. 378–383. ACM (2016). https://doi.org/10.1145/2851613.2851619
10. Filho, M.C.S., Oliveira, R.L., Monteiro, C.C., Inácio, P.R.M., Freire, M.M.: CloudSim plus: a cloud computing simulation framework pursuing software engineering principles for improved modularity, extensibility and correctness. In: IFIP/IEEE Symposium on Integrated Network and Service Management (IM 2017), pp. 400–406. IEEE (2017). https://doi.org/10.23919/INM.2017.7987304
11. Gill, A.Q., Hevary, S.: Cloud monitoring data challenges: a systematic review. In: Hirose, A., Ozawa, S., Doya, K., Ikeda, K., Lee, M., Liu, D. (eds.) ICONIP 2016. LNCS, vol. 9947, pp. 72–79. Springer, Cham (2016). https://doi.org/10.1007/978-3-319-46687-3_8
12. Github: Github actions. https://github.com/features/actions. Accessed 08 Oct 2025
13. Gupta, H., Vahid Dastjerdi, A., Ghosh, S.K., Buyya, R.: iFogSim: a toolkit for modeling and simulation of resource management techniques in the internet of things, edge and fog computing environments. Softw. Pract. Exp. **47**(9), 1275–1296 (2017)
14. Habaebi, M.H., Merrad, Y., Islam, M.R., Elsheikh, E.A., Sliman, F., Mesri, M.: Extending cloudsim to simulate sensor networks. Simulation **99**(1), 3–22 (2023)
15. HDF Group: HDF5. https://www.hdfgroup.org/solutions/hdf5/
16. Hunt, M., Clark, S., Mejia, D., Desai, S., Strachan, A.: Sim2Ls: fair simulation workflows and data. PLoS ONE **17**(3), e0264492 (2022)
17. Jaeger Authors: Jaeger: Open source, end-to-end distributed tracing (2025). https://www.jaegertracing.io/. Accessed 08 Oct 2025
18. Jararweh, Y., Alshara, Z., Jarrah, M., Kharbutli, M., Alsaleh, M.N.: TeachCloud: a cloud computing educational toolkit. Int. J. Cloud Comput. 1 **2**(2-3), 237–257 (2013)
19. Jararweh, Y., Jarrah, M., Alshara, Z., Alsaleh, M.N., Al-Ayyoub, M., et al.: CloudExp: a comprehensive cloud computing experimental framework. Simul. Model. Pract. Theory **49**, 180–192 (2014)

20. Khalil, M., Khomonenko, A., Matushko, M.D.: Measuring the effect of monitoring on a cloud computing system by estimating the delay time of requests. J. King Saud Univ. Comput. Inf. Sci. **34**(7) (2021). https://doi.org/10.1016/j.jksuci.2021.02.001

21. Li, X., Jiang, X., Huang, P., Ye, K.: DartCSim: an enhanced user-friendly cloud simulation system based on cloudsim with better performance. In: 2012 IEEE 2nd International Conference on Cloud Computing and Intelligence Systems, vol. 1, pp. 392–396. IEEE (2012)

22. Mampage, A., Buyya, R.: CloudSimSC: a toolkit for modeling and simulation of serverless computing environments. In: 2023 IEEE International Conference on High Performance Computing & Communications, Data Science & Systems, Smart City & Dependability in Sensor, Cloud & Big Data Systems & Application (HPC-C/DSS/SmartCity/DependSys), pp. 550–557. IEEE (2023)

23. Meta Platforms, Inc.: React: A Javascript library for building user interfaces. https://react.dev/. Accessed 08 Oct 2025

24. Microsoft: What is the azure portal? (2024). https://learn.microsoft.com/en-us/azure/azure-portal/azure-portal-overview. Accessed 08 Oct 2025

25. Muller, S.: Visualization methods for time-dependent data-an overview. In: Proceedings of the 2003 Winter Simulation Conference, 2003, vol. 1, pp. 737–745. IEEE (2003)

26. Nguyen, H.T., Usman, M., Buyya, R.: iQuantum: a toolkit for modeling and simulation of quantum computing environments. Softw. Pract. Exp. **54**(6), 1141–1171 (2024)

27. Nõu, A., Talluri, S., Iosup, A., Bonetta, D.: Investigating performance overhead of distributed tracing in microservices and serverless systems. In: Companion of the 16th ACM/SPEC International Conference on Performance Engineering, pp. 162–166 (2025)

28. OpenTelemetry Authors: OpenTelemetry: High-quality, ubiquitous, and portable telemetry to enable effective observability (2025). https://opentelemetry.io/. Accessed 08 Oct 2025

29. React: React hooks. https://react.dev/reference/react/hooks

30. Shahid, M.A., Alam, M.M., Su'ud, M.M.: A systematic parameter analysis of cloud simulation tools in cloud computing environments. Appl. Sci. **13**(15), 8785 (2023)

31. Shahid, M., Alam, M., Su'ud, M.M.: A systematic parameter analysis of cloud simulation tools in cloud computing environments. Appl. Sci. **13**(15), 8785 (2023). https://doi.org/10.3390/app13158785

32. Sheng, J., et al.: VMAgent: a practical virtual machine scheduling platform. In: IJCAI, pp. 5944–5947 (2022)

33. Son, J., Dastjerdi, A.V., Calheiros, R.N., Ji, X., Yoon, Y., Buyya, R.: CloudSimSDN: modeling and simulation of software-defined cloud data centers. In: 2015 15th IEEE/ACM International Symposium on Cluster, Cloud and Grid Computing, pp. 475–484. IEEE (2015)

34. Sonatype, Inc.: Maven central repository. https://central.sonatype.com/. Accessed 08 Oct 2025

35. Sonatype, Inc.: Sonatype. https://www.sonatype.com/. Accessed 08 Oct 2025

36. Syed, H.J., Gani, A., Nasaruddin, F.H., Naveed, A., Ahmed, A.I.A., Khan, M.K.: CloudProcMon: a non-intrusive cloud monitoring framework. IEEE Access **6**, 44591–44606 (2018). https://doi.org/10.1109/ACCESS.2018.2864573

37. Teixeira Sá, T., Calheiros, R.N., Gomes, D.G.: CloudReports: an extensible simulation tool for energy-aware cloud computing environments. In: Mahmood, Z. (ed.) Cloud Computing. CCN, pp. 127–142. Springer, Cham (2014). https://doi.org/10.1007/978-3-319-10530-7_6
38. Tirana, J., Tsigkari, D., Iosifidis, G., Chatzopoulos, D.: Minimization of the training makespan in hybrid federated split learning. IEEE Trans. Mobile Comput. (2025)
39. TypeScript Team: Typescript: Javascript with syntax for types. https://www.typescriptlang.org/. Accessed 08 Oct 2025
40. Vercel Inc.: Vercel: Develop. Preview. Ship. https://vercel.com/. Accessed 08 Oct 2025
41. VoidZero Inc: Vite: The Build Tool for the Web. https://vite.dev/. Accessed 08 Oct 2025
42. Wickremasinghe, B., Calheiros, R.N., Buyya, R.: CloudAnalyst: a cloudsim-based visual modeller for analysing cloud computing environments and applications. In: 2010 24th IEEE International Conference on Advanced Information Networking and Applications, pp. 446–452. IEEE (2010)
43. Zheng, Y.: The accelerator toolkit: a review of profiling and tracing for GPUs and other co-processor. https://eunomia.dev/en/blog/posts/gpu-profile-tools-analysis. Accessed 08 Oct 2025

Policy Agents for Zero-Trust Kubernetes:
A Comprehensive Survey

Sonika Arora[(⊠)] , Prashanth Josyula , Anant Kumar ,
and Gangadharayya Hiremath

Salesforce, San Francisco, USA
`{sonika.arora,prashanth.chaitanya,anantkumar,ghiremath}@salesforce.com`

Abstract. In this survey, we explore how different policy agents can help implement zero-trust security in Kubernetes environments. To make comparisons more concrete, we propose a new metric called the Policy Effectiveness Score (PES), which considers how well each agent aligns with zero-trust principles, its compatibility with cloud platforms, and the operational effort it requires. We take a closer look at four popular tools Open Policy Agent (OPA), Kyverno, Gatekeeper, and Pod Security Admission and identify three key architectural models they follow: Side-car, Admission Controller, and Operator. Each of these comes with its own strengths and limitations. To test our framework, we draw insights from 14 peer-reviewed studies. Our findings suggest that while no single agent covers all the bases, using a phased, multi-agent setup can strike a good balance between strong security, system performance, and manageable complexity.

1 Introduction

Kubernetes has become the dominant container orchestration platform, with 66% of organizations using it in production [1]. This widespread adoption, combined with multi-cloud deployments, creates significant challenges for maintaining consistent security policies. Zero-trust architecture, adopted by 61% of organizations [2], requires continuous verification and policy enforcement regardless of network boundaries.

Policy agents have emerged as the primary mechanism for implementing security controls in Kubernetes. However, the diversity of available agents, each with different architectural approaches and performance characteristics, makes selection challenging. This paper addresses these challenges through a comprehensive survey of policy agents for zero-trust Kubernetes deployments.

Our key contributions include: (1) a novel Policy Effectiveness Score (PES) framework for quantitative evaluation; (2) systematic analysis of three architectural patterns with quantified trade-offs; (3) empirical validation using data from 14 peer-reviewed studies; (4) practical guidelines for policy agent selection; and (5) identification of future research directions.

We address four research questions: How do different policy agents implement zero-trust principles (RQ1)? What architectural patterns do they follow (RQ2)?

D. Garlisi and D. Chatzopoulos (Eds.): ALGOCLOUD 2025, LNCS 16349, pp. 31–42, 2026.
https://doi.org/10.1007/978-3-032-13744-9_3

How can organizations evaluate and select appropriate agents (RQ3)? What are emerging trends in policy orchestration (RQ4)?

Our methodology combines theoretical analysis with empirical validation. We analyzed over 100 sources (2018–2023) and developed the Policy Effectiveness Score:

$$PES = \sum_{i=1}^{n}(w_i \times f_i) \times \frac{1}{1 + T_{overhead}} \times C_{agnostic} \times Z_{trust} \qquad (1)$$

Where w_i represents criterion weight, f_i is normalized feature score, $T_{overhead}$ is policy evaluation overhead (ms), $C_{agnostic}$ is cloud-agnostic compatibility (0-1), and Z_{trust} is zero-trust implementation score (0-1).

2   Background

2.1   Kubernetes Security Architecture

Kubernetes implements security through multiple control points [13]. The API Server serves as the primary enforcement point for admission control, with admission webhooks enabling policy injection. The admission control pipeline consists of mutating webhooks (modify requests) and validating webhooks (accept/reject requests).

Policy enforcement complexity grows exponentially: $C_{total} = O(n \times p \times r \times c)$ where n is nodes, p is pods, r is rules, and c is cloud providers. This complexity necessitates specialized policy agents providing centralized management, dynamic enforcement, and cloud-agnostic operations [3].

2.2   Zero-Trust Principles

Zero-trust in Kubernetes manifests through four key principles that fundamentally reshape security approaches in distributed systems [17].

Identity-based access control requires that every entity, whether users, services, or pods, must have a verifiable identity. Kubernetes implements this through Service Accounts for pods, with each pod receiving a unique token for API authentication. This identity forms the foundation for all authorization decisions, enabling fine-grained access control based on the principle of "never trust, always verify." Policy agents extend this by enabling complex identity-based rules that consider not just the identity itself but also contextual factors such as time of access, source location, and behavioral patterns.

Least privilege access ensures that permissions are minimal and specific to the task at hand. While Role-Based Access Control (RBAC) provides the foundational layer, it operates at a relatively coarse level. Policy agents add granular controls that can enforce restrictions such as "pods in namespace X can only mount secrets with label Y" or "containers can only pull images from approved registries." This granularity is essential for preventing privilege escalation and limiting the blast radius of potential compromises [11].

Continuous verification represents a departure from traditional perimeter-based security where trust, once established, persists. In zero-trust architectures, trust must be continuously validated throughout the lifecycle of a workload [10]. This requires policy agents that go beyond admission-time checks to monitor runtime behavior, detect anomalies, and respond to policy violations in real-time. The dynamic nature of Kubernetes, with pods constantly being created and destroyed, makes this continuous verification both challenging and critical [19].

Microsegmentation creates security boundaries between workloads, implementing the principle of least privilege at the network level. Policy agents enforce these boundaries through network policies that control traffic flow based on pod labels, namespaces, and other metadata [20]. This prevents lateral movement in case of compromise, ensuring that a breach in one component doesn't automatically grant access to others. Advanced implementations include layer 7 policies that inspect application-level protocols and enforce rules based on API endpoints or data sensitivity.

2.3 Related Work

Previous research explored various aspects of policy management. While formal approaches to policy languages have been extensively studied [4], these works often lack empirical validation in production environments. Sultan et al. [11] analyzed container security challenges but focused primarily on threats rather than policy enforcement. Ma et al. [7] analyzed webhook-based admission control focusing on specific attack scenarios. Our work uniquely combines architectural analysis with empirical validation from 14 production deployments, addressing the gap between theoretical policy frameworks and practical multi-cloud implementation.

3 Policy Agent Architecture Patterns

We identify three fundamental architectural patterns for policy agents, each with distinct characteristics and trade-offs:

3.1 Sidecar Pattern

Deploys enforcement logic alongside application containers, providing fine-grained pod-level control. The sidecar intercepts network traffic, file system access, and system calls. This pattern introduces per-pod resource overhead (50–100 MB RAM, 0.1–0.5 CPU cores) but enables continuous validation essential for zero-trust. Performance impact includes 2–5 ms latency for intercepted operations.

Real-world implementations include Istio/Envoy for service mesh policies and Falco for runtime security monitoring. The pattern excels in scenarios requiring deep application visibility but suffers from scalability challenges in large deployments.

3.2   Admission Controller Pattern

Implements cluster-level enforcement during resource admission through webhooks. The API server sends admission review requests to policy agents, which evaluate and return allow/deny decisions. This pattern offers centralized control with minimal runtime impact (1.5–5 ms latency) but is limited to admission-time checks. Can handle 5,000–10,000 requests/second when properly scaled.

Key considerations include webhook high availability (requires multiple replicas), failure policy configuration (Ignore vs Fail), and TLS certificate management for secure communication.

3.3   Operator Pattern

Uses custom controllers for continuous state reconciliation, enabling complex policy handling through watch loops [14]. Operators compare current state with desired state and take corrective actions. Typically consumes 100–300 MB memory and 0.2–0.5 CPU cores. Provides continuous validation but with eventual consistency limitations.

Advanced capabilities include drift detection, auto-remediation, and complex multi-resource policy orchestration. The pattern suits scenarios requiring continuous compliance but introduces complexity in debugging and race condition management [18].

We evaluate pattern effectiveness using:

$$AES = \frac{P_{enforced}}{P_{total}} \times \frac{1}{O_{overhead}} \times F_{flexibility} \times Z_{alignment} \times C_{portability} \quad (2)$$

Analysis yields: Admission Controller (AES = 0.75), Operator (AES = 0.71), Sidecar (AES = 0.68).

4   Survey of Policy Agents

4.1   Open Policy Agent (OPA) Ecosystem

OPA implements a declarative policy model using the Rego language. Core components include Policy Store (versioned management), Data Store (contextual data), and Query Engine (evaluation with caching). According to the OPA documentation [5], policy evaluation for high-performance use cases targets a budget on the order of 1 ms. Our empirical data shows OPA achieves 4.3 ms latency in production deployments with 1000+ nodes (see Table 1).

The ecosystem includes several key components that extend OPA's capabilities for Kubernetes environments. Gatekeeper provides Kubernetes-native integration through Custom Resource Definitions (CRDs), enabling policy management using familiar kubectl commands. It introduces constraint templates that allow organizations to define reusable policy patterns, significantly reducing duplication and improving consistency. The audit functionality continuously scans existing resources for policy violations, providing both real-time enforcement and compliance reporting capabilities essential for regulatory requirements.

OPA-Envoy extends policy enforcement to the service mesh layer, enabling fine-grained authorization decisions for service-to-service communication. This integration allows policies to consider request headers, JWT tokens, and other L7 information, providing context-aware security that goes beyond simple network-level controls. Organizations report that this capability is particularly valuable for implementing API-level rate limiting and preventing data exfiltration.

Conftest serves as a policy testing framework that integrates seamlessly with CI/CD pipelines. It enables developers to validate their configurations against organizational policies before deployment, shifting security left in the development lifecycle. This proactive approach significantly reduces the number of policy violations that reach production environments, with some organizations reporting a 75% reduction in security-related deployment failures.

Performance characteristics: 10,000+ decisions/second throughput, linear memory growth (1 MB per 100 rules), 0.1–0.3 CPU cores under normal load.

Rego provides powerful policy expression capabilities but requires investment in learning its Datalog-inspired syntax. Organizations report 2–4 week ramp-up time for developers to become proficient [15].

4.2 Kyverno

Kyverno uses YAML for policy definitions, aligning with Kubernetes' native syntax. It operates as a dynamic admission controller supporting validation, mutation, generation, and image verification.

```yaml
apiVersion: kyverno.io/v1
kind: ClusterPolicy
metadata:
  name: require-pod-security
spec:
  validationFailureAction: enforce
  background: true
  rules:
    - name: check-security-context
      match:
        any:
        - resources:
            kinds: ["Pod"]
      validate:
        message: "Security context required"
        pattern:
          spec:
            securityContext:
              runAsNonRoot: "true"
              runAsUser: ">1000"
            containers:
            - name: "*"
```

```
                securityContext:
                  allowPrivilegeEscalation: "false"
                  readOnlyRootFilesystem: "true"
                  capabilities:
                    drop: ["ALL"]


  - name: add-default-labels
    match:
      any:
        - resources:
            kinds: ["Pod"]
    mutate:
      patchStrategicMerge:
        metadata:
          labels:
            managed-by: kyverno
            security-policy: enforced
```

Listing 1.1. Kyverno policy example

Performance: 2–4 ms webhook latency, 150–300 MB memory usage, 5,000+ requests/second throughput. Background scanning processes 100–200 resources/second.

4.3 Pod Security Admission

Built-in admission controller implementing three security levels:

– **Privileged**: Unrestricted policies for system workloads
– **Baseline**: Minimal restrictions preventing privilege escalations
– **Restricted**: Maximum security following current best practices

Each level supports enforce, audit, and warn modes for gradual rollout. Configuration is namespace-scoped using labels, enabling flexible security postures across different workload types [12].

4.4 Cloud Provider Solutions

AWS: Integrates OPA with EKS, providing AWS-specific templates, IAM integration, and Security Hub reporting. Pre-built policies cover common AWS scenarios like S3 bucket access and ECR image sources.

Azure: Native AKS enforcement with Azure Policy definitions, compliance mappings (NIST, CIS), and Arc support. Hierarchical policy assignment enables organization-wide governance.

Google: Anthos Policy Controller with hierarchical management, Binary Authorization, and 200+ policy templates. Config Sync enables GitOps-based policy deployment across clusters [16].

5   Empirical Analysis

We synthesized performance data from 14 peer-reviewed studies and technical reports spanning diverse production environments:

Table 1. Performance Data from Literature

Study	Agent	Nodes	Latency	Memory	Throughput
Kitahara et al. [6]	OPA	1000+	4.3 ms	256 MB	8,500/s
Ma et al. [7]	Webhook	500	5 ms	180 MB	5,000/s
Kim & Kim [8]	Quotas	200	2.1 ms	120 MB	3,000/s
Nirmata/CNCF [9]	Kyverno	300+	3.5 ms	200 MB	5,000/s

Key findings: webhook-based controllers add 1.5–5ms latency; large deployments (1000+ nodes) maintain sub-5 ms evaluation; memory scales linearly with policy count; systems handle 10,000 policies with acceptable performance.

Policy evaluation overhead follows: $T_{eval} = \alpha + \beta \log(P_{count}) + \gamma C_{complexity}$ where α is base latency (1–2 ms), β is policy scaling factor (0.5–1.0), and γ is complexity coefficient (0.1–0.5).

Applying our PES framework (Table 2):

Table 2. Policy Effectiveness Scores

Agent	Features	Overhead	Cloud	Zero-Trust	PES
OPA/Gatekeeper	0.85	0.90	0.95	0.90	0.73
Kyverno	0.75	0.92	0.85	0.85	0.71
Pod Security	0.60	0.98	0.95	0.75	0.68
Cloud-specific	0.70	0.93	0.60	0.85	0.62

Scores correlate with production success metrics (Pearson correlation: 0.82, $p < 0.01$), validating the framework's predictive capability.

6   Multi-cloud Considerations

Implementing consistent policies across cloud providers presents significant challenges (Table 3):

Organizations can adopt three strategies:

Abstraction Layer: Use cloud-agnostic agents (OPA, Kyverno) with provider specific data inputs. This maintains policy logic consistency while accommodating provider differences.

Table 3. Cloud Provider Differences

Feature	AWS	Azure	GCP
Identity	IAM Roles	Managed Identity	Service Accounts
Network	VPC/SG	VNet/NSG	VPC/Firewall
Storage	EBS/EFS	Managed Disks	Persistent Disks
Load Balancers	ELB/ALB/NLB	Azure LB	GCP LB
Secrets	Secrets Manager	Key Vault	Secret Manager

Federation: Deploy provider-specific agents but federate policy management through a central control plane. Tools like Anthos Config Management enable this approach.

Translation: Implement policy translation layers that convert abstract policies to provider-specific implementations. Requires sophisticated mapping logic but provides maximum flexibility.

Each approach has trade-offs in complexity, portability, and feature utilization. Most organizations adopt a hybrid approach based on workload requirements.

7   Practical Guidelines

7.1   Selection Framework

See Table 4.

Table 4. Policy Agent Selection Matrix

Scenario	Recommended Agent
Complex multi-cloud	OPA/Gatekeeper
Simple policies	Kyverno
Baseline security	Pod Security
Single cloud	Cloud-specific
Compliance focus	OPA + Cloud-specific
Developer-friendly	Kyverno
High performance	Pod Security

7.2   Phased Deployment Strategy

Phase 1 establishes the security foundation for the first two weeks. Organizations begin by deploying the Pod Security Admission with the baseline profile across all namespaces, starting with warn mode to identify violations without disrupting workloads. This reveals which pods require exemptions for legitimate system-level access. Simultaneously, teams implement RBAC with least-privilege principles, auditing existing permissions, and creating role templates for common personas such as developers, operators, and CI/CD systems. Monitoring infrastructure using Prometheus and Grafana provides visibility into policy decisions and cluster health. A formal exemption process ensures that security exceptions are documented, time-limited, and regularly reviewed.

Phase 2 enhances policy capabilities during weeks three and four. Kyverno deployment begins with simple validation policies for required labels and resource limits, gradually expanding to mutation policies that automatically add security defaults to pods. Integration with CI/CD pipelines through policy-as-code practices ensures that policy violations are caught before deployment. Background scanning identifies existing resources that violate newly introduced policies, enabling gradual remediation. Compliance dashboards provide stakeholders with real-time visibility into the security posture across namespaces and clusters.

Phase 3 implements advanced controls during weeks five and six. Organizations deploy OPA for complex authorization logic that cannot be expressed in simpler policy languages, such as multi-factor authorization rules or context-aware access controls. Runtime enforcement tools like Falco provide detection of anomalous behavior that static policies cannot catch. Integration with cloud-specific features enables leveraging native security services while maintaining portability for core policies. The transition to full enforcement mode occurs gradually, with careful monitoring of metrics and close collaboration with development teams to ensure minimal disruption to legitimate workloads.

7.3   Best Practices

Policy development requires a systematic approach that balances security requirements with operational efficiency. Organizations should begin with audit or dry-run mode for all new policies, allowing teams to understand the impact before enforcement. This approach reveals unexpected violations and provide an opportunity for remediation without disrupting production workloads. Version control for policies using semantic versioning enables rollback capabilities and clear tracking of policy evolution over time.

Comprehensive testing forms the backbone of reliable policy deployment. Unit tests validate individual policy rules, integration tests ensure policies work correctly with real Kubernetes resources, and end-to-end tests verify the complete policy enforcement pipeline. Documentation should capture not just the technical details of policies but also the business justification, expected behavior, and exemption procedures. This documentation proves invaluable during audits and helps new team members understand the security posture.

Operational excellence in policy management requires continuous monitoring and optimization. Webhook latency monitoring with service level objectives such as p95 latency under 10 ms ensures that policy enforcement doesn't impact cluster performance. Alert fatigue can be avoided by carefully tuning alert thresholds and implementing intelligent grouping of related violations. Regular audits of policy effectiveness help identify obsolete rules that add overhead without security value.

Performance optimization becomes critical as policy complexity grows. Enabling result caching can reduce evaluation time by up to 90% for frequently accessed policies. Request coalescing prevents duplicate evaluations for the same resource, particularly important during deployment rollouts. Horizontal pod autoscaling ensures that policy agents can handle traffic spikes without introducing bottlenecks. Organizations should also implement pod disruption budgets to maintain availability during updates and use leader election for high availability in multi-replica deployments.

8   Implementation Case Studies

To further validate our findings, we examined three real-world implementations that demonstrate the practical application of policy agents in production environments.

A major financial services company with over 1000 nodes has implemented OPA with Gatekeeper to meet PCI-DSS compliance requirements. Their implementation journey revealed several critical insights. Initial deployment faced resistance due to Rego's learning curve, which they addressed through intensive training programs and a library of prebuilt policy templates. Performance optimization became crucial at scale, with the team implementing sophisticated caching strategies that reduced policy evaluation time from 8 ms to 4.3 ms at the 95th percentile. The organization achieved 99.9% policy coverage by adopting a gradual rollout strategy, starting with non-production environments and progressively moving to production with careful monitoring at each stage. Key success factors included executive sponsorship, dedicated policy engineering teams, and a comprehensive monitoring infrastructure that provided real-time visibility into policy decisions.

An e-commerce platform with 500 nodes chose Kyverno for its developer-friendly YAML syntax, significantly reducing the barrier to entry for policy creation. The organization reported a 60% reduction in policy development time compared to their previous Rego-based system. Their implementation leveraged Kyverno's mutation capabilities to automatically inject security configurations, eliminating the need for developers to remember complex security requirements. The platform maintained 3.5 ms latency even with 150 active policies by implementing intelligent policy ordering and leveraging Kyverno's built-in caching mechanisms. The team particularly valued Kyverno's generate rules for creating NetworkPolicies automatically when new namespaces were created, ensuring consistent network segmentation without manual intervention.

A healthcare SaaS provider with 300 nodes implemented a hybrid approach using Pod Security Admission for baseline security and cloud-specific agents for advanced features. This strategy allowed them to achieve HIPAA compliance while maintaining operational efficiency. Pod Security Admission provided immediate protection against common security misconfigurations with minimal overhead (2 ms latency), while AWS-specific policies enforced encryption requirements for data at rest and in transit. The organization found that this layered approach provided defense in depth without overwhelming their operations team. They reported that the combination of native Kubernetes security features with cloud-specific enhancements struck the optimal balance between security, performance, and maintainability.

9   Challenges and Future Directions

Current limitations include performance degradation with complex policies (latency increases from 2 ms to 20 ms beyond 1000 policies), policy language fragmentation (Rego vs YAML vs CEL), debugging complexity, and multi-cluster coordination challenges.

Emerging trends shaping the future include:

AI-Enhanced Policy Management: Natural language for policy generation, anomaly detection for unusual violations, and automated remediation suggestions. Early experiments show 85% accuracy for standard compliance requirements.

WebAssembly Integration: Portable policy execution with near-native performance (10–20% overhead), language-agnostic development, and improved cold-start times.

eBPF-Based Enforcement: Kernel-level policy enforcement with negligible overhead ($<0.1\%$ CPU), enabling real-time security without sidecars or proxies.

Future research should address formal verification for policy correctness, cross-platform standardization efforts, edge computing adaptations, and quantum-safe policy frameworks.

10   Conclusion

This survey presented a comprehensive analysis of policy agents for zero-trust Kubernetes deployments. Through the PES framework and the empirical validation of 13 studies, we demonstrated that the selection of policy agents requires careful consideration of architectural patterns, performance characteristics, and organizational requirements.

Key findings include: (1) three architectural patterns with quantified trade-offs, where Admission Controllers offer the best balance for most scenarios; (2) Validated performance showing sub-5 ms latency achievable at scale; (3) No single agent addresses all multi-cloud requirements optimally; (4) A phased multi-agent approach provides the best path to comprehensive enforcement.

As Kubernetes adoption continues to grow, effective policy orchestration becomes increasingly critical. Future developments in AI, WebAssembly, and eBPF promise to address current limitations while enabling new capabilities. Organizations should focus on clear requirements, systematic evaluation using frameworks like PES, and gradual deployment with careful monitoring.

References

1. CNCF: CNCF annual survey 2023, Technical report (2023)
2. Okta: State of Zero Trust Security 2023, Technical report (2023)
3. Rahman, A., et al.: A systematic mapping study of infrastructure as code research. Inf. Softw. Technol. **108**, 65–77 (2019)
4. Margheri, A., Masi, M., Pugliese, R., Tiezzi, F.: A rigorous framework for specification, analysis and enforcement of access control policies. IEEE Trans. Software Eng. **45**(1), 2–33 (2019)
5. Open Policy Agent Contributors: Open Policy Agent: Policy-based control for cloud native environments, Open Source Project Documentation (2023). https://www.openpolicyagent.org/docs/
6. Kitahara, H., et al.: Highly-scalable container integrity monitoring for large-scale Kubernetes cluster. In: 2020 IEEE International Conference on Big Data, pp. 449–454 (2020)
7. Ma, T., et al.: A mutation-enabled proactive defense against service-oriented man-in-the-middle attack in Kubernetes. IEEE Trans. Comput. **72**(7), 1843–1856 (2023)
8. Kubernetes: Resource Quotas. Kubernetes Documentation (2023). https://kubernetes.io/docs/concepts/policy/resource-quotas/
9. Bugwadia, J., Emara, K.: The need for speed: optimizing Kyverno's performance. CNCF Blog. https://www.cncf.io/blog/2024/02/09/the-need-for-speed-optimizing-kyvernos-performance/
10. Pierantoni, G., et al.: Describing and processing topology and quality of service parameters of applications in the cloud. J. Grid Comput. **18**, 761–778 (2020)
11. Sultan, S., Ahmad, I., Dimitriou, T.: Container security: issues, challenges, and the road ahead. IEEE Access **7**, 52976–52996 (2019)
12. Kubernetes: Pod Security Standards. Kubernetes Documentation (2023). https://kubernetes.io/docs/concepts/security/pod-security-standards/
13. Kubernetes: Kubernetes Docs. https://kubernetes.io/docs/
14. Dobies, J., Wood, J.: Kubernetes Operators. O'Reilly Media (2020)
15. Burns, B., Beda, J., Hightower, K., Evenson, L.: Kubernetes: Up and Running, 3rd edn. O'Reilly Media (2022)
16. CoreOS: etcd Documentation. https://etcd.io/docs/
17. Rose, S., Borchert, O., Mitchell, S., Connelly, S.: Zero trust architecture. NIST Special Publication 800-207, National Institute of Standards and Technology, Gaithersburg (2020)
18. Senjab, K., et al.: A survey of Kubernetes scheduling algorithms. J. Cloud Comput. **12**(1), 87 (2023)
19. Bernstein, D.: Containers and cloud: from LXC to Docker to Kubernetes. IEEE Cloud Comput. **7**(3), 81–84 (2020)
20. CNCF: Kubernetes Network Policy Guide. CNCF Technical Report (2021). https://kubernetes.io/docs/concepts/services-networking/network-policies/

Constrained Adaptive Partial Training for Federated Learning on Heterogeneous Clients

Mohan Xu[1]([✉])[iD] and Lena Wiese[1,2][iD]

[1] Fraunhofer Institute for Toxicology and Experimental Medicine,
Hannover, Germany
[2] Institute of Computer Science, Goethe University Frankfurt,
Frankfurt a. M., Germany
`{mohan.xu,lena.wiese}@item.fraunhofer.de`

Abstract. Federated learning is a distributed paradigm that enables collaborative training across multiple clients while preserving data privacy. However, in practice, it often encounters challenges such as heterogeneous client computing capabilities and varying communication conditions. Additionally, differences in user preferences, data acquisition environments, and devices lead to non-identical data distributions and diverse research tasks across clients. To address these heterogeneity challenges, this paper proposes a constrained Federated Learning Partial Training algorithm (cFedPT), motivated by variations in client data distributions. The algorithm dynamically adjusts the participating submodels in each training round and enables clients with heterogeneous resources to engage in federated learning. Experimental results on the ISIC2019 image dataset and the ICBHI audio dataset demonstrate that cFedPT achieves superior performance compared to baseline models.

Keywords: Federated learning · Heterogeneous clients · Deep learning

1 Introduction

To safeguard the security of technological implementations, prevent user privacy leakage, and mitigate the data silo problem [1,2], Federated Learning [3] has emerged as a privacy-preserving learning paradigm. It enables distributed clients to train models on local datasets while acquiring knowledge from other clients, all without directly sharing raw data, under the coordination of a cloud server.

Although federated learning has made significant progress, mainstream approaches typically assume that all clients use the same neural network architecture and have similar data distributions [4,5]. However, in real-world scenarios, this assumption is often difficult to satisfy due to the diversity of client deployment environments. Specifically, clients may have significantly different data distributions, a challenge known as data heterogeneity [6]. Network conditions also vary across clients, leading to limited communication with the cloud server,

D. Garlisi and D. Chatzopoulos (Eds.): ALGOCLOUD 2025, LNCS 16349, pp. 43–57, 2026.
https://doi.org/10.1007/978-3-032-13744-9_4

referred to as communication heterogeneity [7,8]. Additionally, differences in hardware performance and resource constraints result in varying computational capabilities among clients, known as device heterogeneity [9]. These heterogeneity issues collectively present fundamental challenges in federated learning for heterogeneous clients.

To address the challenges of heterogeneous clients and ensure effective model aggregation on the cloud server, this paper investigates a heterogeneous model aggregation method based on partial training. The method extracts sub-models from a larger global model and distributes them to clients for local training. After training, the optimized sub-model parameters are uploaded to the cloud server for aggregation. This approach is designed to accommodate clients with limited computational resources and communication bandwidth [10–12]. Inspired by the sub-model extraction method based on data distribution proposed in [13], we introduce a constrained adaptive partial training algorithm, cFedPT. During neuron selection, cFedPT considers both current activations and historical activation patterns. This helps prevent specific neurons from being over-trained or persistently ignored. To evaluate the effectiveness of cFedPT, we conduct experiments on two types of tasks: image classification and audio classification. The results demonstrate its applicability and performance in heterogeneous client environments.

2   Related Work

2.1   Partially Trainable Neural Networks in Federated Learning

Partially trainable neural networks have been explored in the field of machine learning and are proved as an effective approach to reducing communication and computation costs in federated learning. [14] proposes an iterative parameter freezing method that initially freezes larger parameter blocks and gradually reduces their size if performance degrades, repeating the process to optimize the model configuration for each client. Federated Dropout [15] achieves both the construction of lightweight submodels and a reduction in communication cost by randomly dropping neurons during training.

To address training time imbalances caused by heterogeneous clients with varying computational capacities, network bandwidths, and availability, TimelyFL [16] dynamically adjusts the proportion of the model trained on each client, adaptively allocating workloads to minimize training time discrepancies and enhance overall efficiency. HeteroFL [7] takes a similar perspective by assigning submodels of varying scales to heterogeneous clients, enabling adaptation to diverse resource conditions while maintaining a unified global model architecture. In contrast, AdaptiveFL [17] utilizes width pruning in conjunction with a reinforcement learning-based device selection strategy to allocate submodels of different sizes, thereby improving resource utilization across clients.

2.2   Neuron-Based Model Pruning

Quantifying neuron-level information is crucial for understanding neural network behavior. This methodology has been applied in model interpretability, knowledge distillation, and efficient model deployment, particularly in heterogeneous federated learning environments. This section focuses on neuron-based model pruning, which plays a key role in optimizing neural networks for devices with limited computational resources.

A variety of methods have been proposed to measure neuron importance and guide pruning strategies. [18] quantifies neuron significance by computing the zero activation ratio after ReLU mapping and applies iterative pruning to remove less important neurons. [19] records neuron activations multiple times during training, tracks their frequency as highly active neurons, and determines whether to retain or prune them based on a voting score. Layer-wise relevance propagation [20] optimizes models by decomposing classification decisions into individual neuron contributions and pruning irrelevant neurons during backpropagation. In heterogeneous client environments, [21] allocates sub-models of different sizes based on each client's computing capacity, excluding neurons with low or no activation to reduce computational overhead.

Furthermore, to enhance pruning effectiveness, [22] employs the transfer entropy redundancy criterion to dynamically remove neurons that contribute minimally to information transfer. By preserving mutual information between adjacent layers, it ensures that the pruned model maintains good trainability and predictive performance.

Previous studies have demonstrated that partial training methods can effectively reduce computational and communication overhead among heterogeneous clients in federated learning, while neuron activation-based model pruning methods have also shown promising performance in model compression and efficiency improvement. Inspired by these insights, we propose a constrained adaptive partial training algorithm (cFedPT). Unlike existing methods, cFedPT integrates both short-term and long-term neuron activation patterns through cross-round backtracking and dynamic analysis of neuron activations, effectively avoiding incorrect exclusion or over-training of important neurons.

3   Methodology

3.1   Preliminaries

Consider N heterogeneous clients, each holding a private dataset D_n. Let $D_n = \{(x_i^n, y_i^n)\}_{i=1}^{|D_n|}$, where x_i^n denotes the i-th input sample of the n-th client, and $y_i^n \in \{1, 2, \ldots, C\}$ represents the corresponding class label from C possible classes. The global dataset, composed of all clients' data, is defined as $D = \bigcup_{n=1}^{N} D_n$, with total size $|D| = \sum_{n=1}^{N} |D_n|$. The objective of federated learning is to collaboratively train a global model with parameters θ based on the combined dataset D, by minimizing the following global loss function:

$$\min_{\theta} F(\theta) = \sum_{n=1}^{N} \frac{|D_n|}{|D|} \mathcal{L}_n(\theta) \tag{1}$$

where the local loss function $\mathcal{L}_n(\theta)$ is defined as:

$$\mathcal{L}_n(\theta) = \frac{1}{|D_n|} \sum_{(x_i^n, y_i^n) \in D_n} l(f(x_i^n; \theta), y_i^n) \tag{2}$$

here $f(\cdot; \theta)$ denotes the global model parameterized by θ, and $l(\cdot, \cdot)$ represents cross-entropy loss function measuring the discrepancy between the model predictions and the true labels.

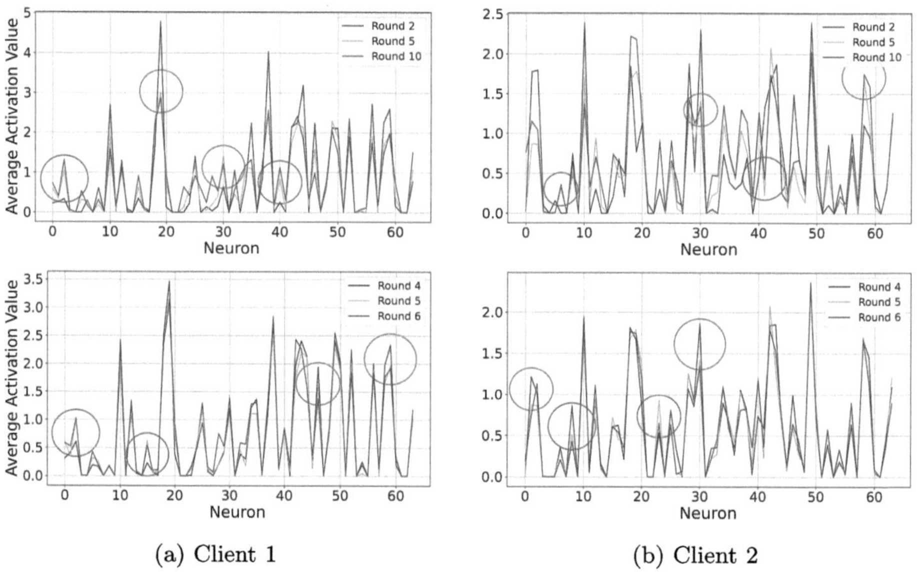

(a) Client 1   (b) Client 2

Fig. 1. Long-term and short-term variations in neuron activation values of the middle layer in a 3-layer MLP on two heterogeneous clients. The first row represents long-term changes, whereas the second row shows short-term changes.

3.2   Motivations

To investigate the evolution of neuron activation values during neural network training, we constructed a Multilayer Perceptron (MLP) on two clients with heterogeneous data distributions. Figure 1 presents trends of activation values in the middle layer. For long-term training analysis, we computed the average activation values of all neurons at the early, middle, and late stages (rounds 2, 5, and 10; first row), excluding round 1 from the analysis due to sharp fluctuations that could compromise trend stability. For short-term analysis, we examined activation values from consecutive rounds (rounds 4, 5, and 6; second row). Red and purple circles denote neurons with relatively high and low activation values, both displaying considerable fluctuations. Based on these results, we identified the following observations:

- Long-term Training: The activation values of neurons in the early stage (round 2, blue line) differ markedly from those in the mid-to-late stages (rounds 5 and 10, orange and green lines). This difference is especially pronounced in neurons marked by the red and purple circles, where activation values in round 2 are substantially higher or lower than in later rounds, while the activation distributions in rounds 5 and 10 are more similar.
- Short-term Training: During consecutive training rounds (rounds 4, 5, and 6), there exist neurons that exhibit significant fluctuations in activation values, regardless of their initial activation levels. For example, neurons marked by red or purple circles show substantial variation across these rounds, even if their activation values are initially high or low.

Based on the above observations, we propose the following propositions to characterize the changes in neuron activation values during training.

Proposition 1. *After t training rounds, the activation value of neuron i, denoted as h_i^t, stabilizes as the neural network parameters θ converge.*

When the objective loss function $L(\theta)$ converges to a local minimum L^*, the neural network satisfies,

$$\lim_{t \to \infty} \|\theta^{t+1} - \theta^t\| = 0. \tag{3}$$

Let θ^* be the optimal parameter set after model convergence. As $t \to \infty$, $\theta^t \to \theta^*$. Since the activation value of neuron i depends on the model parameters θ^t, we define

$$h_i^t = f_i(x; \theta^t) \tag{4}$$

When the model converges to θ^*, it follows that

$$\lim_{t \to \infty} h_i^t = h_i^* = f_i(x; \theta^*) \tag{5}$$

This result indicates that neuron activation values stabilize to a fixed value h_i^* in the later stages of training.

Proposition 2. *The model output probability score p_i is positively correlated with the neuron activation value h_i.*

We use the most common probability normalization function *Softmax*, to demonstrate this property. For a total of C categories, the probability of category i is given by,

$$p_i = \frac{e^{h_i/T}}{\sum_{j=1}^{C} e^{h_j/T}} \tag{6}$$

where $T > 0$ is the temperature parameter, taking the partial derivative of p_i with respect to h_i,

$$\frac{\partial p_i}{\partial h_i} = \frac{p_i}{T}(1 - p_i) > 0. \tag{7}$$

A higher activation value h_i leads to a higher probability score p_i, indicating that variations in neuron activation directly impact the model's predicted output. Therefore, selecting neurons with consistently stable and important activation patterns is beneficial for improving the interpretability of the model's predictions.

Based on the above analysis, the selection of neurons for training should not rely solely on their activation values in the current round, but also take into account their behavior throughout the training process. This helps avoid mistakenly selecting neurons due to a temporary surge in their current activation values.

3.3 cFedPT Design

Motivated by the analysis above, we propose cFedPT, a novel algorithm for federated learning. It dynamically selects a subset of neurons from heterogeneous client models to participate in local training. This design helps prevent over-training and reduces the risk of discarding important neurons.

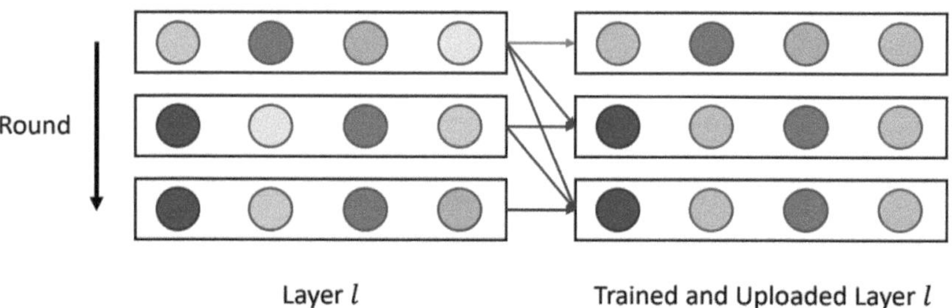

Fig. 2. Neuron selection at layer l in cFedPT with 50% model capacity, based on current and historical rounds. The intensity of green indicates the magnitude of activation values; gray denotes frozen neurons; arrows of different colors represent which historical rounds of neuron activation values considered. (Color figure online)

To illustrate the operational mechanism of cFedPT more intuitively, Fig. 2 depicts the sub-model extraction process for layer l of a specific client model over three consecutive communication rounds. Neurons are selected based on their activation levels on the current local dataset, combined with their performance across up to the three most recent rounds. The left side of Fig. 2 illustrates the activation values of each neuron in layer 1 during the current round using color intensity. For example, when constructing a submodel with 50% of the original model's capacity, the system selects the top 50% of neurons under the dynamic selection rule for local training in that round. The right side of Fig. 2 shows that arrows with different colors indicate which previous rounds' activation values are incorporated into the current selection. The selected neurons participate in local training and upload their parameters to the server, while the remaining neurons are frozen and excluded from forward propagation and gradient updates.

The detailed algorithmic procedures of cFedPT are presented in Algorithm 1. Specifically, before local training begins, client n's model calculates the activation value $h_{n,i}^{(l)}$ of the neuron i in layer l using a subset of the local dataset. Defining the amount of historical tracking rounds as R^h, the variance $Var(h_{n,i}^{(l)})$ of neuron i can be computed based on historical activation values over the most recent R^h communication rounds. If the current round is fewer than R^h, the variance is calculated based on the historical activation values from round 1 to the current round.

Algorithm 1. cFedPT

1: **Input:** local epochs E, clients N, global model $\theta^{(r-1)}$, amount of communication rounds R and historical tracking rounds R^h
2: **Output:** the final global model $\theta^{(r)}$
3: **Server executes:**
4: Initialize θ^1
5: **for** each round $r \in R$ **do**
6:     **for** each client $n \in N$ **in parallel do**
7:         $\theta_n^{(r)} \leftarrow ClientLocalUpdate(n, \theta^{(r-1)})$
8:     **end for**
9:     $\theta^{(r)} \leftarrow Aggregate\left(\{\theta_{n,p}^{(r)}\}_{n=1}^N\right)$ //Aggregate partially overlapping parameters
10: **end for**
11: return $\theta^{(r)}$
12: **function** CLIENTLOCALUPDATE($n, \theta^{(r-1)}$)
13:     The activation value and variance of the i-th neuron in the l-th layer are: $h_{n,i}^{(l)}, Var(h_{n,i}^{(l)})$ which satisfy $Var(h_{n,i}^{(l)}) = \frac{1}{R^h} \sum_{r'=r-R^h+1}^{r} (h_{n,i}^{(l,r')} - \bar{h}_{n,i}^{(l)})^2$
14:     Based on the neuron activation value $h_{n,i}^{(l)}$, variance $Var'(h_{n,i}^{(l)})$, and coefficient k, compute the neuron sampling probability $p_{n,i}^{(l)}$
15:     Partial training parameters according to sampling ratio:
16:     $\theta_{n,p}^{(r)} = \bigcup_{l=1}^{L} \left\{\theta_{n,i}^{(l)} \mid i \in l, i \sim p_{n,i}^{(l)}\right\}$ //Neuron selection rule
17:     **for** each epoch $e \in E$ **do**
18:         $\theta_{n,p}^{(r)} \leftarrow \theta_{n,p}^{(r)} - \eta \nabla \mathcal{L}_n^{(r)}$
19:     **end for**
20:     return partial training parameters $\theta_{n,p}^{(r)}$
21: **end function**

To balance the influence of both the mean activation and its variance over historical rounds on the sampling probability of neurons, we introduce a weighting coefficient k. The sampling probability p of neuron i in layer l on client n is computed as: $p_{n,i}^{(l)} = h_{n,i}^{(l)} + k \cdot Var(h_{n,i}^{(l)})$.

During the r-th communication round, for each training layer $l \in L$ with $|l|$ neurons, given a sample ratio c, the number of neurons to be trained is $l_{select} = \lceil |l| \cdot c \rceil$. These neurons are sampled based on the probability distribution defined above, forming the local parameter set $\theta_{n,p}^{(r)}$ for training at client n. Subsequently, the client performs gradient descent updates on the selected parameters using its local dataset. After training, the updated parameters $\theta_{n,p}^{(r)}$, together with their position indices, are uploaded to the server.

On the server side, the uploaded partial model parameters from clients are aggregated to update the global model. Based on the position indices of the parameters received from each client, the server tracks how many clients have updated each parameter in the current communication round. The contribution of each client to the aggregation is weighted according to the size of its local dataset. Using this information, the server computes the aggregated value for each parameter. Once aggregation is completed, the updated global model parameters are broadcast to all clients to be used as the initialization for the next round of local training.

3.4   Theoretical Analysis

According to the findings in [13], in federated learning, the convergence of algorithms that extract sub-models from a global model depends on the mathematical expectation of the activation error between the sub-model and the full model at the neuron level. To improve the convergence of the global model, it is essential to reduce such activation errors.

To further investigate the factors influencing this activation error, we consider the activation discrepancy at the l-th layer of the n-th client as an example. Following the notation in Algorithm 1, the mathematical expectation of the activation error over the selected neurons in this layer can be expressed as: $\mathbb{E} \sum_{i \in n_{\text{select}}} \|\epsilon_i\|^2$.

The activation error ϵ_i can be decomposed as,

$$\epsilon_i = h_{i,p} - h_i = \left(h_{i,p} - \bar{h}_i \right) + \left(\bar{h}_i - h_i \right) \tag{8}$$

where $h_{i,p}$ and h_i represent the activation values of neuron i in the sub-model and the global model, respectively. $\bar{h}_i$ denotes the historical average activation of neuron i over previous communication rounds under the global model.

Expanding the squared norm of the error,

$$\|\epsilon_i\|^2 = \left\| h_{i,p} - \bar{h}_i \right\|^2 + \left\| \bar{h}_i - h_i \right\|^2 + 2 \left\langle h_{i,p} - \bar{h}_i, \ \bar{h}_i - h_i \right\rangle \tag{9}$$

Taking the mathematical expectation on both sides, and noting that the client's local dataset is fixed while the global model activation h_i is a deterministic output given the current global model and input, we treat the second term $\left\| \bar{h}_i - h_i \right\|^2$ as constant and do not take its expectation. The mathematical expectation of the first term can be written as:

$$\mathbb{E} \left\| h_{i,p} - \bar{h}_i \right\|^2 = \text{Var}(h_{i,p}) \tag{10}$$

For the cross term, we apply the Cauchy–Schwarz and Young's inequalities. For any $\eta > 0$,

$$2\mathbb{E}\left\langle h_{i,p} - \bar{h}_i,\ \bar{h}_i - h_i \right\rangle \leq \eta \cdot \mathrm{Var}(h_{i,p}) + \frac{1}{\eta}\left\|\bar{h}_i - h_i\right\|^2 \tag{11}$$

Combining the results above, the mathematical expectation of the activation error is bounded as

$$\mathbb{E}\sum_{i \in n_{\text{select}}}\|\epsilon_i\|^2 \leq \sum_{i \in n_{\text{select}}}\left[(1+\eta)\cdot\mathrm{Var}(h_i^{(p)}) + \left(1 + \frac{1}{\eta}\right)\cdot\left\|\bar{h}_i - h_i\right\|^2\right] \tag{12}$$

Inequality 12 suggests that to reduce the activation error ϵ_i, the selected neurons for the sub-model should exhibit low variance across rounds and have current activation values close to their historical averages.

4   Experiments

4.1   Experimental Settings

We evaluated the performance of cFedPT in a heterogeneous client environment through experiments on both image and audio datasets. Each experiment was repeated using three different random seed settings. To better reflect data heterogeneity in federated learning, the datasets were partitioned non-overlappingly across clients.

Image Classification. The image classification task is conducted on the ISIC 2019 dermoscopic image dataset, which contains 25,331 images across eight skin lesion categories: melanocytic nevus (12,875), actinic keratosis (867), vascular lesion (253), benign keratosis (2,624), dermatofibroma (239), melanoma (4,522), squamous cell carcinoma (628), and basal cell carcinoma (3,323) [23–25]. The dataset was partitioned by category into four clients: client 1 is assigned melanoma and melanocytic nevus; client 2 is assigned basal cell carcinoma and squamous cell carcinoma; client 3 is assigned actinic keratosis and benign keratosis; client 4 is assigned dermatofibroma and vascular lesion.

All images are resized to 224×224 and processed in batches of 32 using ResNet18 initialized with ImageNet pre-trained weights. Local training uses the Adam optimizer with a learning rate of 0.0003 for 3 epochs per communication round. A total of 10 communication rounds are performed.

Audio Classification. A publicly available respiratory sound dataset, ICBHI [26], was used for the audio classification task. The dataset comprises 6898 respiratory cycles collected from 126 subjects, categorized into four classes: normal (3642), crackle (1864), wheeze (886), and both (506). The dataset is partitioned into two clients by class: client 1 was assigned normal and both, while client 2 received crackle and wheeze. Each audio sample was resampled to 16 kHz and fed into the Wavegram-Logmel-CNN [27] with a batch size of 32. Local training employed the Adam optimizer with a learning rate of 0.0003, running 3 epochs per round over 15 rounds of federated communication.

Due to the significant class imbalance in the datasets, we adopt the widely used F1-weighted score to evaluate model performance on each client, as it better reflects model effectiveness under imbalanced conditions. For each client, the local dataset is divided into 70% for training, 10% for validation, and 20% for testing. To comprehensively assess the overall performance, we report the average results across all clients as an aggregated performance metric.

4.2 Performance Comparison Across Internal Parameters

Since this work focuses on the performance of heterogeneous clients in the sub-model extraction scenario, the training of full models on the client side is not considered. We define the model capacity ratios $c \in (0, 1]$ as the fraction of neurons in each layer that participate in training. For the experiments, ResNet18 was evaluated under three model capacity ratios (c): $\frac{1}{4}, \frac{1}{2}, \frac{3}{4}$, while Wavegram-Logmel-CNN was assessed using a $\frac{3}{4}$ capacity configuration. For historical round information, two settings are evaluated: the most recent 50% and 100% of neuron activation values, including the current round. The weighted ratio between the mean and variance of activation values is further examined. Specifically, the ISIC2019 dataset uses ratios of 1:0, 1:0.25, 1:0.5, 1:2, and 1:4, while the ICBHI dataset uses 1:0, 1:0.1, 1:0.2, 1:0.3, and 1:0.4. Based on the internal parameter configurations of cFedPT, Fig. 3 presents the average F1-weighted scores of each client model on the ISIC2019 and ICBHI test sets.

We use the setting with equal model capacity and without incorporating the fluctuation information of neuron activation values across historical training rounds ($k = 0$) as the baseline model. Experimental results indicate that introducing such fluctuation information, along with a properly designed weighting strategy, consistently improves the F1-weighted scores across all model capacities compared to the baseline. Specifically, for model capacities of $1/4$, $1/2$, and $3/4$, the F1-weighted scores on the ISIC2019 dataset increase by up to 1.43%, 2.05%, and 1.49%, respectively; on the ICBHI dataset, the maximum improvement reaches 1.02%.

On the ISIC2019 dataset, the F1-weighted score shows a consistent improvement as the ResNet18 model capacity increases. This observation suggests that in scenarios with large-scale data and high task complexity, appropriately increasing model capacity can enhance the model's representational ability. However, it is important to note that such increases must be carefully balanced against the client's computational overhead and the risk of model overfitting.

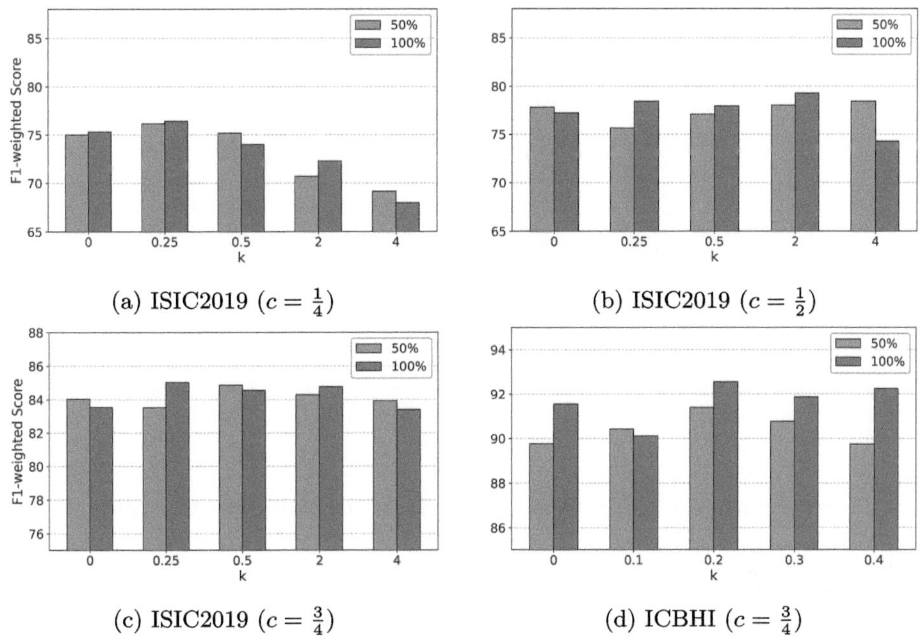

Fig. 3. F1-weighted score under varying mean-to-variance ratios (k) across different model capacity ratios (c) and historical data proportions (50%, 100%)

4.3   Impact of Effective Parameter Ratios on Training and Communication Costs

Based on the above experimental results, cFedPT effectively alleviates the collaboration challenges in federated learning caused by client heterogeneity by training a subset of the model. This section further analyzes the impact of varying the proportion of trainable parameters on communication overhead and model performance using the ResNet18 architecture. Communication cost is defined as the total bytes transferred per client per round, computed as the sum of uplink and downlink payloads and including the transmitted model parameters and metadata (Fig. 4).

As the percentage of parameters involved in training increases from 25% to 100%, the communication cost rises from 55.97 MB to 89.61 MB, while the average F1-weighted score across clients improves from 76.41% to 87.25%. These results indicate that reducing the proportion of trainable parameters can significantly lower communication costs, though it may result in reduced model performance. Therefore, in practical deployments, clients should balance training cost and model accuracy by selecting an appropriate parameter participation ratio based on their computational resources and performance requirements.

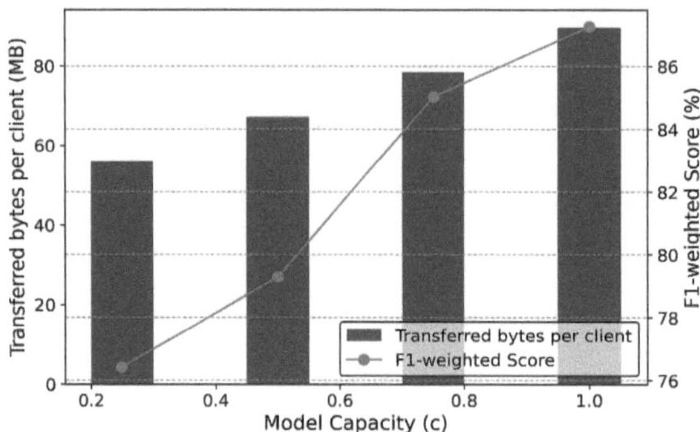

Fig. 4. Communication time, model complexity, and F1-weighted scores under varying effective parameter ratios

4.4   Performance Comparison with State-of-the-Art Methods

To better compare the performance of sub-models extracted by different methods under the same model capacity, we selected four baseline methods: Federated Dropout, FedPrune, HeteroFL, and FedDSE. All these baselines control the sub-model size by selecting channels at each layer, ensuring that the number of trainable parameters remains consistent across methods under the same model capacity.

Table 1. The F1-weighted scores of cFedPT and other state-of-the-art methods.

Method	Homogeneous		Heterogeneous	
	ISIC2019	ICBHI	ISIC2019	ICBHI
Federated Dropout	80.84 ± 0.30	89.58±0.37	70.81 ± 2.71	92.74±1.03
FedPrune	76.60 ± 0.85	90.22±1.07	69.05 ± 1.38	92.52±1.11
HeteroFL	81.28 ± 0.27	91.96±0.29	74.37 ± 1.46	**94.37±0.30**
FedDSE	82.64 ± 0.33	92.03±0.39	74.82 ± 0.91	93.29±0.33
cFedPT	**85.02 ± 0.91**	**92.56±0.47**	**76.13 ± 0.67**	93.98±0.48

Table 1 compares the client-averaged F1-weighted scores of our proposed algorithm, cFedPT, with four baseline methods under both homogeneous and heterogeneous model capacity settings. Under the same model capacity ratio ($c = \frac{3}{4}$), cFedPT achieves performance improvements of 2.38% and 0.53% on the ISIC2019 and ICBHI datasets, respectively. Under heterogeneous capacities ($c=\frac{3}{4}, \frac{1}{2}, \frac{1}{2}, \frac{1}{4}$), cFedPT yields a 1.31% improvement on ISIC2019. Furthermore, in another heterogeneous configuration ($c = \frac{3}{4}, \frac{9}{10}$), cFedPT outperforms all baselines except HeteroFL. These results suggest that submodel selection based on neuron activation values from previous training rounds not only theoretically reduces the expected upper bound of activation error, but also empirically enhances submodel convergence performance.

5   Conclusion

This paper proposes cFedPT, a partial training algorithm for federated learning based on submodel extraction. By analyzing neuron activations across clients during different training rounds, cFedPT enables dynamic submodel extraction, thereby facilitating effective aggregation of important neurons on the server side. Compared with several baseline partial training algorithms, client models using cFedPT not only adapt more flexibly to task differences among clients but also achieve improved performance under varying model capacities.

Acknowledgments. This project has been partially funded by the BMBF and the European Union (NextGenerationEU) under project number 16KISA001K (PrivacyUmbrella).

References

1. Mammen, P.M.: Federated learning: Opportunities and challenges. arXiv preprint arXiv:2101.05428 (2021)
2. Wen, J., Zhang, Z., Lan, Y., Cui, Z., Cai, J., Zhang, W.: A survey on federated learning: challenges and applications. Int. J. Mach. Learn. Cybern. **14**(2), 513–535 (2023)
3. McMahan, B., Moore, E., Ramage, D., Hampson, S., y Arcas, B.A.: Communication-efficient learning of deep networks from decentralized data. In: Artificial Intelligence and Statistics, pp. 1273–1282. PMLR (2017)
4. Ye, M., Fang, X., Du, B., Yuen, P.C., Tao, D.: Heterogeneous federated learning: State-of-the-art and research challenges. ACM Comput. Surv. **56**(3), 1–44 (2023)
5. Fang, X., Ye, M.: Robust federated learning with noisy and heterogeneous clients. In: Proceedings of the IEEE/CVF Conference on Computer Vision and Pattern Recognition, pp. 10072–10081 (2022)
6. Mendieta, M., Yang, T., Wang, P., Lee, M., Ding, Z., Chen, C.: Local learning matters: rethinking data heterogeneity in federated learning. In: Proceedings of the IEEE/CVF Conference on Computer Vision and Pattern Recognition, pp. 8397–8406 (2022)
7. Diao, E., Ding, J., Tarokh, V.: Heterofl: Computation and communication efficient federated learning for heterogeneous clients. arXiv preprint arXiv:2010.01264 (2020)
8. Pfeiffer, K., Rapp, M., Khalili, R., Henkel, J.: Federated learning for computationally constrained heterogeneous devices: a survey. ACM Comput. Surv. **55**(14s), 1–27 (2023)
9. Pei, J., Liu, W., Li, J., Wang, L., Liu, C.: A review of federated learning methods in heterogeneous scenarios. IEEE Trans. Consumer Electr. (2024)

10. Alam, S., Liu, L., Yan, M., Zhang, M.: Fedrolex: model-heterogeneous federated learning with rolling sub-model extraction. Adv. Neural. Inf. Process. Syst. **35**, 29677–29690 (2022)
11. Ilhan, F., Su, G., Liu, L.: Scalefl: resource-adaptive federated learning with heterogeneous clients. In: Proceedings of the IEEE/CVF Conference on Computer Vision and Pattern Recognition, pp. 24532–24541 (2023)
12. Jiang, Z., Zhang, Z., Zhao, Y.: Efficient federated learning mechanism based on layer-wise model pruning. In: 2024 IEEE International Symposium on Parallel and Distributed Processing with Applications (ISPA), pp. 476–483. IEEE (2024)
13. Wang, H., et al.: Feddse: distribution-aware sub-model extraction for federated learning over resource-constrained devices. In: Proceedings of the ACM Web Conference 2024, pp. 2902–2913 (2024)
14. Sidahmed, H., Xu, Z., Garg, A., Cao, Y., Chen, M.: Efficient and private federated learning with partially trainable networks. arXiv preprint arXiv:2110.03450 (2021)
15. Caldas, S., Konečny, J., McMahan, H.B., Talwalkar, A.: Expanding the reach of federated learning by reducing client resource requirements. arXiv preprint arXiv:1812.07210 (2018)
16. Zhang, T., Gao, L., Lee, S., Zhang, M., Avestimehr, S.: Timelyfl: heterogeneity-aware asynchronous federated learning with adaptive partial training. In: Proceedings of the IEEE/CVF Conference on Computer Vision and Pattern Recognition, pp. 5064–5073 (2023)
17. Jia, C., et al.: Adaptivefl: Adaptive heterogeneous federated learning for resource-constrained aiot systems. In: Proceedings of the 61st ACM/ieee Design Automation Conference, pp. 1–6 (2024)
18. Hu, H., Peng, R., Tai, Y.W., Tang, C.K.: Network trimming: A data-driven neuron pruning approach towards efficient deep architectures. arXiv preprint arXiv:1607.03250 (2016)
19. Alqahtani, A., Xie, X., Essa, E., Jones, M.W.: Neuron-based network pruning based on majority voting. In: 2020 25th International Conference on Pattern Recognition (ICPR), pp. 3090–3097. IEEE (2021)
20. Yeom, S.K., et al.: Pruning by explaining: a novel criterion for deep neural network pruning. Pattern Recogn. **115**, 107899 (2021)
21. Munir, M.T., Saeed, M.M., Ali, M., Qazi, Z.A., Qazi, I.A.: Fedprune: towards inclusive federated learning. arxiv preprint arxiv:2110.14205 (2021)
22. Westphal, C., Hailes, S., Musolesi, M.: Mutual information preserving neural network pruning. arXiv preprint arXiv:2411.00147 (2024)
23. Tschandl, P., Rosendahl, C., Kittler, H.: The ham10000 dataset, a large collection of multi-source dermatoscopic images of common pigmented skin lesions. Scientific Data **5**(1), 1–9 (2018)
24. Codella, N.C., et al.: Skin lesion analysis toward melanoma detection: a challenge at the 2017 international symposium on biomedical imaging (isbi), hosted by the international skin imaging collaboration (isic). In: 2018 IEEE 15th international symposium on biomedical imaging (ISBI 2018), pp. 168–172. IEEE (2018)
25. Hernández-Pérez, C., et al.: Bcn20000: Dermoscopic lesions in the wild. Scientific data **11**(1), 641 (2024)

26. Rocha, B., et al.: A respiratory sound database for the development of automated classification. In: Precision Medicine Powered by pHealth and Connected Health: ICBHI 2017, Thessaloniki, Greece, 18-21 November 2017, pp. 33–37. Springer (2018). https://doi.org/10.1007/978-981-10-7419-6_6
27. Kong, Q., Cao, Y., Iqbal, T., Wang, Y., Wang, W., Plumbley, M.D.: Panns: large-scale pretrained audio neural networks for audio pattern recognition. IEEE/ACM Trans. Audio, Speech Lang. Process. **28**, 2880–2894 (2020)

Split Learning Based GAN Training
for Non-IID Federated Learning

Joana Tirana[1]([✉]) [ID], Andreas Chouliaras[1] [ID], Theodoros Aslanidis[1] [ID],
John Byabazaire[1] [ID], Spyridon Mastorakis[2], and Dimitris Chatzopoulos[1] [ID]

[1] University College Dublin, Dublin, Ireland
{joana.tirana,andreas.chouliaras,theodoros.aslanidis}@ucdconnect.ie,
{john.byabazaire,dimitris.chatzopoulos}@ucd.ie
[2] Microsoft, Redmond, USA
smastorakis@microsoft.com

Abstract. One crucial issue in Federated Learning (FL) is the fact that
the participating devices, i.e., the *data owners*, are expected to collect
non-Independent-and-Identically-Distributed (non-IID) data. This dete-
riorates training performance, i.e., delaying training or not reaching convergence. Consequently, additional methods, such as data augmentation,
are applied to address this problem. In fact, producing synthetic data
using GAN models has been proven to be an effective method against
non-IID FL. However, the data owners need to participate in an additional FL training to train GANs in a privacy-preserving manner. Yet,
this is not expected to be always feasible due to data owners' resource
limitations. In this position paper, we identify the issues that occur
when training GANs with FL for data augmentation, and propose a
lightweight alternative that utilizes Split Learning (SL) to offload the
computational load into a *compute node*. Further, we highlight the gap
of cloud-based FL-SL integration and propose a microservice architecture based on existing tools that could significantly enhance the FL-SL
deployment and orchestration, while balancing the energy and the financial cost.

Keywords: Federated Learning · Split Learning · Edge Computing

1 Introduction

Federated Learning (FL) [1,2] is a widely used, distributed Machine Learning (ML) paradigm that has been proposed for training ML models, usually
Neural Networks (NN), in a distributed manner. In detail, the idea of FL is
that several small devices (e.g., IoT, mobile devices, etc.), characterized as *data
owners*, collaborate to train one global ML model without sharing their data.
This is realized by allowing all data owners, in parallel, to train *on-device* the
model using their local data. Their results are synchronized at the end of each

J. Tirana, A. Chouliaras, T. Aslanidis, and J. Byabazaire—Equal contribution.

D. Garlisi and D. Chatzopoulos (Eds.): ALGOCLOUD 2025, LNCS 16349, pp. 58–72, 2026.
https://doi.org/10.1007/978-3-032-13744-9_5

training round by applying an aggregation algorithm, like `FedAvg()` [1]. FL has demonstrated effectiveness [2], attracting growing research interest and numerous publications. However, one of the main challenges in FL is data heterogeneity, a direct consequence of its distributed nature. Since data owners operate independently, their locally stored data is often non-Independent-and-Identically-Distributed (non-IID), which leads to a degraded training performance – lower model accuracy and requiring substantially more training rounds, with convergence sometimes remaining unattained [3].

One emerging solution to the non-IID distribution of data owners' datasets is *data augmentation* using synthetic data. This synthetic data can be generated via typical data augmentation techniques, such as mix-up, or an even more effective approach is to train Generative Adversarial Networks (GANs) [4–8]. In practice, the idea is to train GANs using samples from multiple data owners, which results in a generator that produces synthetic data that follows the distribution of the merged data from all data owners. The server can use this synthetic data as a warm-up dataset [4,6] or by the data owners to augment their dataset [8,9] locally. A natural question is, *how is the GAN trained without violating the data owners' privacy?* This question is answered by [4], which proposes a solution for training GANs using FL. Nevertheless, this comes at a cost: substantial computing capacity is required. In detail, the computing cost for training large and complex NN models cannot always be supported by all data owners [10]. To this end, Split Learning (SL) [11–16] has been proposed, which significantly drops the computing requirements at the data owners. This is achieved by vertically splitting the model into one or multiple parts and offloading the most computationally intensive ones to more powerful *compute nodes*. This approach enables resource-constrained devices with limited computing and memory resources to participate in training while preserving their privacy; data owners only share intermediate activations and not their raw data. *Therefore, in this position paper, we explore how SL can be leveraged within an FL system to enable GAN-based data augmentation.*

Furthermore, we have noticed that in the existing literature, there is no discussion regarding the deployment and implementation of frameworks that can support both SL and FL training with on-demand resources, i.e., the system should be able to dynamically scale the number of compute nodes according to the system's demands. We believe that a cloud-based implementation following the architecture of microservices can fully support the demands of a system that uses both FL and SL. Such architectures can provide many benefits while considering the energy and financial costs. *Hence, we present a microservices-based architecture that meets the aforementioned goals while utilizing well-known and already established tools.*

In summary, this position paper has the following contributions:

(i) Proposes a new system design to train Federated GANs using SL.

(ii) Presents a cloud-based architecture by utilizing existing microservice tools for supporting the simultaneous use of scalable SL and FL training.

(iii) Contains a thorough discussion of further open research questions that determine a promising future work.

2   Related Work

2.1   Non-IID in Federated Learning

Data heterogeneity introduces substantial difficulties in training, manifesting in issues such as model bias, slower convergence rates, and diminished accuracy [17]. In response to this challenge, a range of aggregation techniques have been proposed, including FedProx [18], SCAFFOLD [19], and FedNova [20]. While these approaches offer promising results under certain conditions, they tend to struggle when faced with extreme non-IID scenarios. A comprehensive evaluation [3] reveals that no single aggregation method consistently outperforms the others across all situations. Consequently, a universally robust aggregation-based solution capable of effectively handling the full spectrum of non-IID data in FL remains to be identified. A promising approach to mitigate the challenges posed by non-IID data in FL is *data sharing*, introduced in [21]. In this approach, data owners send a small subset of their data to the central server, which then constructs a globally shared dataset that approximates an IID distribution. Following each training round, after aggregating the local updates, the server further trains the global model using this shared dataset before redistributing the updated model to the data owners. Evaluations of this technique [21–23] show notable improvements in model accuracy, with gains of up to 30%. However, while effective, this method undermines one of the foundational principles of FL—namely, the privacy of data owners' information. Sharing data, even in small amounts, compromises the local data privacy that FL is designed to preserve. An alternative approach involves utilizing publicly available IID datasets that are large enough to meet the training needs of non-IID FL systems. Yet, such datasets cannot always be assumed to be available.

Alternatively, data augmentation can be employed in FL to construct a global IID dataset for use in data sharing [24,25]. Rather than sharing raw data, data owners utilize various augmentation methods to generate synthetic datasets. A related development is PP-FedGAN [4], a FL framework designed to train Differentially Private (DP) GANs. This approach effectively combines data sharing, data augmentation, and DP GANs to mitigate the challenges posed by non-IID data in FL. Several studies [5–7] have demonstrated the effectiveness of this strategy, where data owners collaboratively train GAN generators, after which the server employs the trained generator to produce a global IID dataset. Conversely, [8,9] propose an alternative approach, wherein data owners use local generators to modify their datasets independently. Even though GAN-generated synthetic data offers notable benefits, it comes with a trade-off: federated GAN training requires substantial computational and networking resources. This demand effectively restricts participation to data owners with sufficiently capable devices. Consequently, a significant research gap exists in developing scalable federated GAN training solutions. In this position paper, we seek to address this gap by exploring a potential solution based on SL.

2.2 Cloud-Based Federated and Split Learning

The implementation of FL-SL systems in a cloud-based scheme can bring many opportunities. First of all, since many entities are involved in the system, the management of energy consumption should be thoroughly considered. In fact, several studies highlight the significant energy consumption involved in training large deep NNs, particularly GANs [26]. For instance, the cost analysis in [26] illustrates that training large language models on new datasets can incur prohibitively high costs. To address these challenges, [27] introduced GANPU, an energy-efficient processor for on-device GAN training, offering superior energy efficiency compared to previous methods. Another example is [28], which focuses on domain-specific optimization of GANs. However, on-device solutions may not always be applicable and could result in reduced precision. Further, for certain IoT devices, the energy consumption for communication can be lower than for computation operations [29]. Therefore, we argue that SL (which is mainly based on communication) offers a promising "in-the-middle" solution, reducing on-device energy consumption while maintaining convergence guarantees. However, although in SL the computing burden is offloaded to the server side, the energy consumption and utilization of the compute nodes should still be considered. Practically, as the number of data owners grows, the number of compute nodes should increase proportionally [29]. Yet, *there has been little research addressing dynamic and smooth scale-up/scale-down mechanisms for compute nodes.* On the other hand, the seamless scaling of resources based on demand is one of the attributes of the cloud-based system. Hence, FL-SL frameworks that follow a cloud-based implementation could easily manage these scaling demands.

Further, several frameworks support FL-based training, but there has been limited work addressing scenarios where offloading is essential and SL-based training is required. Examples of open-source FL frameworks include Flower[1], FATE[2], and PySyft [30], which, when combined with PyGrid [31], offer private and secure data science applications. While these frameworks provide useful APIs for FL applications, they are not ML-as-a-Service (MLaaS) tools, as they do not extensively address software challenges or provide cloud-based implementations. In contrast, the only MLaaS framework supporting SL-based training is [10], but it lacks dynamic scale-in/out capabilities. Additionally, structured software architecture designs for FL and SL systems have been largely overlooked [32]. On the other hand, cloud providers such as Google Cloud[3] and AWS[4] have discussed the use of FL with services like SageMaker Pipelines and IoT solutions. *In light of this, we believe that a fully cloud-based deployment, leveraging a microservice design, can effectively address the energy and deployment challenges in FL-SL.*

---

[1] https://flower.dev/.

[2] https://fate.fedai.org.

[3] https://cloud.google.com/architecture/federated-learning-google-cloud.

[4] https://aws.amazon.com/sagemaker-ai/pipelines/.

3 Using SL to Train GANs

Figure 1 illustrates how the training of GANs can be implemented using an SL framework. At first glance, our approach differs from existing methods discussed in Sect. 2.1. In the following, we present the design and workflow of the proposed method.

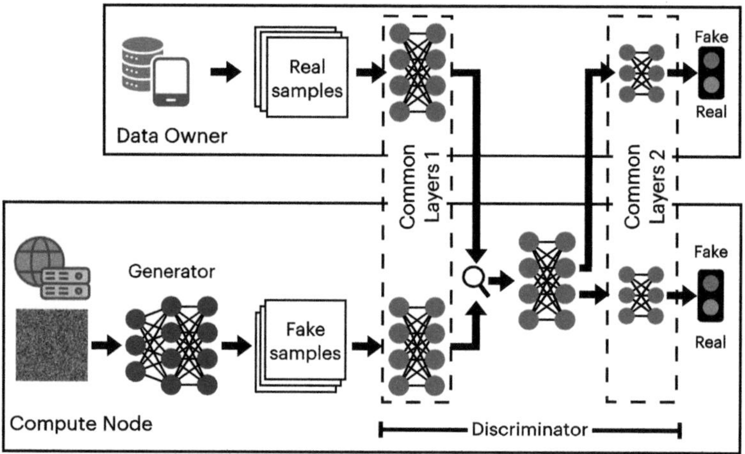

Fig. 1. Training generator using SL.

3.1 Design

We propose offloading the entire burden of training the GAN generator to the compute node. Unlike some prior works, including [8,9], our method enables data owners to collaboratively train a single global generator, which is updated using data from all participants. This update occurs implicitly through adversarial learning. Conversely, the discriminator is trained using an SL approach, where part of its computation is offloaded to the compute node. This choice stems from privacy concerns: while the generator only handles fake data, which does not contain privacy-sensitive information, the discriminator processes both real and fake data. Consequently, it is crucial to keep parts of the discriminator on the data owner's device to maintain privacy. In particular, we adopt the USplit setup [11], which ensures that the most privacy-sensitive layers (e.g., the input and output layers) remain exclusively managed by the data owners.

A critical aspect of GAN training is that the generator's output must be passed into the discriminator, potentially increasing communication costs due to the data owner's control over the discriminator's input and output layers. To mitigate this, we introduce the concept of "common layers". This allows the data owners and the compute node to update the discriminator simultaneously.

In this configuration, data owners update the discriminator with real samples from their local datasets, while the compute node updates it using the generator's output (see the workflow in Fig. 1). A natural question is *how should the common layers be handled?* A straightforward approach might involve using an averaging algorithm, such as `Fedavg()` [1], similar to what is done in Parallel SL [10]. We discuss this and other considerations in Sect. 5.

3.2   Workflow

Figure 2 presents the workflow of the SL-based GAN training. Particularly, the training contains three key phases: *(i)* the GAN training phase, *(ii)* the fine-tuning phase, and *(iii)* the main training phase of the model.

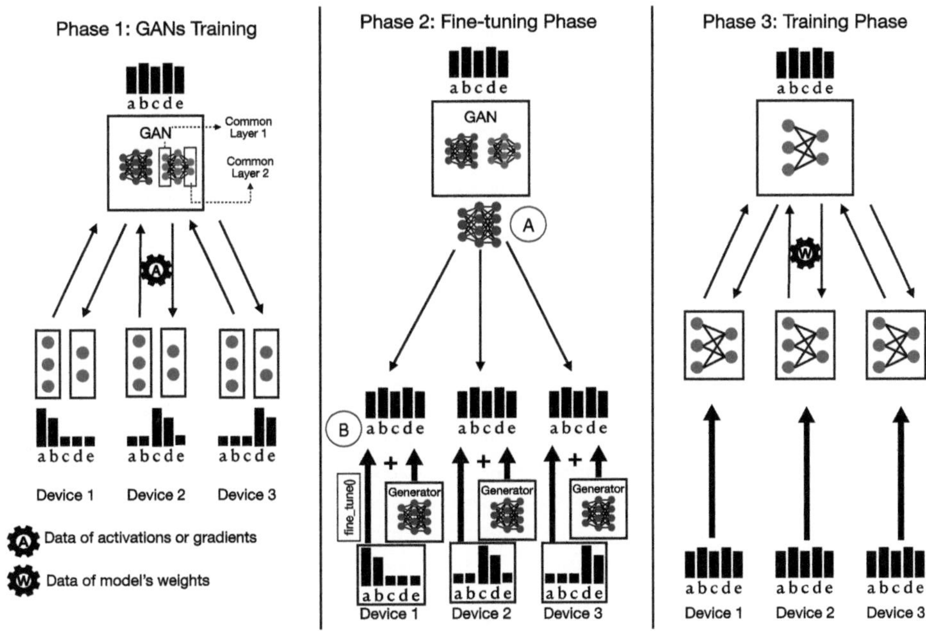

Fig. 2. Steps of the proposed training protocol. The blue model parts correspond to the Discriminator part of the GAN, the dark red to the Generator, whereas the green model parts belong to the model of the main training task. (Color figure online)

In the GAN training phase, we adhere to the principles described in Sect. 3.1. Once the generator is sufficiently trained, the fine-tuning phase begins. In this phase, the compute node distributes the final version of the generator to all data owners (step A of phase 2 in Fig. 2). Following this, each data owner, in parallel, generates synthetic data locally to augment their respective datasets by invoking the `fine_tuner` function (step B of phase 2). This step introduces several key research challenges that could pave the way for future exploration, as discussed in Sect. 5. For instance, one fundamental question is: *Which synthetic samples should each data owner select?* The objective is for data owners to become IID, addressing intra-client non-IID challenges. However, the local biases inherent in each data owner's dataset, coupled with their limited view of the global dataset, complicate this goal. For example, approaches like IoTSL [8] generate separate generators for each label, managed centrally by the server. So, the server having the whole view of the merged distribution, can orchestrate how the data owners will augment their data. However, note that having a different generator for each label, restricts the approach for label-skewness scenarios, and fails to tackle other forms of non-IID data, where explicitly defined groups are difficult to determine [17]. In contrast, training a shared generator, as proposed in our approach, enables the creation of a generator that reflects the distribution across all datasets, irrespective of non-IID type. A subsequent question arises: *Can GANs be leveraged to stabilize inter-client non-IID issues?* We caution that if the overall dataset is biased, GANs alone cannot guarantee IID augmentation.

In the final phase, the main model is trained using both the original and synthetic data. This phase can either be executed within a traditional FL framework or take advantage of the SL infrastructure established in the earlier phases. *The choice between FL and SL should be dynamically determined, based on system characteristics such as the computational capacity of the data owners and available network bandwidth.*

4   Cloud-Based FL-SL

In this section, we propose a novel cloud-based design leveraging existing microservices tools to support an MLaaS capable of handling the three phases of the training process, and facilitating the choice between FL or SL for the final training phase, based on system characteristics. Specifically, we consider the AWS services to illustrate a potential cloud-based system, as depicted in Fig. 3. The system is structured into two main components: *(i)* the compute nodes, running as part of the AWS infrastructure, and *(ii)* the data owners, which are computationally constrained nodes, such as mobile IoT devices, mobile phones, and similar devices.

The number of compute nodes should scale in proportion to the system demand (e.g., the number of data owners). This is crucial for resource optimization; otherwise, the system may become either over-utilized or under-utilized. In an over-utilized system, there are more requests than resources, leading to training delays. Conversely, an under-utilized system has redundant resources, resulting in wasted capacity. A more efficient configuration could reduce resource usage without affecting delivery times, as noted by [33]. Typically, the system includes a single aggregator, as aggregation does not require significant computational power. The components and interactions of the proposed protocol are illustrated in Fig. 3. Specifically, the system is organized into the following logical components, each with its respective interactions:

Init. Data owners first use the `profiler` to collect measurements regarding the computational cost of training the model on their devices. This data is then

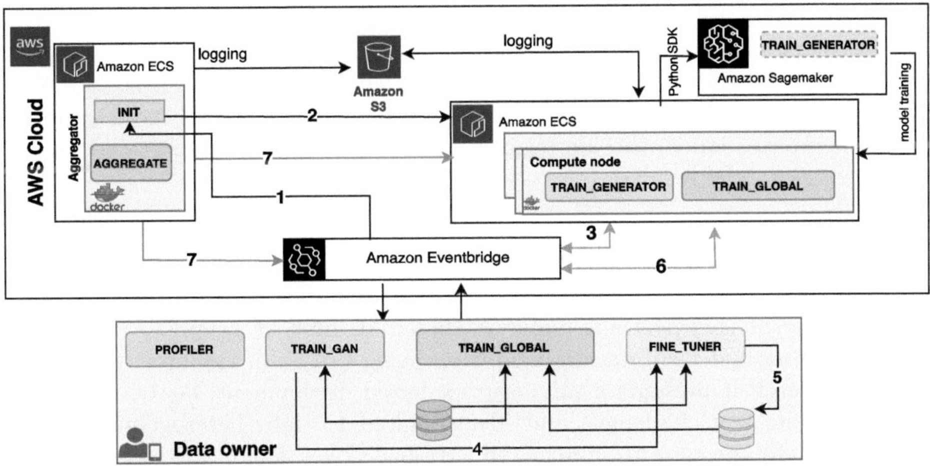

Fig. 3. Proposed cloud-based architecture. Modules illustrated in the same color, belong in the same logical part.

sent to the aggregator via the `init` module (steps 1–2 in Fig. 3). All communications between the data owners and the cloud node are event-driven and managed through AWS EventBridge. This module determines critical system parameters: *(i)* the splitting points for the model, *(ii)* the selection of compute nodes, and *(iii)* the allocation of data owners across compute nodes, especially in scenarios involving multiple compute node containers to ensure scalability. This step is vital because the choice of system parameters directly impacts the training delay [29]. Thus, the system needs to be modeled to jointly optimize these parameters, focusing on minimizing the training delay. Additional optimization objectives, such as energy consumption, could also be considered.

Training GANs. The compute nodes, in collaboration with the data owners, will train the GAN discriminator. To ensure scalability, especially when dealing with increasingly large offloaded models, compute nodes can leverage two key AWS services: (1) offloading model training to AWS SageMaker and (2) utilizing Amazon ECS's auto-scaling feature for other processes running on the compute nodes. Throughout the training process and upon completion, the compute nodes use Amazon S3 buckets to store intermediate results and maintain comprehensive logs, thus improving the fault tolerance of the system.

Fine-Tuning. During this phase, data owners generate synthetic data using the generator they received from the compute nodes via the `fine_tuner` operation (steps 4–5). Each data owner uses the generator to produce synthetic data instances, to address local distribution imbalances. By generating synthetic data tailored to the specific data owner's needs, this phase facilitates the convergence of the data owners' datasets toward a more IID state. The creation of a balanced, globally consistent dataset is crucial for efficient model training. Further details on potential approaches for the `fine_tuner` function are discussed in Sect. 5.

Training the Global Model. In this final phase, the data owners will train the global model either in collaboration with the compute nodes or using FL (step 6). At the end of each communication round, all nodes send their models to the aggregator (step 7), which combines them into a global model. Similar to the compute nodes, the aggregator utilizes Amazon S3 buckets to archive intermediate model results.

5   Discussion and Open Questions

The purpose of this position paper is threefold: first, it proposes a potential alternative method for data augmentation using GANs in resource-constrained devices; second, it presents a microservice-based deployment; lastly, it explores and highlights key challenges and ideas related to data heterogeneity in FL, considering the two new approaches (SL trained GAN, and cloud-based FL-SL). In Sect. 2, we reviewed existing approaches, identifying their limitations and open questions. Having now introduced our proposed approach, it is important to outline the new research questions that emerge. We believe these questions will shape an intriguing direction for future work.

5.1   GAN Training Phase

We emphasize that training GANs in an SL framework represents a novel direction within existing approaches. While SL has been explored for CNNs [10], LSTMs [34], and more recently for LLMs [35], its application to GANs remains largely unexplored. This raises several open challenges that warrant further investigation.

(i) What is the most efficient approach for training GANs in an SL setting, balancing both accuracy and training delay? A fundamental constraint is that data owners' datasets cannot be shared. Moreover, considering the design in Fig. 2, a new challenge is the training of the shared layers, as both collaborating entities (i.e., data owners and compute nodes) must maintain a consistent view at all times. One possible solution is to leverage aggregation techniques, similar to those used in Parallel SL [10], but this approach requires careful consideration of aggregation frequency to ensure stability and performance.

(ii) How will the generated data be labeled? GANs are inherently trained in an unsupervised manner, and the synthetic data produced by the generator lacks explicit labels. Therefore, a novel *distributed* pseudo-labeling approach must be developed. Unlike prior works discussed in Sect. 2.1, which typically assume a centralized entity managing the final generator, our scenario is more complex: the generator is shared among multiple data owners. This necessitates a distributed labeling method that ensures convergence across participants. Several potential approaches exist, including conditional GANs [6] and pseudo-labeling techniques [7]. Another promising strategy, particularly suitable for SL/FL systems, involves utilizing the main ML model for labeling. However, this requires

continuous label updates as the model evolves throughout training, i.e., the third phase in Fig. 2.

(iii) How should the discriminator be split? The choice of where to split the discriminator in SL has far-reaching implications, not only for model accuracy and training efficiency [36] but also for data privacy. The selection of the cut layer directly influences how much information is exposed, which is a critical factor in privacy-preserving learning [37–39]. Designing an optimal split strategy that balances privacy, performance, and training delay remains an open research challenge.

5.2 Synthetic Data Selection

For the fine-tuning phase (i.e., finding the optimal data distribution of the desired data classes), reinforcement learning (RL) [40] can be used. Concretely, each data owner can maintain and train an RL agent to learn the optimal distribution of synthetic data instances. RL has been extensively proposed for resource management in cloud and cloud-edge environments, including tasks such as allocation, auto-scaling, load balancing, and job placement [41–43], highlighting its ability to adapt to complex, dynamic systems. However, standard RL algorithms can be computationally heavy and may exceed the limited resources available on data owners' devices. Therefore, more computationally efficient RL algorithms, such as SARSA [44], NPG [45], or modern lightweight RL frameworks with small memory footprints, such as TinyRL [46] or Small-Batch DRL [47], are preferable for performing the fine-tuning process.

Solving this problem using RL involves framing it as a Markov decision process, defining the state space, action space, and reward function. The state space refers to the set of all possible states that the agent can encounter. For example, in the case of label skewness (i.e., the distribution of the labels among the clients is non-IID), the state space consists of all combinations of class distributions across all data owners' datasets. The action space contains the available classes that the RL agent can request from the generator at each time. The reward function serves as feedback for the RL agent, i.e., evaluating its actions. The goal of the agent is to find and generate the optimal distribution of classes that brings the current distribution closer to IID. A training step consists of requesting a batch of classes for generation from the generator and receiving a reward based on the new distribution. Once the final dataset is generated, it is compared with the intended IID distribution using an appropriate evaluation metric. This process defines a training epoch, which is executed iteratively to refine the agent's behavior, maximizing reward and minimizing non-IID.

For example, in the case of label skewness, we can have the following formulation:
- *State Space:* The current label distribution of the data owner's local dataset $d_{ct} \in \Re^L$, where L is the total number of labels, of the label set $\mathcal{L}$.
- *Action Space:* Each action corresponds to requesting a synthetic sample of a specific class label. In case of conditional GANs, this means choosing a specific

label, but in the case of unconditional GANs, the action could represent a noise vector with a latent class embedding.

- *Reward Function:* We can use a simple, but effective reward function like the following,

$$r_t = -||d_{ct}^l - d_c^{IID}||, \forall l \in \mathcal{L} \tag{1}$$

This, essentially, measures the negative distance of the label distribution at step t and a target IID distribution.

5.3   Dynamic Scale-in/out of the Compute Nodes

Scaling dynamically the compute nodes not only benefits the data owners (i.e., handling the data owners' load without compromising their QoS), but it also profits the server-side because it directly affects their energy and financial costs. A microservice design like the one presented in Fig. 3 and Sect. 4 decomplexes several aspects of the dynamic scale-in/out challenges. Particularly, the main questions in a dynamic system are:

(i) How to scale safely and efficiently? In the proposed solution, each compute node runs as a containerized service managed by AWS ECS, which supports the Auto Scaling service. Having this service, the number of running tasks can be scaled without any user intervention. In other words, we can leverage a SOTA framework to support complex functionalities, like the one studied here. Moreover, users do not have to decide which entity should make such decisions during runtime, since this is entirely handled from the server side.

(ii) How is the state migrated? One of the key issues of dynamic scaling spotted in [29] is the state handover across compute nodes. Recall that during training, the compute nodes preserve a training state for each data owner, e.g., the updated weights and the intermediate activations, etc., which requires a non-negligible memory. Transferring this load during training can significantly increase the training time [29]. But, this can be tackled smoothly when using S3 buckets, as the handover of state between compute nodes is implemented directly by the cloud system internally and efficiently.

(iv) What metrics to monitor and when to scale? Even though the auto scaling service of ECS offers plenty options for the user to monitor (e.g., CPU/memory usage, or custom CloudWatch metrics – model training time, queue length, number of connected clients, or Event-driven triggers – EventBridge rule indicating a new client has joined.), it remains an open research question which is the best to be used. This decision is not trivial/straightforward, and it depends on plenty of parameters (e.g., the QoS of the system, the type of training and devices, etc.). Therefore, a future direction of this architecture would be to study the impact of these parameters in order to find the most suitable.

(v) How to predict the needs of scale-in/out? This is another open research question that cannot just be answered with the support of microservice design. Note that according to [29] the *response time* of the system to the changes can

increase the overhead. Hence, if the system requires a significant time to find the best new solution, then there is no point in switching to this new state. Of course, this depends on the frequency of changes, e.g., if changes are not often, then even a slow auto-scaling mechanism could be tolerated. On the other hand, when changes are frequent (which is the expected case [29]), the auto-scaling mechanism needs to have a fast response time. However, using intelligent RL agents or, in general, ML models to make predictions of system changes could be a new direction in the future, because it will allow obviation. Some preliminary studies (e.g., [48–50]) mainly focus on predicting the next best split point. Yet, the dynamic scaling of compute nodes remains a not-widely-studied area.

6   Conclusions

In this position paper, we have discussed key challenges associated with non-IID data in FL and highlighted critical open issues. Additionally, we proposed a novel data augmentation approach by leveraging SL for training GANs, an area that has received limited attention in existing research. Furthermore, considering the growing adoption of microservices for ML system deployment, we outlined a potential framework that integrates these concepts to enhance scalability and efficiency. Finally, we provided a comprehensive discussion on future research directions, emphasizing the need for further exploration of distributed labeling, optimization of SL-based GAN training, and reinforcement learning for synthetic data selection.

Acknowledgments. This work has been supported by the Horizon Europe research and innovation program of the European Union, under grant agreement no 101092912, project MLSysOps.

References

1. McMahan, B., Moore, E., Ramage, D., Hampson, S., y Arcas, B.A.: Communication-efficient learning of deep networks from decentralized data. In: AISTATS, pp. 1273–1282. PMLR (2017)
2. Wen, J., Zhang, Z., Lan, Y., Cui, Z., Cai, J., Zhang, W.: A survey on federated learning: challenges and applications. Int. J. Mach. Learn. Cybern. **14**(2), 513–535 (2023)
3. Zhu, H., Xu, J., Liu, S., Jin, Y.: Federated learning on non-iid data: a survey. Neurocomputing **465**, 371–390 (2021)
4. Ghavamipour, A.R., Turkmen, F., Wang, R., Liang, K.: Federated synthetic data generation with stronger security guarantees. In: Proc. of the 28th ACM Symposium on Access Control Models and Technologies, pp. 31–42 (2023)
5. Cheng, Y., Zhang, L., Li, A.: Gfl: federated learning on non-iid data via privacy-preserving synthetic data. In: 2023 IEEE International Conference on Pervasive Computing and Communications (PerCom), pp. 61–70. IEEE (2023)

6. Wijesinghe, A., Zhang, S., Ding, Z.: Pfl-gan: When client heterogeneity meets generative models in personalized federated learning, arXiv preprint arXiv:2308.12454 (2023)
7. Li, Z., Shao, J., Mao, Y., Wang, J.H., Zhang, J.: Federated learning with gan-based data synthesis for non-iid clients. In: International Workshop on Trustworthy Federated Learning. Springer, pp. 17–32 (2022)
8. Feng, X., et al.: Iotsl: Towards efficient distributed learning for resource-constrained internet of things. IEEE Internet of Things J. (2023)
9. Jeong, E., Oh, S., Kim, H., Park, J., Bennis, M., Kim, S.-L.: Communication-efficient on-device machine learning: Federated distillation and augmentation under non-iid private data, arXiv preprint arXiv:1811.11479 (2018)
10. Tirana, J., Lalis, S., Chatzopoulos, D.: Mp-sl: Multihop parallel split learning, arXiv preprint arXiv:2402.00208 (2024)
11. Vepakomma, P., Gupta, O., Swedish, T., Raskar, R.: Split learning for health: Distributed deep learning without sharing raw patient data, arXiv preprint arXiv:1812.00564 (2018)
12. Thapa, C., Arachchige, P.C.M., Camtepe, S., Sun, L.: Splitfed: when federated learning meets split learning. In: Proc. of the AAAI Conference on Artificial Intelligence, vol. 36(8), pp. 8485–8493 (2022)
13. Jeon, J., Kim, J.: Privacy-sensitive parallel split learning. In: International Conf. on Information Networking, pp. 7–9. IEEE (2020)
14. Cai, Y., Wei, T.: Efficient split learning with non-iid data. In: 2022 23rd IEEE International Conference on Mobile Data Management (MDM), pp. 128–136. IEEE (2022)
15. Palanisamy, K., Khimani, V., Moti, M.H., Chatzopoulos, D.: Spliteasy: a practical approach for training ml models on mobile devices. In: Proc. of the 22nd International Workshop on Mobile Computing Systems and Applications, ser. HotMobile 2021, pp. 37–43. Association for Computing Machinery, New York (2021). https://doi.org/10.1145/3446382.3448362
16. Tirana, J., Chatzopoulos, D.: Split learning and synergetic inference: When iot collaborates with the cloud-edge continuum. In: Advances in the Internet of Things, pp. 203–227. CRC Press (2025)
17. Jimenez, D.M., et al.: Non-iid data in federated learning: a systematic review with taxonomy, metrics, methods, frameworks and future directions, arXiv preprint arXiv:2411.12377 (2024)
18. Li, X., Huang, K., Yang, W., Wang, S., Zhang, Z.: On the convergence of fedavg on non-iid data,’ arXiv preprint arXiv:1907.02189 (2019)
19. Karimireddy, S.P., Kale, S., Mohri, M., Reddi, S., Stich, S., Suresh, A.T.: Scaffold: stochastic controlled averaging for federated learning. In: International Conference on Machine Learning, pp. 5132–5143. PMLR (2020)
20. Wang, J., Liu, Q., Liang, H., Joshi, G., Poor, H.V.: Tackling the objective inconsistency problem in heterogeneous federated optimization. Adv. Neural. Inf. Process. Syst. **33**, 7611–7623 (2020)
21. Zhao, Z., et al.: Federated learning with non-iid data in wireless networks. IEEE Trans. Wireless Commun. **21**(3), 1927–1942 (2021)
22. Seo, E., Niyato, D., Elmroth, E.: Resource-efficient federated learning with non-iid data: an auction theoretic approach. IEEE Internet of Things J. **9**(24), 25506–25524 (2022)

23. Yoshida, N., Nishio, T., Morikura, M., Yamamoto, K., Yonetani, R.: Hybrid-fl for wireless networks: Cooperative learning mechanism using non-iid data. In: ICC 2020-2020 IEEE International Conference On Communications (ICC), pp. 1–7. IEEE (2020)

24. Zhang, H., Hou, Q., Wu, T., Cheng, S., Liu, J.: Data augmentation based federated learning. IEEE Internet of Things Journal (2023)

25. Jeong, E., Oh, S., Park, J., Kim, H., Bennis, M., Kim, S.-L.: Multi-hop federated private data augmentation with sample compression, arXiv preprint arXiv:1907.06426 (2019)

26. Strubell, E., Ganesh, A., McCallum, A.: Energy and policy considerations for modern deep learning research. In: Proceedings of the AAAI Conference on Artificial Intelligence, vol. 34(09), pp. 13 693–13 696 (2020)

27. Kang, S., et al.: Ganpu: an energy-efficient multi-dnn training processor for gans with speculative dual-sparsity exploitation. IEEE J. Solid-State Circ. **56**(9), 2845–2857 (2021)

28. Kim, S., Kang, S., Han, D., Kim, S., Kim, S., Yoo, H.-J.: An energy-efficient gan accelerator with on-chip training for domain-specific optimization. IEEE J. Solid-State Circ. **56**(10), 2968–2980 (2021)

29. Tirana, J., Tsigkari, D., Iosifidis, G., Chatzopoulos, D.: Minimization of the training makespan in hybrid federated split learning. IEEE Trans. Mobile Comput. (2025)

30. Ziller, A., et al.: PySyft: a library for easy federated learning. In: Rehman, M.H., Gaber, M.M. (eds.) Federated Learning Systems. SCI, vol. 965, pp. 111–139. Springer, Cham (2021). https://doi.org/10.1007/978-3-030-70604-3_5

31. Samir, M., et al.: Pygrid: a software development and assessment framework for grid-aware software defined networking. Int. J. Network Manage **28**(5), e2033 (2018)

32. Lo, S.K., Lu, Q., Zhu, L., Paik, H.-Y., Xu, X., Wang, C.: Architectural patterns for the design of federated learning systems. J. Syst. Softw. **191**, 111357 (2022)

33. Koutsovasilis, P., Parasyris, K., Antonopoulos, C.D., Bellas, N., Lalis, S.: Dynamic undervolting to improve energy efficiency on multicore x86 cpus. IEEE Trans. Parallel Distrib. Syst. **31**(12), 2851–2864 (2020)

34. Abedi, A., Khan, S.S.: Fedsl: federated split learning on distributed sequential data in recurrent neural networks, arXiv preprint arXiv:2011.03180 (2020)

35. Sadeepa, S., Kavinda, K., Hashika, E., Sandeepa, C., Gamage, T., Liyanage, M.: Disllm: distributed llms for privacy assurance in resource-constrained environments. In: 2024 IEEE Conference on Communications and Network Security (CNS), pp. 1–9. IEEE (2024)

36. Dachille, J., Huang, C., Liu, X.: The impact of cut layer selection in split federated learning, arXiv preprint arXiv:2412.15536 (2024)

37. Lee, J., Seif, M., Cho, J., Poor, H.V.: Exploring the privacy-energy consumption tradeoff for split federated learning. IEEE Netw. (2024)

38. Optimizing privacy and latency tradeoffs in split federated learning over wireless networks. IEEE Wireless Commun. Lett. (2024)

39. Lee, J., Cho, J., Lee, W., Seif, M., Poor, H.V.: Game-theoretic joint incentive and cut layer selection mechanism in split federated learning, arXiv preprint arXiv:2412.07813 (2024)

40. Sutton, R.S., Barto, A.G.: Reinforcement learning: an introduction, 2nd edn. adaptive computation and machine learning (2018)

41. Aslanidis, T., Chouliaras, A., Chatzopoulos, D.: Reinforcement learning techniques for optimizing system configuration on the cloud: A taxonomy and open problems.

In: Proceedings of the 2023 International Conference on Embedded Wireless Systems and Networks, EWSN, pp. 25–27 (2023)

42. Mao, H., Alizadeh, M., Menache, I., Kandula, S.: Resource management with deep reinforcement learning. In: Proceedings of the 15th ACM Workshop on Hot Topics in Networks, pp. 50–56 (2016)

43. Aslanidis, T., Kosta, S., Lalis, S., Chatzopoulos, D.: Cross-domain drl agents for efficient job placement in the cloud-edge continuum. In: Proceedings of the 5th Workshop on Machine Learning and Systems, pp. 276–285 (2025)

44. Rummery, G.A., Niranjan, M.: On-line Q-learning using connectionist systems University of Cambridge, Department of Engineering Cambridge, UK, vol. 37 (1994)

45. Kakade, S.M.: A natural policy gradient. Adv. Neural Inform. Processing Syst., vol. 14 (2001)

46. Szydlo, T., Jayaraman, P.P., Li, Y., Morgan, G., Ranjan, R.: Tinyrl: towards reinforcement learning on tiny embedded devices. In: Proceedings of the 31st ACM International Conference on Information & Knowledge Management, pp. 4985–4988 (2022)

47. Obando Ceron, J., Bellemare, M., Castro, P.S.: Small batch deep reinforcement learning. Advances in Neural Information Processing Syst. **36** (2024)

48. Wu, D., Ullah, R., Harvey, P., Kilpatrick, P., Spence, I., Varghese, B.: Fedadapt: adaptive offloading for iot devices in federated learning. IEEE Internet of Things J. **9**(21), 20889–20901 (2022)

49. Li, E., Zeng, L., Zhou, Z., Chen, X.: Edge ai: on-demand accelerating deep neural network inference via edge computing. IEEE Trans. Wireless Commun. **19**(1), 447–457 (2020)

50. Fan, W., Chen, P., Chun, X., Liu, Y.: Madrl-based model partitioning, aggregation control, and resource allocation for cloud-edge-device collaborative split federated learning. IEEE Trans. Mobile Comput. (2025)

Task Orchestration in the Cloud Continuum via Multi-objective Evolutionary Algorithms

Konstantinos Karathanasis[1,3]([✉]) [iD], Spyros Kontogiannis[1,2] [iD],
and Christos Zaroliagis[1,2] [iD]

[1] Department of Computer Engineering and Informatics, University of Patras,
Patras, Greece
`k_karathanasis@ac.upatras.gr`, `spyridon.kontogiannis@upatras.gr`,
`zaro@ceid.upatras.gr`
[2] Computer Technology Institute and Press "Diophantus", Patras, Greece
[3] PIKEI New Technologies, Patras, Greece

Abstract. As IoT ecosystems expand, the need for efficient computational offloading becomes increasingly critical. Traditional cloud-based solutions often suffer from latency and bandwidth limitations, prompting the emergence of cloud-fog/edge-IoT architectures where processing can also occur closer to the data source (edge of the network). This flexibility, introduces new challenges in orchestrating task execution under diverse and dynamic conditions. In this work, we provide a new multi-objective optimization model for the transparent task orchestration problem across the cloud-continuum, aiming to minimize latency, energy consumption, and load imbalance. Our model incorporates task dependencies, task priorities, heterogeneous communication and execution models, making it well-suited for practical deployment. We evaluate state-of-the-art multi-objective evolutionary algorithms (MOEAs), including `NSGA-II`, `NSGA-III`, `MOEA/D`, and `SPEA2`. We also introduce `NS-CSA`, a new evolutionary approach inspired by `Cuckoo Search` and `NSGA-II`. Extensive experiments across diverse configurations demonstrate the advantages of `NS-CSA` and provide valuable insights into the strengths and limitations of different MOEAs for realistic IoT offloading scenarios.

Keywords: Multi-objective Optimization · Cloud Continuum · Task Allocation and Scheduling · Evolutionary Algorithms

1 Introduction

The convergence of Internet of Things (IoT) technologies and artificial intelligence (AI) is transforming how modern societies operate, particularly within urban environments. Cities worldwide are embedding intelligence into infrastructure and services, in an effort to become more efficient, safe, and sustainable. This ongoing digital transformation is powered by a growing ecosystem of connected

D. Garlisi and D. Chatzopoulos (Eds.): ALGOCLOUD 2025, LNCS 16349, pp. 73–93, 2026.
https://doi.org/10.1007/978-3-032-13744-9_6

devices—ranging from environmental sensors and autonomous vehicles to smart homes and wearable technologies—each continuously generating vast volumes of data. These devices not only monitor and react to real-world conditions but also enable data-driven decisions through real-time analytics and predictive modeling. AI plays a pivotal role in enhancing the value of IoT by turning raw sensor data into actionable insights, thereby enabling applications such as predictive maintenance, adaptive traffic control, smart energy distribution, and responsive emergency services.

However, the potential of these intelligent systems hinges critically on the ability to process the massive data streams they produce. Traditional cloud-centric architectures often introduce latency and bandwidth bottlenecks. Meanwhile, edge devices alone may lack the computational capacity to handle complex workloads. To address this, computation is increasingly distributed across the cloud-edge continuum, where tasks are dynamically offloaded among cloud servers, edge nodes, and end devices [14]. This approach balances performance, responsiveness, and resource efficiency, but introduces a major challenge which we shall refer to as the *Task Orchestration Problem*: how to orchestrate task placement optimally across a heterogeneous and dynamic environment. Task placement decisions must consider multiple conflicting objectives, such as minimizing latency and energy consumption and maintaining system resilience. The complexity of these decisions grows with the scale and diversity of IoT deployments, making effective orchestration a critical problem.

Related Work. Computation offloading in the cloud-edge (or cloud-fog) continuum has been extensively studied in recent years. A prominent line of research relies on mathematical programming methods. These include linear programming [2], mixed-integer nonlinear programming (MINLP) [20], and quadratic programming [13]. Given the computational complexity of these optimization formulations, many researchers have turned to evolutionary and genetic algorithms [1,3,12,19,21]. Beyond evolutionary techniques, machine learning-based approaches have emerged [6,17,22], as well as heuristic algorithms, due to their adaptability and reduced computational overhead [10]. Moreover, a range of metaheuristic approaches has been explored [8,11,16,18]. A formulation of the Task Orchestration Problem in cloud—edge—IoT architectures as a multi-objective optimization problem was presented in [9]. That work proposed the use of `NSGA-II` [4] combined with an ϵ-approximation method [15] as a solution approach, but did not provide any experimental validation or evidence on the practicality of the method.

Our Contribution. In this work, we introduce a new and more efficient multi-objective optimization model that solves the task orchestration problem, using only linear constraints. Our model explicitly captures realistic constraints of modern IoT systems, such as task dependencies, task prioritization, and the limited energy budgets for computation of IoT devices. The proposed orchestrator aims to simultaneously optimize three critical objectives: (i) minimizing total execution delay, (ii) minimizing total energy consumption, and (iii) achieving effective load balancing across computational nodes. We evaluate several state-of-the-art evolutionary algorithms, including NSGA-II [4], NSGA-III [5], MOEA/D [23], and SPEA2 [24] and we introduce a new algorithm, NS-CSA, which integrates the non-dominated sorting mechanism of NSGA-II with the exploratory capabilities of the Cuckoo Search Algorithm (CSA) [7]. Finally, we conduct an extensive experimental evaluation to compare the performance of all algorithms under various configurations. Our experimental evaluation demonstrates the advantages of NS-CSA and provides insights into the performance trade-offs of the different algorithms in realistic IoT offloading scenarios.

2   System Architecture

We consider a hierarchical computing architecture composed of three layers: the **IoT Layer**, the **Edge (Fog) Layer**, and the **Cloud Layer**; see Fig. 1.

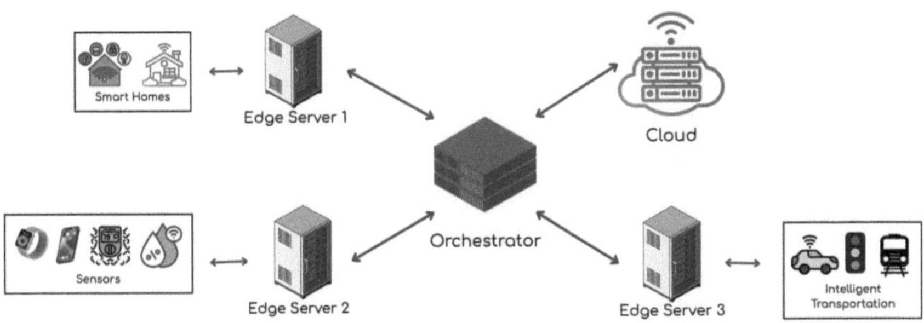

Fig. 1. System architecture.

- **IoT Layer:** This layer comprises a set of resource-constrained IoT devices responsible for data generation and local sensing. These devices initiate computation requests by generating tasks, but typically lack the processing power and battery life to handle complex workloads. Each device communicates with a designated edge server, usually the geographically nearest one.
- **Edge (Fog) Layer:** This intermediate layer consists of multiple edge servers positioned closer to the IoT devices. Among these edge servers, one node is elected as the *orchestrator*, responsible for centralized task scheduling and orchestration across the continuum.
- **Cloud Layer:** The cloud layer offers virtually unlimited computing and storage resources. It serves as a fallback option for executing tasks that cannot be efficiently processed at the edge due to resource constraints, task complexity, or current system load.

This architecture supports a *transparent computing model*, which allows for the separation of code segments from data segments, as individual entities, so that both data migration (closer to programs) and code migration (closer to data sources) are possible. The system operates in a coordinated manner across the cloud–edge continuum, with the orchestrator playing a central role in managing task execution. When an IoT device generates a computational task—triggered by sensing data or an application-specific event—it first sends a task request to its associated edge server. This edge server acts as the device's access point to the broader computing infrastructure. Each edge server forwards incoming task requests to the designated *orchestrator*, an edge node with enhanced processing and communication capabilities. The orchestrator maintains a global view of the system's state, including resource availability, task queues, and network conditions. Using this information, it performs centralized scheduling and determines the optimal execution site for each task.

Tasks may be assigned to the originating IoT device if the task is lightweight and local execution is feasible. Alternatively, the orchestrator may choose to offload the task to an edge server, depending on factors such as current load, proximity to the device, and available resources. In cases where the task is computationally intensive or edge resources are insufficient, the task may be forwarded to the cloud for execution. Once execution is completed, the computing server (either an edge node or the cloud) returns the results to the orchestrator. The orchestrator then routes the response to the corresponding edge server, which in turn delivers the final result back to the originating IoT device.

3   Multi-objective Optimization Model

The task allocation and scheduling problem, can be effectively modeled as a multi-objective optimization problem. The optimization aims to determine optimal task assignments across available resources while respecting task dependencies, priorities and the limited energy of IoT devices. Our model specifically focuses on three key objectives: minimizing total latency, reducing total energy consumption, and promoting load balancing across servers by minimizing the variance in their computational loads. Table 1, presents the notation used in the optimization model along with their descriptions.

3.1   Computing Tasks

IoT devices continuously generate a stream of computational tasks, some of which are lightweight and can be processed locally, while others require offloading to more powerful edge or cloud servers. Offloading such tasks involves transferring the associated data or code segments, which introduces communication overhead. In practice, tasks often exhibit logical or data dependencies. When dependent tasks are executed on different nodes, additional data transfer is required to satisfy these dependencies. Furthermore, tasks can vary in priority—for instance, healthcare-related tasks may demand quicker processing than others. Accounting for such dependencies and priorities introduces additional complexity into the orchestration process. We consider a set of tasks T and of IoT devices I, where each task $i \in T$ is generated by an IoT device $e_i \in I$, and is described by the following attributes:

Table 1. Notation Table

Symbol	Meaning
T	Set of all tasks
S	Set of all servers (size n); server $n-1$ is the cloud server
I	Set of all IoT (edge devices)
D_i^{in}	Input data of task i
D_i^{out}	Output data of task i
R_i	CPU operations required by task i
λ_i	Priority of task i
$Pred_i$	Set containing the predecessors of task i
e_i	The IoT device that generated task i
F_j	Processing rate (CPU frequency) of server j
C_j	CPU energy per operation on server j
P_j	Transmission power of server j
$Trans_j$	Transmission rate of server j
f_e	Processing rate (CPU frequency) of IoT device e
c_e	CPU energy per operation on IoT device e
x_{ij}	Binary variable: 1 if task i is assigned to server j, 0 otherwise
z_i	Binary variable: 1 if task i is executed at its IoT device
$Time_i^{in}$	Transmission time of the input data of task i
$Time_i^{out}$	Transmission time of the output of task i
$Time_i^{trans}$	Total transmission time of task i
$Time_i^{deal}$	Processing time of task i
$Time_i^{start}$	Start time of task i
$Time_i^{total}$	Total execution time of task i
E_j^{trans}	Total transmission energy of server j
E_j^{deal}	Total processing energy of server j
E_{IoT}^{deal}	Total processing energy of all IoT devices
E_j^{total}	Total energy consumption of server j
E_e^{max}	Energy budget for computation of IoT device e
E_{total}	Total system energy consumption
L_j	Load on server j (based on processing time)
$\bar{L}_j$	Average load across all servers
LBV	Load balancing variance across servers
M	A large constant to deactivate constraints

- D_i^{in}: Size of the input data for task i.
- D_i^{out}: Size of the output data produced by task i.
- R_i: Total number of operations required to execute task i.
- λ_i: Priority level of task i, where a higher value indicates higher importance.

- $Pred_i$: Set of predecessor tasks for task i, which must be completed, and their results transmitted before task i can begin execution.

Each task must be assigned to exactly one execution site—either an IoT device, an edge server, or the cloud. The set of available servers is denoted by S, where $|S| = n$. We assume a single cloud server indexed as $n - 1$, and edge servers indexed from 0 to $n-2$. This indexing convention is used consistently throughout the model to distinguish between edge and cloud resources. To represent task allocation, we define two sets of binary decision variables:

- $x_{ij} = 1$, if task i is assigned to server j; 0 otherwise.
- $z_i = 1$, if task i is executed locally on its originating IoT device; 0 otherwise.

3.2   Time Cost Model

We model the execution time of each task $i \in T$ as the sum of communication and processing delays, which depend on its assigned execution location. Each task has an associated start time $Time_i^{start}$, which captures the queuing delay incurred due to data dependencies, task priorities, and resource availability. The constraints regarding $Time_i^{start}$ are detailed later in the problem formulation.

Transmission Time. If a task is offloaded to a server $j \in S$, its input and output data must be transmitted between that server and the orchestrator. We denote by $Trans_j$ the available transmission bandwidth (in bits per sec) between server j and the orchestrator. The respective transmission times are:

$$Time_i^{in} = \sum_{j \in S} x_{ij} \cdot \frac{D_i^{in}}{Trans_j}, \quad Time_i^{out} = \sum_{j \in S} x_{ij} \cdot \frac{D_i^{out}}{Trans_j} \tag{1}$$

Computation Time. The time $Time_i^{deal}$ required to execute task i depends on its execution location. If assigned to a server j, the processing frequency is F_j; if executed on the originating IoT device e_i, the frequency is f_{e_i}:

$$Time_i^{deal} = \sum_{j \in S} x_{ij} \cdot \frac{R_i}{F_j} + z_i \cdot \frac{R_i}{f_{e_i}} \tag{2}$$

Total Task Time. The overall time to complete task i, including waiting, computation, and result transmission, is:

$$Time_i^{total} = Time_i^{start} + Time_i^{deal} + Time_i^{out} \tag{3}$$

Total Time. The total system processing time is defined as the sum of all individual task times:

$$Time_{total} = \sum_{i \in T} Time_i^{total} \tag{4}$$

3.3   Energy Cost Model

To evaluate the energy efficiency of the system, we model the energy consumed by both the servers (edge and cloud) and the IoT devices. The energy cost includes transmission and computation components.

Server-Side Energy. For each server $j \in S$, the energy required to transmit the input and output data of all assigned tasks (E_j^{trans}) and the energy to execute these tasks (E_j^{deal}) are measured by:

$$E_j^{trans} = \sum_{i \in T} x_{ij} \cdot \frac{D_i^{in} + D_i^{out}}{Trans_j} \cdot P_j, \quad E_j^{deal} = \sum_{i \in T} x_{ij} \cdot R_i \cdot C_j \qquad (5)$$

where P_j is the server's transmission power consumption and C_j is the energy consumed per operation. The total energy consumption of server j is the sum of its transmission and computation costs:

$$E_j^{total} = E_j^{trans} + E_j^{deal} \qquad (6)$$

IoT-Side Energy. For tasks executed locally on IoT devices, no transmission is required, so only computation energy is considered. Let c_{e_i} denote the energy consumed per operation by the IoT device e_i that generated task i. The total energy consumed by all IoT devices is given by:

$$E_{IoT}^{total} = \sum_{i \in T} z_i \cdot R_i \cdot c_{e_i} \qquad (7)$$

Total System Energy. The total energy consumption of the system is:

$$E_{total} = E_{IoT}^{total} + \sum_{j \in S} E_j^{total} \qquad (8)$$

3.4   Load Balancing Cost Model

To ensure fairness and efficiency in resource utilization across all servers, we introduce a load balancing objective. The computational load L_j assigned to each server $j \in S$ and the average load $\bar{L}$ across all servers, are measured by:

$$L_j = \sum_{i \in T} x_{ij} \cdot R_i, \quad \bar{L} = \frac{1}{|S|} \sum_{j \in S} L_j \qquad (9)$$

To quantify the degree of load imbalance, i.e., how much each server's load deviates from the average, we define the Load Balance Variance (LBV) as follows:

$$LBV = \frac{1}{|S|} \sum_{j \in S} (\bar{L} - L_j)^2 \qquad (10)$$

A lower *LBV* indicates a more balanced distribution of tasks, thus avoiding overloading certain servers while others remain underutilized. This objective is crucial in maintaining system stability and preventing performance bottlenecks.

3.5 Problem Formulation

Building on the previous analysis, we now formally define the *Multi-Objective Task Orchestration* problem. The goal is to minimize total time and energy consumption while maintaining effective load balancing among the edge servers. The problem can be expressed as:

$$\textbf{minimize}\ \{\ Time_{total},\ E_{total},\ LBV\ \}$$

subject to:

$$[\text{C1}]\quad z_i + \sum_{j \in S} x_{ij} = 1, \quad \forall i \in T$$

$$[\text{C2}]\quad Time_i^{start} \geq Time_i^{in}, \quad \forall i \in T$$

$$[\text{C3}]\quad Time_i^{start} \geq Time_m^{start} + Time_m^{deal} + Time_m^{out} + Time_i^{in},$$
$$\forall i \in T,\ \forall m \in Pred_i$$

$$[\text{C4}]\quad Time_i^{start} \geq Time_m^{start} + Time_m^{deal} + Time_m^{out} + Time_i^{in}$$
$$-(2 - x_{ij} - x_{mj}) \cdot M, \quad \forall i, m \in T : \lambda_m > \lambda_i,\ \forall j \in S$$

$$[\text{C5}]\quad Time_i^{start} \geq Time_m^{start} + Time_m^{deal} + Time_m^{out} + Time_i^{in}$$
$$-(2 - z_i - z_m) \cdot M, \quad \forall i, m \in T : e_m = e_i,\quad \lambda_m > \lambda_i$$

$$[\text{C6}]\quad \sum_{i \in T} z_i \cdot R_i \cdot c_{e_i} \leq E_e^{\max}, \quad \forall e \in E,\ \forall i \in T : e_i = e$$

The constraints are interpreted as follows. Constraint **C1** ensures that each task is assigned to exactly one execution location—either a server or its originating IoT device. **C2** requires that a task's start time is no earlier than its input transmission time, while **C3** enforces precedence by allowing dependent tasks to begin only after their predecessors have completed and transmitted their results. **C4** and **C5** impose priority-based ordering within servers and IoT devices, respectively: if two tasks are assigned to the same node, the one with higher priority must execute first, enforced using a large constant M to linearize the constraint. Finally, IoT devices are typically battery-powered and resource-constrained; allowing them to process too many tasks locally risks depleting their energy and hindering their primary sensing roles. To address this, **C6** limits each device's computational energy usage to a predefined budget $E_e^{\max}$.

4 Solution Approaches

In multi-objective problems, the goal is not to find a single optimal solution but rather a set of solutions that represent different trade-offs among the objectives. In this section, we evaluate the proposed problem formulation using four well-known multi-objective evolutionary algorithms (MOEAs): NSGA-II [4], NSGA-III [5], MOEA/D [23] and SPEA2 [24]. Additionally, we introduce NS-CSA, a new algorithm which inherits mechanisms from NSGA-II and Cuckoo Search Algorithm (CSA) [7].

4.1 Baseline MOEAs and Cuckoo Search Algorithm

All four MOEAs (NSGA-II, NSGA-III, MOEA/D, and SPEA2) follow the general evolutionary computation framework. They operate on a population of candidate solutions, which are evolved over generations through the application of variation operators (see Sect. 4.2). Selection mechanisms are employed to guide the search toward high-quality and diverse solutions. While they share this structure, each algorithm adopts a distinct strategy for fitness assignment, diversity preservation, and selection.

NSGA-II maintains a population of N candidate solutions and evaluates their fitness through fast non-dominated sorting, which organizes the population into hierarchical fronts based on Pareto dominance: individuals in the first front (rank-1) are not dominated by any other, those in the second front are dominated only by rank-1 solutions, and so on. To preserve diversity, NSGA-II uses a crowding distance metric, which estimates how close a solution is to its neighbors in objective space; individuals in less crowded regions are preferred to encourage spread across the Pareto front. Selection is performed to form the new population of size N, by combining dominance rank and crowding distance: individuals from better-ranked fronts are selected first, and within the same front, those with higher crowding distance are favored.

NSGA-III is an extension of NSGA-II for many-objective optimization by modifying its diversity preservation mechanism. While it still uses non-dominated sorting for fitness assignment, it replaces crowding distance with a reference point-based approach. A predefined set of uniformly distributed reference points in the objective space guides the selection process. Each solution is associated with the nearest reference point, and the algorithm selects a subset of N solutions that ensures a balanced representation across these reference points, promoting diversity and improving coverage of the Pareto front.

MOEA/D decomposes the multi-objective problem into N scalar subproblems using aggregation functions, such as Tchebycheff or weighted sum (we use Tchebycheff in our implementation). Fitness is assigned independently for each subproblem by evaluating its aggregated objective value. To maintain diversity, MOEA/D uses neighborhood structures: each subproblem is associated with a local neighborhood, and variation operators (crossover and mutation) are applied within this group to encourage localized exploration. In addition to the working population of N solutions, MOEA/D maintains an external archive that stores all non-dominated solutions found during the search. This archive, which can exceed size N, is returned as the final Pareto front approximation.

SPEA2 evaluates fitness based on dominance strength and density estimation. Each individual in the population of size N receives a fitness score based on the sum of the strengths of individuals that dominate it, where a solution's strength is defined as the number of individuals it dominates. Lower fitness values indicate better solutions (i.e., those that are weakly dominated or non-dominated). To preserve diversity, SPEA2 incorporates a k-nearest neighbor density estimator, penalizing individuals in crowded regions of the objective space. Selection is performed from a combined set of the current population and an external archive that stores non-dominated solutions. The top N individuals—based on fitness and density—are selected to form the next generation, promoting both convergence and diversity.

It is worth noting that NSGA-II, NSGA-III, and SPEA2 maintain a fixed-size population of N individuals throughout the search process, resulting in at most N solutions. In contrast, MOEA/D maintains an external archive to store all non-dominated solutions, which is independent of the working population and may grow beyond size N.

Cuckoo Search Algorithm (CSA) is a population-based metaheuristic inspired by the breeding behavior of certain cuckoo species. Some cuckoos lay their eggs in the nests of other host birds. Hosts that discover these foreign eggs may either discard them or abandon the nest entirely. In our task orchestration setting, each *nest* represents a complete task-to-node assignment for all tasks, and each *egg* corresponds to a single task mapping decision. CSA explores the solution space by having each cuckoo lay a new egg (i.e., propose a modified assignment) in a randomly chosen nest. If the new solution improves the objective, it replaces the old one. The new solutions are guided by Lévy flights, which produce random step sizes drawn from a heavy-tailed distribution: frequent short steps result in minor adjustments to the solution, while rare long steps enable significant jumps in the search space. To tailor CSA for our problem, we implement three rules: (i) each cuckoo lays one egg in a random nest, (ii) the best nests are retained across generations, and (iii) a fraction of poor nests is replaced with random solutions based on a discovery probability p_a.

4.2   Variation Operators

All baseline algorithms, as well as our proposed method, use crossover and mutation as variation operators to explore the search space. Both operators are designed to ensure that any newly generated solution remains feasible with respect to all problem constraints.

Our *crossover* operator creates an offspring by combining two parent solutions, p_1 and p_2. Specifically, the first half of the task-to-node assignments is inherited from p_1, and the second half from p_2. Since this may lead to constraint violations, we apply a repair procedure. First, we check energy constraints (C6) for all IoT devices. If any device exceeds its budget, tasks are iteratively reassigned randomly to edge or cloud servers until feasibility is restored. Then, tasks are sorted by descending priority, and for each task, we enforce: (i) task start time constraint (C2), (ii) precedence constraints (C3), if it has predecessors; and (iii) priority-based ordering (C4, or C5), depending on the execution location (edge/cloud, or IoT respectively).

Our *mutation* operator modifies a candidate solution s by selecting a task t at random and relocating it to a new feasible location—either its originating IoT device (if energy budget permits), an edge server, or the cloud. After relocation, we update t's start time to satisfy all precedence constraints (C3), making sure it executes only after all predecessors have completed and any required data transmission is accounted for. We then enforce priority constraints at the new location: if t now has a higher priority than existing tasks on the same node, those tasks are rescheduled to maintain proper execution order (constraints C4, C5). This may cascade to dependent tasks, requiring further schedule adjustments to preserve feasibility. Finally, the removal of t from its original location may allow other lower-priority tasks there to start earlier, improving resource utilization.

4.3   New Algorithm: NS-CSA

In this section, we present NS-CSA (cf. Algorithm 2), a new evolutionary multi-objective optimization algorithm, which combines the exploratory power of CSA with the dominance-based selection and diversity preservation mechanisms of NSGA-II. The algorithm begins by initializing the population P with N randomly generated task-to-node assignment solutions (which adhere to all constraints), where each solution represents a complete mapping of tasks across cloud, edge, and IoT nodes. An external Pareto archive A is maintained to store all currently non-dominated solutions. At first, A is initialized with the solutions of P. In each generation, new candidate solutions are produced via Lévy flight-based mutation. Specifically, for each solution s in the population, we randomly select an elite solution from the Pareto archive and apply Lévy flight mutation to generate an offspring o.

In our NS-CSA, the Lévy flight returns a step size that determines the exact number of mutations performed on the elite solution: a small step size (which is more frequent) results in performing only a few mutations, causing a relatively small change to the solution; a large step size leads to more mutations being applied, which produces a larger overall change. This approach creates an adaptive search behavior where most offsprings undergo a small number of mutations for fine-grained exploration, while less frequently, a larger number of mutations enables broader jumps in the search space. If after the mutations, the offspring o dominates s, it replaces s in the population, and the update-Pareto-Archive algorithm updates the Pareto archive as follows: all solutions dominated by o are removed, and o is added. If o does not dominate s, s is retained.

To maintain diversity (cf. Algorithm 1), a fraction $p_a \cdot N$ of the worst solutions in the population are replaced by new random solutions, simulating the nest abandonment behavior in CSA. These worst solutions are identified using the non-dominated sorting mechanism of NSGA-II to rank the population into dominance fronts. Starting from the worst front (with the highest rank), all solutions in that front are selected for replacement, if the size of the front does not exceed the limit of $p_a \cdot N$. If the limit is not yet reached, the algorithm proceeds to the next worst front and repeats the process. When a front contains more solutions than remaining slots for replacement, the crowding distance metric of NSGA-II is used to rank solutions within that front. Solutions with the smallest crowding distance, i.e., those in more crowded regions, are chosen for removal until the replacement limit is reached.

The algorithm runs for a predefined number of generations, or until a time limit is reached. The final output is the external Pareto archive containing a set of non-dominated solutions. Similar to `MOEA/D`, this external Pareto archive is independent of the working population of size N. As a result, it may return more than N non-dominated solutions in the final output.

Algorithm 1: DiversityMaintenance(P, N, p_a)

Input: Population P, size N and abandonment probability p_a
Output: Updated population P

```
 1  F ← NonDominatedSort(P);          // F contains all dominance fronts
 2  S ← ∅; remaining ← p_a · N;
 3  for i ← |F| to 1 do
 4      if |F_i| ≤ remaining then
 5          S ← S ∪ F_i;
 6          remaining ← remaining − |F_i|;
 7      else
 8          F_i ← Sort-By-Crowding-Distance(F_i);
 9          S ← S ∪ F_i[: remaining];
10          break;
11      end
12  end
13  foreach s ∈ S do
14      replace s with a new randomly generated solution in P;
15  end
16  return P;
```

Algorithm 2: NS-CSA(tasks, servers, IoTs, generations)

Input: Set of tasks, servers and IoT devices, number of generations
Output: A Pareto set of task-assignment solutions

```
 1  P ← Initialize population with N randomly generated solutions;
 2  A ← P;
 3  for gen ← 1 to generations do
 4      foreach solution s ∈ P do
 5          mutations ← Lévy flight step size;
 6          o ← copy of a random solution from A;
 7          for i in 1 to mutations do
 8              o ← Mutate(o, tasks, servers, IoTs)
 9          end
10          if o dominates s then
11              replace s with o in P;
12              A ← update-Pareto-Archive(o);
13          end
14      end
15      P ← DiversityMaintenance(P, N, p_a)
16  end
17  return A
```

Table 2. Value ranges used for synthetic data generation.

Entity	Parameter	Range/Description
Task	Input data size D_i^{in}	10 KB – 1 MB
	Output data size D_i^{out}	10 KB – 1 MB
	Operations R_i	1,000 – 100,000
	Priority λ_i	Integer in [1, 10]
IoT Device	CPU frequency f_e	50 – 1000 MHz
	Energy per operation c_e	0.001 – 0.01 energy units
Server	CPU frequency F_j	1 – 5 GHz
	Energy per operation C_j	0.01 – 0.1 energy units
	Transmission power P_j	100 – 400 W
	Transmission rate $Trans_j$	1 Mbps – 10 Gbps

5 Experimental Evaluation

In this section, we present the results of our experiments comparing all five algorithms. All experiments were conducted on a single core of an Intel Core i7-10700 CPU @ 2.90 GHz with 16 GB of RAM, running Ubuntu 22.04 LTS.

5.1 Data Sets

Due to lack of real-world data, we created synthetic data sets that simulate real-world edge computing environments. Tasks, IoT devices, and servers were generated using value ranges based on real hardware specifications and values from existing studies. Each task was assigned random values for computation size, input/output data, and priority to produce a heterogeneous workload. Task dependencies were introduced probabilistically, and priorities were adjusted to ensure logical consistency (i.e., a task that depends on another cannot have a higher priority). For IoT devices, we used realistic CPU frequencies and energy consumption per operation. The energy budget for each device was scaled based on the total number of tasks and IoT devices in the problem instance. Server parameters such as CPU frequency, energy consumption, and bandwidth were also set within practical ranges to represent diverse hardware configurations. Table 2 summarizes all the value ranges.

5.2 Metrics

In all experiments, we construct a *global Pareto set* by aggregating the non-dominated solutions from all algorithms. For each algorithm, we evaluate its performance by measuring how many of its solutions contribute to this global front. In this context, True Positives (TP) are the solutions returned by the algorithm that are part of the global Pareto set. False Positives (FP) are the solutions returned by the algorithm that are dominated and therefore not part of the global Pareto set. False Negatives (FN) are the non-dominated solutions in the global Pareto set that were not found by the algorithm. Using these definitions, we compute the following standard classification metrics:

$$\text{Precision} = \frac{\text{TP}}{\text{TP} + \text{FP}}, \ \text{Recall} = \frac{\text{TP}}{\text{TP} + \text{FN}}, \ \text{F1-score} = 2 \cdot \frac{\text{Precision} \cdot \text{Recall}}{\text{Precision} + \text{Recall}}$$

High precision means most of the algorithm's returned solutions are of high quality (i.e., non-dominated), while high recall indicates that the algorithm discovers a large portion of the global Pareto front. The F1-score provides a balanced measure of both aspects. In Tables 3, 4 and 5, for each algorithm, except for the above metrics, we also report the size of the global Pareto set, along with key metrics for each algorithm: the total number of solutions it returned (column "Total"), how many of those are part of the global Pareto set (column "Undom"), and the total execution time. All reported values are averaged over 5 independent runs, each performed on a distinct randomly generated dataset with identical problem settings (same number of tasks, servers and IoT devices).

5.3   Experimental Results

We designed three experimental settings: In the first, (*Fixed Population Experiment*) all algorithms use a fixed population size and run over the same number of generations. As discussed earlier, NSGA-II, NSGA-III, and SPEA2 return at most N non-dominated solutions, while MOEA/D and NS-CSA, which use external Pareto archives, may return more. The second experiment introduces a time limit (*Time Limit Experiment*), evaluating the quality of solutions each algorithm produces under constrained computational time. In the third experiment, we adjust the population sizes of the algorithms to ensure that they all output approximately the same number of solutions (*Same Result Size Experiment*). Below, we discuss in detail the results for each experiment.

Fixed Population Experiment. Table 3 reports the results of all algorithms using a fixed population size $N = 100$, over 250 generations across various instance configurations. The results demonstrate that NS-CSA consistently outperforms the other algorithms in terms of F1-score across all problem instances. Its high recall and strong precision, (which in all but one instance is higher than 0.8), indicate both broad coverage of the global Pareto front and high-quality solutions. However, it's important to note that NS-CSA generates significantly more solutions than the other methods, which contributes to its higher recall. Among the rest, SPEA2 maintains a solid balance between recall and precision, though with longer runtimes. NSGA-III achieves high precision but generally lower recall, suggesting it finds fewer Pareto-optimal solutions overall. NSGA-II is consistent but modest across all metrics. MOEA/D, despite being the fastest, consistently underperforms in coverage and F1-score.

Time Limit Experiment. Table 4 reports the results of all algorithms using a population size $N = 50$, but with a time limit set to each instance. NS-CSA

Table 3. *Fixed Population Experiment.* Performance comparison of all algorithms using a fixed population size ($N{=}100$), running for 250 generations across various instance configurations.

Algorithm	Total	Undom	Recall	Precision	F1-score	Time(s)
Tasks: 10, Servers: 2, IoT: 5, Global Pareto Size $\approx$ 304						
NSGA-II	92.40	73.80	0.243	0.798	0.373	13.98
NSGA-III	72.20	52.80	0.174	0.732	0.281	18.62
MOEA/D	60.20	5.40	0.018	0.089	0.030	**9.47**
SPEA2	100.00	79.80	0.263	0.798	0.394	60.19
NS-CSA	**209.80**	**187.40**	**0.617**	**0.894**	**0.730**	15.62
Tasks: 20, Servers: 2, IoT: 5, Global Pareto Size $\approx$ 320						
NSGA-II	97.20	43.80	0.137	0.451	0.210	24.25
NSGA-III	84.60	20.40	0.067	0.236	0.104	28.82
MOEA/D	51.60	0.80	0.003	0.017	0.006	**20.01**
SPEA2	100.00	70.00	0.219	0.700	0.334	78.89
NS-CSA	**225.20**	**184.20**	**0.576**	**0.861**	**0.690**	28.94
Tasks: 20, Servers: 5, IoT: 5, Global Pareto Size $\approx$ 472						
NSGA-II	98.60	38.80	0.083	0.393	0.132	26.62
NSGA-III	96.40	67.20	0.143	0.697	0.237	31.10
MOEA/D	114.40	18.60	0.039	0.169	0.063	**23.46**
SPEA2	100.00	88.60	0.189	**0.886**	0.314	92.67
NS-CSA	**291.80**	**257.40**	**0.545**	0.880	**0.673**	33.36
Tasks: 30, Servers: 5, IoT: 10, Global Pareto Size $\approx$ 446						
NSGA-II	99.40	51.40	0.116	0.514	0.188	44.43
NSGA-III	98.80	70.60	0.159	0.714	0.260	49.10
MOEA/D	105.20	8.40	0.019	0.078	0.030	**41.75**
SPEA2	100.00	84.20	0.189	0.842	0.307	114.67
NS-CSA	**267.00**	**234.60**	**0.526**	**0.851**	**0.646**	54.85
Tasks: 50, Servers: 10, IoT: 10, Global Pareto Size $\approx$ 600						
NSGA-II	100.00	40.20	0.067	0.402	0.114	104.18
NSGA-III	99.40	89.40	0.149	**0.899**	0.253	107.90
MOEA/D	186.00	89.60	0.149	0.482	0.226	**103.73**
SPEA2	100.00	85.20	0.142	0.852	0.243	172.72
NS-CSA	**351.60**	**295.40**	**0.492**	0.840	**0.619**	126.29
Tasks: 100, Servers: 10, IoT: 20, Global Pareto Size $\approx$ 562						
NSGA-II	100.00	40.80	0.073	0.408	0.124	**366.63**
NSGA-III	99.60	91.00	0.162	**0.914**	0.276	368.30
MOEA/D	208.80	144.40	0.257	0.692	0.373	374.70
SPEA2	100.00	69.60	0.124	0.696	0.210	443.50
NS-CSA	**291.60**	**222.20**	**0.395**	0.762	**0.520**	431.02

Table 4. *Time Limit Experiment.* Performance comparison of all algorithms using a fixed time limit, across various instance configurations (population $N = 50$).

Algorithm	Total	Undom	Recall	Precision	F1-score	Limit(s)
Tasks: 10, Servers: 2, IoT: 5, Global Pareto Size $\approx$ 230						
NSGA-II	47.40	31.80	0.138	0.671	0.227	
NSGA-III	42.40	30.40	0.132	0.717	0.222	
MOEA/D	32.60	1.20	0.005	0.037	0.009	10
SPEA2	49.80	39.40	0.171	0.791	0.281	
NS-CSA	**178.00**	**160.00**	**0.696**	**0.899**	**0.784**	
Tasks: 20, Servers: 2, IoT: 5, Global Pareto Size $\approx$ 246						
NSGA-II	49.60	19.40	0.079	0.391	0.130	
NSGA-III	47.60	29.20	0.119	0.613	0.198	
MOEA/D	38.60	0.00	0.000	0.000	0.000	20
SPEA2	50.00	33.20	0.135	0.664	0.222	
NS-CSA	**191.20**	**170.80**	**0.694**	**0.894**	**0.780**	
Tasks: 20, Servers: 5, IoT: 5, Global Pareto Size $\approx$ 205						
NSGA-II	49.40	22.00	0.107	0.445	0.171	
NSGA-III	49.20	38.40	0.187	0.780	0.301	
MOEA/D	63.40	14.20	0.069	0.224	0.107	20
SPEA2	50.00	41.40	0.202	0.828	0.325	
NS-CSA	**205.40**	**190.20**	**0.928**	**0.926**	**0.927**	
Tasks: 30, Servers: 5, IoT: 10, Global Pareto Size $\approx$ 155						
NSGA-II	49.40	24.80	0.160	0.503	0.243	
NSGA-III	49.00	39.80	0.257	0.813	0.391	
MOEA/D	65.40	6.60	0.043	0.101	0.060	30
SPEA2	50.00	41.00	0.265	0.820	0.401	
NS-CSA	**154.20**	**142.60**	**0.920**	**0.923**	**0.922**	
Tasks: 50, Servers: 10, IoT: 10, Global Pareto Size $\approx$ 205						
NSGA-II	50.00	22.40	0.109	0.448	0.176	
NSGA-III	50.00	41.60	0.203	0.832	0.327	
MOEA/D	112.60	71.80	0.350	0.638	0.452	50
SPEA2	50.00	42.60	0.208	**0.852**	0.331	
NS-CSA	**201.20**	**167.60**	**0.818**	0.833	**0.825**	
Tasks: 100, Servers: 10, IoT: 20, Global Pareto Size $\approx$ 142						
NSGA-II	50.00	29.40	0.207	0.588	0.310	
NSGA-III	50.00	43.40	0.306	**0.868**	0.453	
MOEA/D	136.00	83.00	0.585	0.610	0.597	100
SPEA2	50.00	31.00	0.218	0.620	0.325	
NS-CSA	**137.00**	**110.40**	**0.778**	0.806	**0.792**	

outperforms all other algorithms across nearly all instance configurations. While NSGA-III and SPEA2 often deliver competitive precision, occasionally outperforming NS-CSA in that regard, their lower recall results in a less balanced overall performance. NSGA-II and MOEA/D show mixed results: NSGA-II provides moderate precision with low recall, while MOEA/D improves for larger instances but still underperforms in earlier scenarios.

Same Result Size Experiment. Table 5 presents the performance of all algorithms over 100 generations, with population sizes adjusted to yield approximately 100 final solutions per run. The population size for NSGA-II, NSGA-III, and SPEA2 is fixed at 100, while for MOEA/D and NS-CSA, the population size is selected manually for each instance through trial and error (column "Pop"). The results indicate that NS-CSA performs particularly well on smaller instances, achieving both high precision and recall—even with small populations. However, as instance complexity increases, its effectiveness diminishes due to the limited population size, failing to explore a larger solution space. Nevertheless, its small population makes it the fastest algorithm in most cases. MOEA/D exhibits similar behavior to prior experiments: it struggles with smaller problem sizes but shows improvement as the problem scale increases. Overall, NSGA-III demonstrates the most consistent and high-quality performance across all instances, with NSGA-II and SPEA2 generally trailing, though in one case NSGA-II outperforms the rest.

Results Overview. Table 6 presents the average Recall, Precision, and F1-score of all algorithms across the three experiments, summarizing Tables 3–5. The results indicate that NS-CSA outperforms all other methods in the *Fixed Population* and *Time Limit* experiments, achieving the highest average Recall and Precision, leading to the best F1-scores. In these two experiments, SPEA2 and NSGA-III follow as the next best performers, though with a notable gap compared to NS-CSA. In the *Same Result Size* experiment, NS-CSA's performance declines due to its smaller population size, but still achieves the highest Recall and ranks as the second-best overall, just behind NSGA-III.

Practical Implications. The true value of using such algorithms that generate diverse Pareto sets lies in empowering the decision maker with flexibility and insight. Once this set of high-quality trade-off solutions is available, one can dynamically select the most appropriate outcome based on current system conditions, priorities, or operational constraints. For example, if the system is experiencing high energy costs, solutions that emphasize energy minimization can be favored—even if they slightly compromise on execution time or load balancing. The decision maker can impose preference weights on the objectives or define thresholds (e.g., maximum acceptable energy consumption), and then filter or rank the Pareto solutions accordingly. This approach contrasts with aggregating objectives into a single weighted-sum formulation, which would require re-solving the entire optimization problem from scratch each time preferences change—a computationally expensive and inflexible process. In this way, the precomputed Pareto set serves not only as a collection of optimal configurations but also as a

Table 5. *Same Result Size Experiment.* Performance comparison of all algorithms across various instance configurations. Each algorithm is executed for 100 generations, with population sizes tuned to produce approximately 100 final solutions.

Algorithm	Pop	Total	Undom	Recall	Precision	F1-score	Time(s)
Tasks: 10, Servers: 2, IoT: 5, Global Pareto Size ≈ 285							
NSGA-II	100	99.50	77.50	0.272	0.779	0.402	5.97
NSGA-III	100	95.50	75.00	0.263	0.785	0.394	7.76
MOEA/D	250	107.00	21.00	0.074	0.196	0.107	9.98
SPEA2	100	100.00	85.50	0.300	0.855	0.445	26.72
NS-CSA	30	103.60	**96.50**	**0.339**	**0.931**	**0.497**	**2.49**
Tasks: 20, Servers: 2, IoT: 5, Global Pareto Size ≈ 159							
NSGA-II	100	96.50	42.00	0.264	0.435	0.329	10.38
NSGA-III	100	92.00	34.50	0.217	0.375	0.274	12.18
MOEA/D	250	95.00	0.00	0.000	0.000	0.000	20.83
SPEA2	100	100.00	39.00	0.245	0.390	0.300	28.01
NS-CSA	50	94.50	**73.00**	**0.459**	**0.773**	**0.575**	**4.52**
Tasks: 20, Servers: 5, IoT: 5, Global Pareto Size ≈ 319							
NSGA-II	100	99.50	51.00	0.160	0.513	0.248	11.13
NSGA-III	100	97.50	**90.00**	**0.282**	**0.923**	**0.430**	12.80
MOEA/D	120	97.50	31.50	0.099	0.323	0.151	11.41
SPEA2	100	100.00	54.50	0.171	0.545	0.260	32.23
NS-CSA	30	102.00	**90.00**	**0.282**	0.882	0.426	**5.17**
Tasks: 30, Servers: 5, IoT: 10, Global Pareto Size ≈ 291							
NSGA-II	100	100.00	41.50	0.143	0.415	0.211	19.58
NSGA-III	100	99.00	**87.50**	**0.301**	**0.884**	**0.448**	21.00
MOEA/D	170	110.00	41.50	0.143	0.377	0.208	30.46
SPEA2	100	100.00	75.50	0.260	0.755	0.387	44.77
NS-CSA	30	99.00	61.00	0.210	0.616	0.314	**9.08**
Tasks: 50, Servers: 10, IoT: 10, Global Pareto Size ≈ 262							
NSGA-II	100	100.00	**78.50**	**0.300**	**0.785**	**0.435**	42.58
NSGA-III	100	99.50	75.50	0.288	0.759	0.415	43.79
MOEA/D	100	110.00	35.50	0.136	0.323	0.193	42.53
SPEA2	100	100.00	59.00	0.225	0.590	0.326	67.59
NS-CSA	30	98.50	43.50	0.166	0.442	0.240	**20.47**
Tasks: 100, Servers: 10, IoT: 20, Global Pareto Size ≈ 351							
NSGA-II	100	100.00	64.50	0.184	0.645	0.286	147.97
NSGA-III	100	99.00	**87.50**	**0.249**	**0.884**	**0.389**	149.15
MOEA/D	40	110.00	80.00	0.228	0.727	0.345	**60.28**
SPEA2	100	100.00	66.00	0.188	0.660	0.293	176.85
NS-CSA	30	99.00	63.50	0.181	0.641	0.281	69.02

Table 6. Average Recall, Precision, and F1-score of all algorithms for each experiment

Algorithm	Fixed Population			Time Limit			Same Result Size		
	Rec.	Prec.	F1-score	Rec.	Prec.	F1-score	Rec.	Prec.	F1-score
NSGA-II	0.129	0.494	0.204	0.133	0.507	0.210	0.220	0.595	0.321
NSGA-III	0.142	0.698	0.235	0.200	0.770	0.317	0.266	**0.768**	**0.395**
MOEA/D	0.080	0.314	0.127	0.175	0.268	0.211	0.113	0.320	0.167
SPEA2	0.187	0.795	0.302	0.198	0.762	0.314	0.231	0.632	0.330
NS-CSA	**0.525**	**0.840**	**0.646**	**0.805**	**0.880**	**0.840**	**0.272**	0.714	0.393

powerful tool for responsive, informed, lightweight and context-aware decision-making.

6   Conclusion

In this work, we formulated the task orchestration problem across the cloud continuum as a multi-objective optimization problem, capturing realistic trade-offs involved in practical deployments. We demonstrated how state-of-the-art evolutionary algorithms can be effectively applied to tackle this problem, and we introduced NS-CSA, a new multi-objective evolutionary algorithm. Through extensive comparative experiments, we highlighted the strengths and limitations of each algorithm under different configurations. As future work, we plan to investigate additional evolutionary strategies and meta-heuristic techniques.

Acknowledgments. This work was partially supported by the EU I3 Instrument under GA No 101115116 (project AMBITIOUS) and by the University of Patras under GA No 83770 (programme "MEDICUS").

References

1. Ali, I.M., Sallam, K.M., Moustafa, N., Chakraborty, R., Ryan, M., Choo, K.K.R.: An automated task scheduling model using non-dominated sorting genetic algorithm ii for fog-cloud systems. IEEE Trans. Cloud Comput. **10**(4), 2294–2308 (2020)
2. Chang, Z., Liu, L., Guo, X., Sheng, Q.: Dynamic resource allocation and computation offloading for IoT fog computing system. IEEE Trans. Ind. Inform. **17**(5), 3348–3357 (2021). https://doi.org/10.1109/TII.2020.2978946
3. Chen, J., Du, T., Xiao, G.: A multi-objective optimization for resource allocation of emergent demands in cloud computing. J. Cloud Comput. **10**(1), 20 (2021). https://doi.org/10.1186/S13677-021-00237-7
4. Deb, K., Agrawal, S., Pratap, A., Meyarivan, T.: A fast and elitist multiobjective genetic algorithm: NSGA-II. IEEE Trans. Evol. Comput. **6**(2), 182–197 (2002). https://doi.org/10.1109/4235.996017

5. Deb, K., Jain, H.: An evolutionary many-objective optimization algorithm using reference-point-based nondominated sorting approach, part I: solving problems with box constraints. IEEE Trans. Evol. Comput. **18**(4), 577–601 (2014). https://doi.org/10.1109/TEVC.2013.2281535

6. Fan, W., Li, S., Liu, J., Su, Y., Wu, F., Liu, Y.: Joint task offloading and resource allocation for accuracy-aware machine-learning-based iiot applications. IEEE Internet Things J. **10**(4), 3305–3321 (2023). https://doi.org/10.1109/JIOT.2022.3181990

7. Gandomi, A.H., Yang, X., Alavi, A.H.: Cuckoo search algorithm: a metaheuristic approach to solve structural optimization problems. Eng. Comput. **29**(1), 17–35 (2013). https://doi.org/10.1007/S00366-011-0241-Y

8. Hussein, M., Mousa, M.: Efficient task offloading for Iot-based applications in fog computing using ant colony optimization. IEEE Access **8**, 37191–37201 (2020). https://doi.org/10.1109/ACCESS.2020.2975741

9. Karathanasis, K., Kontogiannis, S., Zaroliagis, C.: Optimizing task orchestration across the cloud continuum. In: Artificial Intelligence Applications and Innovations. AIAI 2025 IFIP WG 12.5 International Workshops, pp. 209–222. Springer Nature Switzerland, Cham (2025). https://doi.org/10.1007/978-3-031-97317-8_16

10. Li, K.: Heuristic computation offloading algorithms for mobile users in fog computing. ACM Trans. Embed. Comput. Syst. **20**(2), 11:1–11:28 (2021).https://doi.org/10.1145/3426852

11. Liu, C., Wang, J., Zhou, L., Rezaeipanah, A.: Solving the multi-objective problem of IoT service placement in fog computing using cuckoo search algorithm. Neural Process. Lett. **54**(3), 1823–1854 (2022). https://doi.org/10.1007/S11063-021-10708-2

12. Liu, Q., Mo, R., Xu, X., Ma, X.: Multi-objective resource allocation in mobile edge computing using PAES for internet of things. Wirel. Networks **30**(5), 3533–3545 (2024). https://doi.org/10.1007/S11276-020-02409-W

13. Mukherjee, M., Kumar, S., Zhang, Q., Matam, R., Mavromoustakis, C.X., Lv, Y., Mastorakis, G.: Task data offloading and resource allocation in fog computing with multi-task delay guarantee. IEEE Access **7**, 152911–152918 (2019). https://doi.org/10.1109/ACCESS.2019.2941741

14. Naha, R.K., et al.: Fog computing: Survey of trends, architectures, requirements, and research directions. IEEE Access **6**, 47980–48009 (2018). https://doi.org/10.1109/ACCESS.2018.2866491

15. Papadimitriou, C.H., Yannakakis, M.: On the approximability of trade-offs and optimal access of web sources. In: 41st Annual Symposium on Foundations of Computer Science, FOCS 2000, 12-14 November 2000, Redondo Beach, California, USA, pp. 86–92. IEEE Computer Society (2000). https://doi.org/10.1109/SFCS.2000.892068

16. Potu, N., Jatoth, C., Parvataneni, P.: Optimizing resource scheduling based on extended particle swarm optimization in fog computing environments. Concurr. Comput. Pract. Exp. **33**(23) (2021). https://doi.org/10.1002/CPE.6163

17. Razaq, M.M., Rahim, S., Tak, B., Peng, L.: Fragmented task scheduling for load-balanced fog computing based on q-learning. Wirel. Commun. Mob. Comput. **2022**(1), 4218696 (2022). https://doi.org/10.1155/2022/4218696

18. Saif, F.A., Latip, R., Hanapi, Z.M., Kamarudin, S.: Multi-objective grey wolf optimizer algorithm for task scheduling in cloud-fog computing. IEEE Access **11**, 20635–20646 (2023). https://doi.org/10.1109/ACCESS.2023.3241240

19. Sun, Y., Lin, F., Xu, H.: Multi-objective optimization of resource scheduling in fog computing using an improved NSGA-II. Wirel. Pers. Commun. **102**(2), 1369–1385 (2018). https://doi.org/10.1007/S11277-017-5200-5
20. Vu, T.T., Nguyen, D.N., Hoang, D.T., Dutkiewicz, E.: Optimal task offloading and resource allocation for fog computing. CoRR **abs/1906.03567** (2019). http://arxiv.org/abs/1906.03567
21. Xu, H., Zeng, W., Zhang, D., Zeng, X.: MOEA/HD: a multiobjective evolutionary algorithm based on hierarchical decomposition. IEEE Trans. Cybern. **49**(2), 517–526 (2019). https://doi.org/10.1109/TCYB.2017.2779450
22. Yang, Z., Bai, W.: Distributed computation offloading in mobile fog computing: a deep neural network approach. IEEE Commun. Lett. **26**(3), 696–700 (2022). https://doi.org/10.1109/LCOMM.2021.3138800
23. Zhang, Q., Li, H.: MOEA/D: a multiobjective evolutionary algorithm based on decomposition. IEEE Trans. Evol. Comput. **11**(6), 712–731 (2007). https://doi.org/10.1109/TEVC.2007.892759
24. Zitzler, E., Laumanns, M., Thiele, L.: Spea2: Improving the strength pareto evolutionary algorithm. TIK report **103** (2001)

Duplication-Based Workflow Scheduling
with Communication Awareness
for Heterogeneous Cloud Computing
Environments

Yani Ping$^{(\boxtimes)}$ and Rizos Sakellariou

Department of Computer Science, University of Manchester, Manchester, UK
{yani.ping,rizos}@manchester.ac.uk

Abstract. Workflow scheduling in heterogeneous environments presents significant challenges due to complex task dependencies, particularly for data-intensive workflows where data transmission time substantially affects scheduling performance and consumes considerable bandwidth. This paper introduces a Communication-aware Duplication-based Workflow Scheduling algorithm (CDWS) that enhances scheduling efficiency through strategically duplicating critical predecessors of tasks and co-locating them on the same computational resources, followed by an elimination phase to remove redundant resource occupancy. The key idea is to reduce costly data transfers thereby improving overall makespan. Extensive simulation using synthetic data from four real-world scientific workflows shows that CDWS outperforms other approaches across key metrics such as normalized schedule length, data transmission volume and resource utilization, while maintaining low computational complexity.

Keywords: Workflow Scheduling · Task Duplication · Heterogeneous Cloud Computing

1 Introduction

Cloud computing systems integrate heterogeneous computing resources to support a range of different workloads. Scientific workflow applications running on such systems typically model their workloads as Directed Acyclic Graphs (DAGs), where vertices represent tasks and directed edges indicate data dependencies. These dependencies establish a critical constraint: a task can only be scheduled after all its predecessor tasks have completed and transmitted their output data. Under this constraint, workflow scheduling inevitably introduces waiting periods, resulting in idle time slots on computing resources and overall system underutilization. This inefficiency becomes particularly pronounced in data-intensive workflows, which handle large volumes of data and therefore data transmission time is significant [13].

D. Garlisi and D. Chatzopoulos (Eds.): ALGOCLOUD 2025, LNCS 16349, pp. 94–107, 2026.
https://doi.org/10.1007/978-3-032-13744-9_7

Workflow scheduling is known to be an NP-hard problem. The heterogeneous nature of modern distributed computing environments introduces an additional dimension of complexity as one needs to choose among a range of diverse resources. To address the challenge, numerous heuristic approaches have been developed, generally categorized into list-based, clustering-based, and duplication-based [2]. Among these, duplication-based methods are promising approaches that optimize both makespan and the amount of transmitted data by selectively duplicating tasks across multiple resources. Genez et al. [12] propose a duplication method that selects the earliest-scheduled predecessor of a task for duplication. While this method performs better than the widely used HEFT [17] and the Lookahead variant of HEFT [4] in terms of makespan and data transmission volume, it suffers from a higher computational complexity compared to HEFT. It can also be observed that certain scheduled tasks may become obsolete after subsequent task duplications, resulting in a waste of computing resources. Inspired by this, this paper introduces an improved static workflow scheduling algorithm that achieves performance benefits while addressing the complexity limitations. The main contributions of this paper are as follows:

1. Analyze the limitations of exiting duplication-based methods and explore areas for improvement.
2. Introduce a Communication-aware Duplication-based Workflow Scheduling algorithm (CDWS) comprising scheduling and elimination phases that optimize both normalized schedule length and data transmission volume, while maintaining low computational complexity.
3. Evaluate the performance of CDWS against various baselines and show its improvements using synthetic data from four real-world scientific workflows.

The remainder of this paper is organized as follows. Section 2 reviews related work; Sect. 3 presents the mathematical formulation of the workflow scheduling problem; Sect. 4 outlines the motivation for our research; Sect. 5 introduces the proposed algorithm with illustrative examples; Sect. 6 presents and analyzes the experimental results; and Sect. 7 concludes the paper.

2   Related Work

Workflow scheduling in cloud computing has attracted extensive attention from researchers, with the majority of studies focusing on optimizing performance metrics such as makespan, cost, and energy consumption [9,14,18]. However, most existing studies overlook the impact of data transmission, which has become increasingly critical as the scale of data in cloud computing grows exponentially [3]. Large-scale data transmission places a greater burden on computing, cooling and switching devices, not only causing energy waste [5] but also significantly increasing cloud computing costs [8].

Given the practical importance of data transmission, there has been research on reducing communication in workflow scheduling. In [13], a list-based algorithm is proposed that balances communication and computation cost by adjusting the weight of communication to increase its impact when scheduling, thereby avoiding communication wherever possible. Alternatively, clustering-based algorithms [6,10] optimize makespan and reduce communication costs by grouping tasks into clusters, then scheduling them as cohesive units.

Duplication-based heuristics take a different approach by duplicating selected tasks across additional resources. These methods are proposed under the assumption that communication between tasks executed on the same resource is typically negligible. In [16], a computation capacity heterogeneity factor is introduced to set the weights of task nodes and edges. The algorithm attempts to duplicate all predecessor tasks to improve the earliest completion time of each task, at the cost of increased computational complexity. Other approaches employ more selective duplication strategies. For example, the method proposed in [1] only duplicates the entry tasks, while several methods [7,11] duplicate a critical predecessor for each task. In [7], the critical predecessor is defined as the predecessor whose data has the latest arrival time on the computing resource where the current task is scheduled. The work in [11] proposes a new task priority method and duplicates the highest-priority predecessor task. These selective approaches achieve good performance in makespan optimization while maintaining reasonable computational complexity.

However, these methods have not explicitly demonstrated reductions in data transmission, which can be an important optimization metric. The algorithm proposed in [12], which is referred to as DECP (Duplicate Earliest-scheduled Critical Predecessor) throughout the remainder of this paper, performs well in both makespan and data transmission and can be considered as a starting basis for further improvements and comparison. Yet, despite its effectiveness, careful analysis of DECP suggests that it has certain limitations which will be discussed in Sect. 4, and leaves place for a new and improved algorithm.

3 Problem Formulation

Scientific workflows are commonly modelled as directed acyclic graphs (DAGs), denoted by $G = (V, E)$. Here, V represents the set of tasks, each of which is atomic and non-preemptive. z_i denotes the computational instructions required for the task v_i. $E = \{e_{ij} \mid i, j \in \{1, \ldots, |V|\}\}$ represents the set of directed edges, and $d_{i,j}$ is the data volume transmitted from task v_i to its successor v_j. The function $pred(v)$ returns the set of predecessors for any given task v, and $succ(v)$ returns the set of successors. Resources (which are assumed to be heterogeneous and part of a cloud data center) are denoted by $R = \{r_1, \ldots, r_k\}$. Each resource r_m has processing capacity c_m, and all resources are fully interconnected with varied bandwidth. $b_{m,n}$ denotes the bandwidth between resource r_m and r_n.

To establish the mathematical framework, task v_i is assumed to be scheduled on resource r_m. Its execution time ct_i^m is calculated as:

$$ct_i^m = \frac{z_i}{c_m} \tag{1}$$

Denote $DAT_{p,i}$ the data arrival time from a predecessor task v_p of task v_i. $duplist(v)$ is the function that outputs all duplicates of a task. Assume v_k is one element from the union of v_p and its duplicates, and is scheduled on resource r_n. $DAT_{p,i}$ can be computed by Eq. 2, where $d_{k,i} = d_{p,i}$. The earliest start time EST_i of task v_i is the maximum data arrival time across all its predecessor tasks and can be computed using Eq. 3. Its earliest finish time EFT_i can be obtained from Eq. 4.

$$DAT_{p,i} = \min_{v_k \in duplist(v_p) \cup \{v_p\}} \begin{cases} EFT_k + \frac{d_{k,i}}{b_{m,n}}, & m \neq n \\ EFT_k, & m = n \end{cases} \tag{2}$$

$$EST_i = \max_{v_p \in pred(v_i)} DAT_{p,i} \tag{3}$$

$$EFT_i = EST_i + ct_i^m \tag{4}$$

The optimization objective is to minimize the makespan, defined as in Eq. 5.

$$makespan = \max_{v_i \in V} EFT_i \tag{5}$$

4   Motivation

The main idea of DECP [12] is to select the earliest scheduled predecessor of each task as critical predecessor (CP) for duplication. When scheduling a task, DECP first uses HEFT to select the optimal resource and obtains a result without duplication. It then attempts to duplicate the task's CP on other resources except the one selected by HEFT. After each duplication, HEFT is reapplied to schedule the task. If duplication enables an earlier task finish time compared to no duplication, the duplicate of the critical predecessor is retained. While the above allows DECP to demonstrate good performance in terms of both makespan and data transmission volume, it also has some limitations that present opportunities for improvement. Some of these limitations are listed below.

i) **The selection of the CP is not always effective.** DECP selects the predecessor of a task with the highest rank (earliest-scheduled) as its CP, but this predecessor's data transmission time may not actually determine the task's start time. Instead, the predecessor whose data arrives latest at the resource where the task is scheduled determines the task's earliest start time. Duplicating this predecessor task may be more effective.

ii) **A resource excluded from the duplication process may still be a valuable candidate.** DECP first selects a resource for a task using HEFT, and then attempts to duplicate CPs on resources other than the selected one. However, duplicating CPs on that excluded resource as well may contribute to optimizing makespan. This means that all resources should be considered during the duplication process.

iii) **Checking all resources to schedule a task after each duplication significantly increases the computational complexity.** In DECP, after duplicating a task's CP on a given resource, the task must be scheduled by

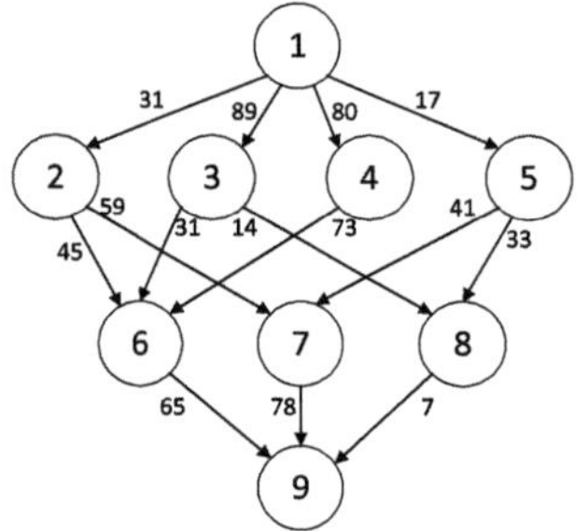

Task	R1	R2	R3	rank
1	19	19	19	365.67
2	28	46	20	246.67
3	36	30	34	232.33
4	15	25	37	266.67
5	30	8	8	212.67
6	33	35	59	168.00
7	12	20	21	156.33
8	13	22	24	87.33
9	41	68	73	60.67

Fig. 1. An example workflow and execution time table on three resources.

iterating through all resources again. Furthermore, the selected resources for the task and its duplicated CP may differ, which may undermine the anticipated reduction in data transmission. To improve this, both the task and its duplicated CP can be scheduled on the same computing resource, thereby reducing both computational complexity and data transmission.

To illustrate the above, consider the example workflow shown in Fig. 1. The workflow (DAG) on the left-hand side consists of 9 tasks; the values next to the edges represent the size of data transmitted between tasks. For simplicity, assume the bandwidth between resources is 1 unit of data per unit of time. The execution time of each task on three resources (R1, R2, R3) and the rank of each task are in the table. The ranks are calculated using HEFT's upward ranking [17]; then the scheduling order of tasks is: 1, 4, 2, 3, 5, 6, 7, 8, 9.

Three different ways to build a schedule for the example workflow are shown in Fig. 2. Figure 2(a) shows the schedule obtained using HEFT [17]. Figure 2(b) shows the schedule obtained using DECP [12]. Figure 2(c) shows the improvements that can be made to DECP's schedule that motivate the work in this paper.

In the schedule obtained by DECP, the CPs for tasks 2 through 9 are identified as tasks 1, 1, 1, 1, 4, 2, 3 and 6, respectively. Among these, only the duplication of task 1 on R2 and R3 results in an improved makespan, enabling the earlier execution of task 2 with an earliest finish time (EFT) of 39 and task 3 with 49. Without duplication, the EFTs for tasks 2 and 3 on R1 would be 62 and 98, respectively. However, duplicating additional tasks can also be effective, as shown in Fig. 2(c). For example, duplicating task 2 on R1 improves task 6's start time from 84 to 80 because task 2 is the bottleneck determining when task 6 can start. Similarly, duplicating task 5 on R2 allows task 8 to be scheduled on R2 rather than R3, reducing its start time from 68 to 57. For task 9, rescheduling task 7 from R3 to R1 advances task 9's start time from 146 to 125. After completing the scheduling process, tasks remaining on R3 become redundant and can be removed, still satisfying all workflow dependency constraints, thereby reducing overall resource usage. Thus, the makespan is reduced to 166,

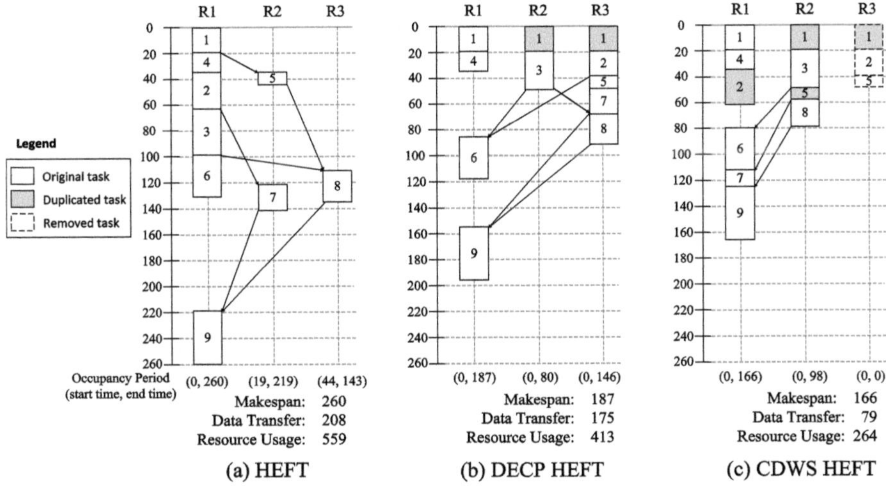

Fig. 2. Scheduling using HEFT, DECP and CDWS for the workflow in Fig. 1.

with a data transmission volume of 79 and total resource usage of 264, achieving significant performance improvements compared to HEFT and DECP.

Note that the start time of the occupancy period for each resource is defined as the earliest finish time among all predecessors of tasks assigned to that resource. This is based on the assumption that when a task completes execution, it immediately transmits data to its successor task, and this successor task simultaneously begins receiving the data. Correspondingly, the end time is defined as the latest data transmission completion time among all tasks assigned to that resource. The resource usage (displayed for each schedule in Fig. 2) is the sum of the occupancy period of all resources. As resource usage directly correlates to the cloud rental period required (hence, monetary cost), it is an important indicator of the efficiency of the schedule.

5   Duplication Based Workflow Scheduling

This section provides a detailed description of the proposed Communication-aware Duplication-based Workflow Scheduling (CDWS) algorithm, which consists of two phases: the scheduling phase and the elimination phase. The pseudocode of each phase is presented in Algorithms 1 and 2, respectively. The algorithm accepts three inputs: workflow structure, computation cost matrix, and bandwidth matrix. The output is a schedule, which allocates tasks onto the resources.

In the scheduling phase, tasks are first sorted using HEFT's upward ranking (line 1). The algorithm then initializes *dupSched* to store scheduling results and schedules tasks sequentially by rank. During each task's scheduling process, the local variables *EFT* (minimum earliest finish time), *copySched* (intermediate scheduling results), and *bestRes* (selected resource) are initialized (line 4). Next,

---

Algorithm 1. CDWS scheduling phase

Require: W: workflow, cM: computation matrix, bM: bandwidth matrix
Ensure: $dupSched$: final scheduling result
1: $taskList, Res \leftarrow sortTask(W, cM, bM)$
2: $dupSched \leftarrow \emptyset$
3: **for** t in $taskList$ **do**
4:     $EFT \leftarrow \infty$, $copySched \leftarrow dupSched$, $bestRes \leftarrow None$
5:     **for** r in Res **do**
6:         $EST_{noDup} \leftarrow$ Earliest start time of t without any duplication or reschedule
7:         $cp \leftarrow$ The predecessor of t whose data arrives latest on r
8:         $EFT_{noDup} \leftarrow$ Earliest finish time of t on r based on EST_{noDup}
9:         $updatedSched \leftarrow$ The schedule obtained by rescheduling cp on r when
$outDegree(cp) = 1$, or by duplicating cp when $outDegree(cp) > 1$
10:        $EFT_{Dup} \leftarrow$ Earliest finish time of t on r with duplication or reschedules of cp
11:        **if** $EFT_{noDup} < EFT$ **then**
12:           $EFT \leftarrow EFT_{noDup}$, $bestRes \leftarrow r$
13:        **end if**
14:        **if** $cp \neq Null$ and $EFT_{Dup} < EFT$ **then**
15:           $EFT \leftarrow EFT_{Dup}$, $bestRes \leftarrow r$, $copySched \leftarrow updatedSched$
16:        **end if**
17:     **end for**
18:     $dupSched \leftarrow copySched$
19:     $dupSched.add(ev)$ ▷ Create a schedule event for task t and add it to $dupSched$
20: **end for**
21: $dupSched \leftarrow eliminationPhase(W, bM, dupSched, taskList)$ ▷ Algorithm 2

---

the algorithm iterates over all resources to find the optimal one for each task (lines 5–17). For each resource, the algorithm calculates the task's earliest start time (EST_{noDup}) without any duplication or reschedule on the resource (line 6), and identifies its critical predecessor cp as the predecessor with the latest data arrival time (line 7). The earliest finish time of the task (EFT_{noDup}) is then calculated based on EST_{noDup} (line 8). For a non-entry task (cp is not null), the algorithm attempts to duplicate its cp on the current resource if its out-degree is greater than 1. Otherwise, cp is rescheduled to that resource and its obsolete schedule is removed (line 9). Then, schedule task t on the same resource as its cp and calculate the resulting finish time EFT_{Dup} (line 10). After comparing EFT_{noDup} and EFT_{Dup} against the current EFT, the algorithm updates EFT and $bestRes$ if a better solution is found (lines 11–16). Once all resources are evaluated, $copySched$ is copied to $dupSched$ (line 18), and the final scheduling event for task t is created and added to $dupSched$ (line 19). This process repeats for all tasks, followed by an elimination phase to remove redundant schedules (line 21). Note that lines 8 and 10 compute EFT according to HEFT [17] (a variant called CDWS-HEFT). This computation can be replaced with the minimum EFT of the successors of each task according to HEFT-Lookahead [4] (a variant called CDWS-Lookahead).

Algorithm 2. CDWS elimination phase

Require: $W, bM, dupSched, taskList$
Ensure: $dupSched$: pruned scheduling results
 1: $checklist = \{t_{exit}\}, usefulTaskList = \emptyset$
 2: **while** $checklist \neq \emptyset$ **do**
 3:     $t = checklist.pop()$ ▷ Pop the task with the lowest rank
 4:     **for** p in $W.pred(t)$ **do**
 5:         $duplicates \leftarrow duplist(p)$ ▷ Get the duplicates of task p, including itself
 6:         $usefulDup \leftarrow getUsefulDup(duplicates, t, W, bM)$
 7:         $checklist.insert(usefulDup, taskList)$ ▷ Insert $usefulDup$ into $checklist$
    in ascending order according to their ranks
 8:     **end for**
 9:     $usefulTaskList.add(t)$
10: **end while**
11: **for** ev in $dupSched$ **do**
12:     **if** $ev.task \notin usefulTaskList$ **then**
13:         $dupSched.remove(ev)$
14:     **end if**
15: **end for**

The elimination phase (Algorithm 2) follows a bottom-up approach, starting from the exit tasks. The algorithm initializes two variables (line 1). *checklist* contains tasks whose predecessors need to be examined. It is initialized with all exit tasks arranged in ascending order according to their ranks. *usefulTaskList* maintains the set of tasks determined to be useful for the final schedule. The main processing occurs in a while loop that continues until *checklist* is empty, indicating all potentially useful tasks have been examined (lines 2–10). Within the loop, the algorithm pops the task t with the lowest rank (line 3) and iterates over its predecessors (line 4). For each predecessor, the algorithm determines which duplicate is useful using two criteria: either a duplicate executing on the same resource as t and completing before t begins, or if no such duplicate exists, the one whose data arrives latest while still preceding t's start time. This latter criterion minimizes resource usage by allowing data reception to begin at the latest possible time (lines 5-6). The identified useful predecessors are inserted into the *checklist* while maintaining ascending rank order (line 7), and once all useful predecessors are determined, task t is added to *usefulTaskList* (line 9). Finally, the algorithm iterates through all scheduling events, removing those corresponding to tasks not in *usefulTaskList* (lines 11–15).

The complexity of CDWS relates to the number of tasks v, edges e and resources r. For the scheduling phase, computing rank values and sorting tasks requires $O(vlogv)$ time, identifying and duplicating critical predecessors and scheduling all tasks requires time similar to HEFT, that is $O(re)$, or commonly reduced to $O(rv^2)$ for dense graphs [17], but noting that in the case of CDWS the number of tasks now includes duplicates. The elimination phase requires $O(v+ed)$ operations to determine all useful tasks, where d is the average number of duplicates per task (a value of $d = 1$ means no duplicates). Thus, the overall complexity of the CDWS algorithm is $O(vlogv) + O(r(vd)^2) + O(v + ed)$ or simply $O(r(vd)^2)$; clearly, the complexity is dominated by the scheduling phase and relates to the number of duplicates. Compared to HEFT, whose computational complexity is $O(rv^2)$ [17], CDWS has a higher complexity. However, this is not as high as DECP (based on HEFT) [12], which has a complexity $(r + c)$ times higher than HEFT, where c is the average number of all ancestors per task.

6   Performance Evaluation

6.1   Experimental Setup

For evaluation, CDWS was implemented making use of both HEFT (CDWS-HEFT) and HEFT-Lookahead (CDWS-Lookahead). Performance is compared against the baselines: HEFT [17], HEFT-Lookahead [4], DECP-HEFT [12], and DECP-Lookahead [12]. Experiments were conducted using synthetic data from four structurally diverse real-world workflows [15]: Montage, CyberShake, LIGO and Sipht. All implementations were developed in Python and executed on an Intel i7-13700F CPU.

The experimental settings are consistent with those presented in [12]. For each workflow application, a DAG of 100 tasks was generated using the Pegasus group workflow generator[1]. Task computation requirements were randomly generated between 500 and 5000 million instructions, while data transmission volumes (in MB) for directed edges were randomly selected from (500, 5000) and scaled according to communication-to-computation ratios (CCR) of 0.5, 1, 2, and 5. Simulations were conducted in a heterogeneous environment of 15 resources with processing capacity (100–500 MIPS) and network bandwidth (100–500 MB/s), which is also consistent with what was used in [12]. The simulations were run 100 times for each workflow and CCR combination with different generated settings, and the average results were used for analysis. In each simulation, the same workflow and resource settings were used to test CDWS and the baselines.

Three metrics were used to evaluate algorithm performance: average normalized schedule length (NSL), data transmission volume, and resource utilization rate. Among these, NSL is defined as the ratio of makespan to the length of critical path of the DAG, where the critical path is computed as the longest path from an entry node to an exit node [16]. Data transmission volume is the total amount of data transmitted across resources. Resource utilization rate is the ratio of the sum of actual task execution times to the total resource usage, which has been defined in Sect. 4.

6.2   Results and Analysis

(a) Montage: Figure 3 presents results for the Montage workflow. Both CDWS implementations achieve lower NSL than baselines, with improvements increasing at higher CCR values. CDWS-HEFT reduces NSL by 2.2–10% versus HEFT

---

[1] https://github.com/pegasus-isi/WorkflowGenerator.

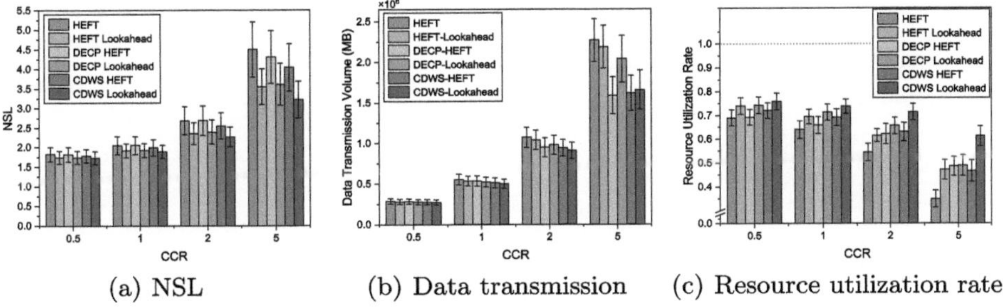

(a) NSL   (b) Data transmission   (c) Resource utilization rate

Fig. 3. Results for Montage with 100 tasks on 15 resources.

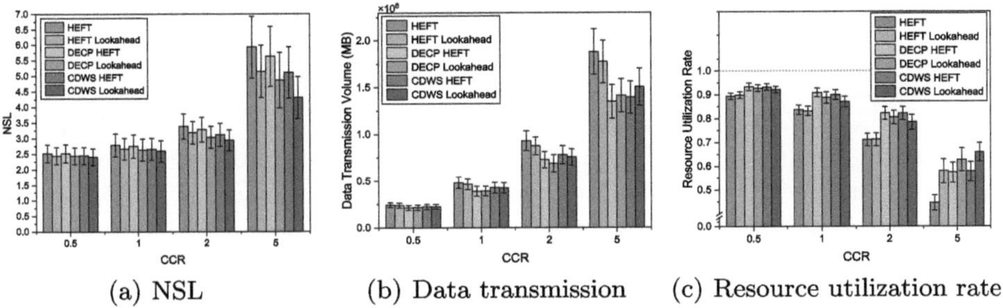

(a) NSL   (b) Data transmission   (c) Resource utilization rate

Fig. 4. Results for CyberShake with 100 tasks on 15 resources.

and 2.2–6% versus DECP-HEFT across increasing CCRs. CDWS-Lookahead achieves up to 9% reduction versus HEFT-Lookahead and 10.7% versus DECP-Lookahead at CCR=5.

For data transmission, both CDWS implementations show modest reductions (3.7%, 2.6%) at CCR=0.5 but substantial improvements (28.6%, 24%) at CCR=5 compared to HEFT and HEFT-Lookahead. Against DECP-HEFT, CDWS-HEFT shows minimal improvement and slightly higher volume at CCR=5. This is likely due to CDWS-HEFT's increased duplications, as newly added duplicates require data thereby generating additional data transmission. However, CDWS-Lookahead achieves up to 18.6% reduction versus DECP-Lookahead at CCR=5, highlighting how different scheduling mechanisms between HEFT and HEFT-Lookahead affect duplication strategy effectiveness.

Regarding resource utilization, CDWS-HEFT outperforms HEFT and DECP-HEFT with one exception (4% lower than DECP-HEFT at CCR=5). This slight decrease may be due to idle time slots generated by CDWS's elimination phase. CDWS-Lookahead consistently exceeds both HEFT-Lookahead and DECP-Lookahead, with significant improvements (30%, 25%) at CCR=5.

(b) CyberShake: Figure 4 presents results for the CyberShake workflow. CDWS-HEFT reduces NSL by 2.8–13.8% versus HEFT and 2.8–9.2% versus DECP-HEFT across increasing CCRs. CDWS-Lookahead achieves more sub-

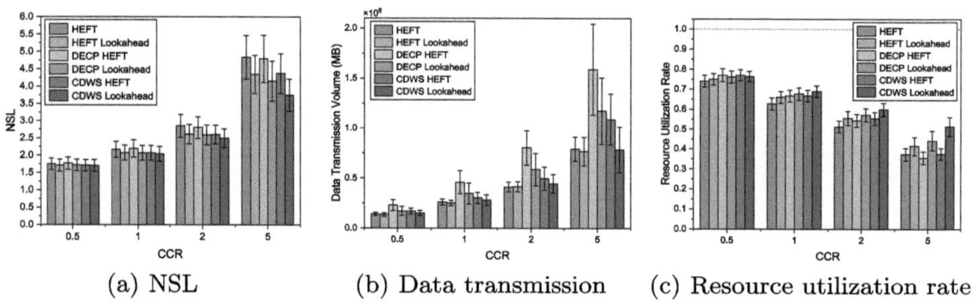

(a) NSL   (b) Data transmission   (c) Resource utilization rate

Fig. 5. Results for LIGO with 100 tasks on 15 resources.

stantial improvements (1.6–16.3% versus HEFT-Lookahead, 1.2–11.5% versus DECP-Lookahead), with most significant gains at CCR=5.

For data transmission, both CDWS implementations achieve substantial reductions compared to HEFT and HEFT-Lookahead (CDWS-HEFT: 8.2–26%, CDWS-Lookahead: 5.9–15.3%), but show increased volume versus DECP implementations. DECP evaluates all resources to schedule a task after duplicating its critical predecessor, enabling them to be assigned to different resources, while CDWS co-locates tasks with their duplicated critical predecessors on the same resource to reduce complexity. This gives DECP greater flexibility in task placement, enabling more entry task duplications and lower transmission volumes.

Regarding resource utilization, CDWS-HEFT shows 4.5–28.9% improvement over HEFT, with minimal differences from DECP-HEFT. CDWS-Lookahead demonstrates 2.2–13.8% higher utilization than HEFT-Lookahead, with slight decreases versus DECP-Lookahead at lower CCRs but a notable 4.8% improvement at CCR=5.

(c) LIGO: Figure 5 presents results for the LIGO workflow. For NSL, CDWS-HEFT achieves reductions of 1.7–9.7% versus HEFT and 2.8–9.0% versus DECP-HEFT. CDWS-Lookahead performs even better with reductions of 0.6–13.8% versus HEFT-Lookahead and 0.6–9.9% versus DECP-Lookahead, with most significant gains at higher CCRs.

For data transmission, both CDWS implementations show higher volumes than HEFT and HEFT-Lookahead but substantial reductions versus DECP (CDWS-HEFT: 25.9–38.3% lower than DECP-HEFT). Since both CDWS and DECP duplicate join tasks, there is an increased data transmission to these tasks. For other tasks, each task has only one successor, resulting in task rescheduling instead of duplication. CDWS co-locates tasks with their rescheduled critical predecessors, resulting in significantly lower data transmission than DECP.

Regarding resource utilization, CDWS-HEFT shows modest improvements (2.7–7.8%) over HEFT with similar performance to DECP-HEFT. CDWS-Lookahead demonstrates more substantial gains, particularly at CCR=5 (21.4% over HEFT-Lookahead, 15.9% over DECP-Lookahead), highlighting CDWS-

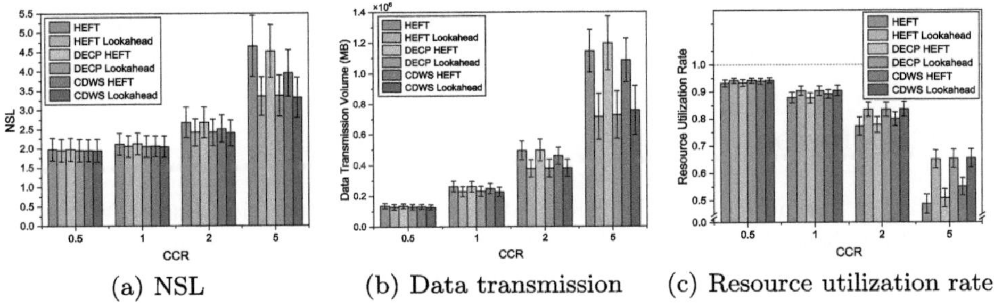

(a) NSL   (b) Data transmission   (c) Resource utilization rate

Fig. 6. Results for Sipht with 100 tasks on 15 resources.

Lookahead's particular effectiveness in improving resource utilization for the LIGO workflow at high communication.

(d) Sipht: Figure 6 presents results for the Sipht workflow. Lookahead-based algorithms generally outperform HEFT-based algorithms across all metrics, while duplication-based approaches yield more significant relative improvements when applied to HEFT than to HEFT-Lookahead. For NSL, CDWS-HEFT achieves significant reductions (1.5–15.1%) over HEFT and comparable improvements against DECP-HEFT. CDWS-Lookahead shows more modest gains (0.5–0.9%) versus both HEFT-Lookahead and DECP-Lookahead, indicating CDWS provides greater NSL benefits when implemented within HEFT for Sipht.

Regarding data transmission, CDWS-HEFT achieves moderate reductions versus both HEFT (3.6–7.3%) and DECP-HEFT (3.2-9.3%). CDWS-Lookahead shows minimal improvements at lower CCRs and actual increases at higher CCRs compared to both HEFT-Lookahead and DECP-Lookahead, suggesting duplication-based approaches implemented within HEFT-Lookahead offer limited data transmission benefits for Sipht workflows, particularly at higher communication intensities.

Regarding resource utilization, CDWS-HEFT demonstrates modest improvements (1.1-12.2%) over HEFT and similar gains versus DECP-HEFT, while CDWS-Lookahead shows minimal differences versus both HEFT-Lookahead and DECP-Lookahead.

Execution Time: Regarding execution time of our implementations, HEFT executes within milliseconds, while CDWS-HEFT requires two orders of magnitude longer but DECP-HEFT demands three orders of magnitude longer, across all workflow types. Both HEFT-Lookahead and CDWS-Lookahead complete within seconds but DECP-Lookahead requires an additional order of magnitude in execution time. These results indicate that CDWS incurs higher execution time than HEFT, which can be attributed to the additional computational overhead introduced by the task duplication and elimination phase. Meanwhile, CDWS achieves shorter execution time than DECP, which requires iterating over all resources again after each duplication operation to schedule tasks. Although some of the extra execution time costs are due to data structure manipulation overheads, the performance differences between the three implementations are broadly consistent with the complexity analysis presented in Sect. 5.

7   Conclusion

This paper introduced a Communication-Aware Duplication-based Workflow Scheduling algorithm for heterogeneous cloud resources, CDWS, which, through critical predecessor identification, selective duplication and redundancy elimination, outperforms baselines, achieving improvements in normalized schedule length, data transmission volume, and resource utilization rate, particularly at higher CCR values where communication costs dominate. Furthermore, CDWS reduces execution time by one to two orders of magnitude compared to DECP while still offering competitive performance benefits. Future work will focus on applying CDWS to more complex scenarios, including resource-constrained environments as well as exploring its potential integration with other scheduling optimization techniques.

Acknowledgments. Yani Ping acknowledges the financial support from the China Scholarship Council.

References

1. Ahmad, W., Alam, B.: An efficient list scheduling algorithm with task duplication for scientific big data workflow in heterogeneous computing environments. Concurr. Comput.: Pract. Exper. **33**(5), e5987 (2021). https://doi.org/10.1002/cpe.5987
2. Ahmad, W., Gautam, G., Alam, B., Bhati, B.S.: An analytical review and performance measures of state-of-art scheduling algorithms in heterogeneous computing environment. Arch. Comput. Methods Eng. **31**(5), 3091–3113 (2024). https://doi.org/10.1007/s11831-024-10069-8
3. Berisha, B., Mëziu, E., Shabani, I.: Big data analytics in Cloud computing: an overview. J. Cloud Comput. **11**(1), 24 (2022). https://doi.org/10.1186/s13677-022-00301-w
4. Bittencourt, L.F., Sakellariou, R., Madeira, E.R.M.: DAG scheduling using a lookahead variant of the heterogeneous earliest finish time algorithm. In: 2010 18th Euromicro Conference on Parallel, Distributed and Network-based Processing, pp. 27–34 (2010). https://doi.org/10.1109/PDP.2010.56
5. Choudhary, A., Govil, M.C., Singh, G., Awasthi, L.K., Pilli, E.S.: Energy-aware scientific workflow scheduling in cloud environment. Clust. Comput. **25**(6), 3845–3874 (2022). https://doi.org/10.1007/s10586-022-03613-3
6. Chowdhary, S.K., Rao, A.: A task clustering based QoS aware scheduling algorithm for task execution in cloud-Iot model for education services. Multimed. Tools Appl. **82**(29), 44783–44800 (2023). https://doi.org/10.1007/s11042-023-15392-z
7. Dogan, A., Ozguner, R.: LDBS: a duplication based scheduling algorithm for heterogeneous computing systems. In: Proceedings International Conference on Parallel Processing, pp. 352–359 (2002). https://doi.org/10.1109/ICPP.2002.1040891

8. Gu, R., et al.: Fluid-Shuttle: efficient cloud data transmission based on serverless computing compression. IEEE/ACM Trans. Netw. **32**(6), 4554–4569 (2024). https://doi.org/10.1109/TNET.2024.3402561

9. Karathanasis, K., Kontogiannis, S., Zaroliagis, C.: Optimizing task orchestration across the cloud continuum. In: IFIP International Conference on Artificial Intelligence Applications and Innovations, pp. 209–222. Springer (2025). https://doi.org/10.1007/978-3-031-97317-8_16

10. Li, F., Tan, W.J., Seok, M.G., Cai, W.: Clustering-based multi-objective optimization considering fairness for multi-workflow scheduling on clouds. J. Parall. Distrib. Comput. **194**, 104968 (2024). https://doi.org/10.1016/j.jpdc.2024.104968

11. Liu, C.H., Li, C.F., Lai, K.C., Wu, C.C.: A dynamic critical path duplication task scheduling algorithm for distributed heterogeneous computing systems. In: 12th International Conference on Parallel and Distributed Systems - (ICPADS'06), vol. 1, pp. 8 pp.– (2006). https://doi.org/10.1109/ICPADS.2006.37

12. Lopes Genez, T.A., Sakellariou, R., Bittencourt, L.F., Mauro Madeira, E.R., Braun, T.: Scheduling scientific workflows on clouds using a task duplication approach. In: 2018 IEEE/ACM 11th International Conference on Utility and Cloud Computing (UCC), pp. 83–92 (2018). https://doi.org/10.1109/UCC.2018.00017

13. Pietri, I., Sakellariou, R.: Scheduling data-intensive scientific workflows with reduced communication. In: Proceedings of the 30th International Conference on Scientific and Statistical Database Management, pp. 1–4 (2018). https://doi.org/10.1145/3221269.3221298

14. Qin, S., Pi, D., Shao, Z.: AILS: a budget-constrained adaptive iterated local search for workflow scheduling in cloud environment. Expert Syst. Appl. **198**, 116824 (2022). https://doi.org/10.1016/j.eswa.2022.116824

15. Silva, R.F.d., Chen, W., Juve, G., Vahi, K., Deelman, E.: Community resources for enabling research in distributed scientific workflows, In: 2014 IEEE 10th International Conference on e-Science, pp. 177–184 (2014). https://doi.org/10.1109/eScience.2014.44

16. Tang, X., Li, K., Liao, G., Li, R.: List scheduling with duplication for heterogeneous computing systems. J. Parall. Distrib. Comput. **70**(4), 323–329 (2010). https://doi.org/10.1016/j.jpdc.2010.01.003

17. Topcuoglu, H., Hariri, S., Wu, M.Y.: Performance-effective and low-complexity task scheduling for heterogeneous computing. IEEE Trans. Parallel Distrib. Syst. **13**(3), 260–274 (2002). https://doi.org/10.1109/71.993206

18. Vamsheedhar Reddy, P., Ganesh Reddy, K.: An energy efficient RL based workflow scheduling in cloud computing. Expert Syst. Appl. **234**, 121038 (2023). https://doi.org/10.1016/j.eswa.2023.121038

Secure Management of a Water Distribution Network in Multi-tenant Scenarios

Pierluigi Locatelli$^{(\boxtimes)}$, Tiziana Cattai , Pietro Spadaccino ,
and Francesca Cuomo

Department of Information Engineering, Electronics and Telecommunications,
Sapienza University of Rome, Rome, Italy
`{pierluigi.locatelli,tiziana.cattai,pietro.spadaccino,`
`francesca.cuomo}@uniroma1.it`

Abstract. Water Distribution Networks (WDNs) are key infrastructures for water supply for domestic, public and industrial use. Efficient WDN monitoring is essential to have a sustainable and reliable service, especially in the critical scenarios of water scarcity exacerbated by poor water infrastructure maintenance. Water operators are distinct from the water utility itself, and are responsible for the deployment and management of sensors. This generates a fragmented management structure, especially in areas where multiple operators share different parts of the WDNs. In this context, trust represents an essential challenge. Since each operator manages their own sensors and data, there is no unified view of the entire system. This fragmentation can cause issues, especially when one operator needs to route water through infrastructure owned by another. Here, we propose a trustworthy water network monitoring framework based on blockchain and specifically on DeLoRaN, a decentralized network model built for LoRaWAN environments. By decentralizing the sensor management and enabling verifiable logging, DeLoRaN presents a useful tool for smart water networks in multiple independent operators.

Keywords: WDN Monitoring · IoT security · Blockchain

1 Introduction

WDNs are fundamental infrastructures for the distribution of drinking water for domestic, public and industrial use. The efficient WDNs monitoring is today paramount to ensure a sustainable and reliable service in the critical scenario caused by water scarcity and exacerbated by poor water infrastructure maintenance [10].

The estimation of the precise volume of water flowing through the WDN and the demand from users is crucial for forecasting future consumption [23], identifying and treat leakages [9], and enabling dynamic water pricing through

D. Garlisi and D. Chatzopoulos (Eds.): ALGOCLOUD 2025, LNCS 16349, pp. 108–121, 2026.
https://doi.org/10.1007/978-3-032-13744-9_8

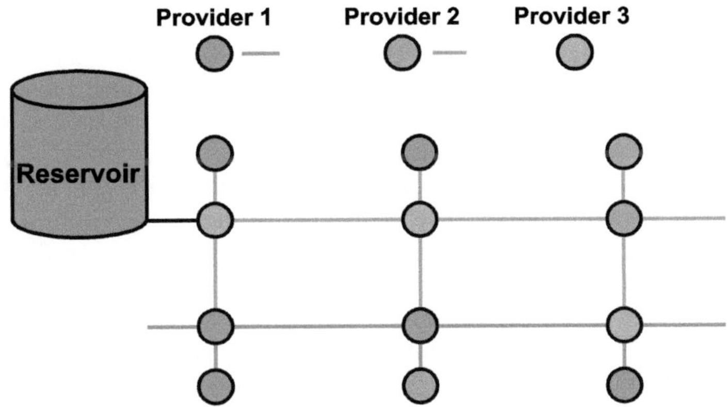

Fig. 1. A representation of a multi-tenant WDN. In particular we have 3 different providers owning different sections of the pipes (lines) and a slice of the costumers (dots). Additionally, every provider gets his share of water from a reservoir owned by Provider 1, instead of having each one their own reservoir.

smart contracts [17]. This is a difficult task due to inconsistencies in how data is collected and reported and differences in deployment in different areas. Traditionally, water network monitoring have been realized by manual operations or over-simplified models, which are expensive, slow and with high error risk [11].

To this end, water sensors may be placed throughout the WDN to monitor flows and water demands from users, transmitting the collected data to a centralized system. Regarding sensor technology, no specific solution has emerged as a standard for WDN monitoring. Internet of Things (IoT) systems that offer low power usage and long-range wireless communication, such as those based on a Low Power Wide-Area Network (LPWAN), are particularly well-suited for this application. Among the available LPWAN technologies, Long Range Wide Area Network (LoRaWAN) has gained significant interest in WDN monitoring due to its advantages in energy efficiency, wide coverage, operational and deployment simplicity [15].

1.1 Multi-tenant Smart Water Distribution Network

Water operators are typically independent entities, distinct from the water utility itself, and are solely responsible for the deployment and management of sensors. This creates a fragmented management structure, especially in areas where multiple operators oversee different parts of the WDNs. While multi-tenant arrangements in water distribution are still rare, we are beginning to see pilot projects that experiment with shared infrastructure and collaborative monitoring in IoT-based water management systems, with scenarios similar to Fig. 1. For example, in Far North Queensland, Australia, a Water Ledger pilot tested blockchain technology to streamline water rights trading among multiple stakeholders [7], creating a shared infrastructure where parties with competing interests could securely share data and collaborate on water usage without compromising trust or transparency. Similarly, in Liège, Belgium, the CILE and NTT collaboration deployed a LoRaWAN-based IoT system for smart water grid monitoring [13], where multiple entities (utilities, contractors, and municipal bodies) share data for more efficient water management.

Despite these innovative pilot projects, full-scale multi-tenant systems for WDNs are not yet widespread. The challenges of data ownership, security, and integrity still present significant barriers to their adoption in traditional water utilities. Water operators are generally reluctant to share real-time data, particularly when this data could be used to influence water pricing or operational decisions. As a result, current monitoring systems tend to be siloed, with each operator responsible for specific segments of the network, leading to a lack of transparency and limited cooperation.

1.2   Trust in a Multi-tenant Water Distribution Network Environment

Trust becomes a major issue when multiple independent operators manage different sections of the same water network. Since each operator is responsible for their own sensors and data, there is no unified view of the entire system. This fragmentation can lead to disputes, especially when one operator needs to route water through infrastructure owned by another. In such cases, fees are charged based on usage, which relies heavily on accurate and trustworthy data about flow rates, volumes, and other metrics. But without a shared source of truth, it's difficult to verify whether reported data is correct. Operators may doubt whether others are accurately measuring or honestly reporting their usage, especially when financial interests are involved. This lack of transparency can lead to mistrust, data manipulation, and disagreements over billing or responsibility in the case of failures or shortages. An independent trustworthy third-party entity, such as a government or alliances, may not be practical when operators are autonomous or competitive. As an alternative, technologies like distributed blockchains, offer a way to build shared trust. These systems make it possible to record data and transactions in a secure, tamper-proof, and transparent way, allowing all stakeholders to verify information without needing to rely on a central authority.

To address the need for trust, auditability, and data integrity in multi-operator WDNs, it is important to allow all stakeholders to independently verify the authenticity and origin of data, even when it comes from infrastructure they do not control. If data is only stored after decoding or aggregation, there is no way to confirm whether reported values reflect the original sensor readings, which can lead to disputes or manipulation, especially when financial agreements depend on accurate flow measurements. Anchoring these original packets or their cryptographic fingerprints to a blockchain at the point of reception allows for a tamper-evident, time-stamped log that all parties can access, creating a shared record supporting fairness, transparency, and future audits.

A possible solution of an architecture that supports this approach is DeLo-RaN [12], a decentralized network model built for LPWAN environments. It allows packet payloads to be stored on the blockchain early in the communication chain, preserving the integrity of the data across different stakeholders. By distributing trust and enabling verifiable logging without relying on centralized servers, DeLoRaN aligns well with the needs of smart water networks that involve multiple independent operators.

The main contributions of our work are the following:

- We identify, present and investigate the problem of creating trustworthy and collaborative monitoring systems for multi-tenant water networks, with particular focus on the integrity and verifiability of WDN status data exchanged between the parties;
- We propose DeLoRaN as a framework to add trust to a multi-tenant WDN, demonstrating how decentralized blockchain-based control can ensure data integrity between non-trusted parties;
- We analyze the trade-off between working in a sampled sensor measurement environment, showing the impact of non-trusted devices from third-party tenant on data accuracy, and demonstrate that DeLoRaN ensures the integrity of the data until the Byzantine device threshold of 33%, beyond which analytical network reconstruction methods offer a better solution for data reliability.

2   Related Works

In recent years, applied research on IoT sensor networks has increasingly focused on WDNs, driven by the need to improve efficiency in a critical context where infrastructure is aging, significant water losses occur due to leakages, and ensuring a reliable water supply to users is becoming ever more crucial [14, 15]. In this scenario, deploying IoT sensors can be challenging due to geographic constraints and high deployment costs, including both personnel and infrastructure/material expenses. In this scenario of typical sample-based measurements, it is necessary to identify methods for signal reconstruction [4] or for integration across different tenants [18].

In this direction, trust-enhancing mechanisms, such as decentralized access control, transparent audit trails, and secure data provenance, can provide an additional security layer. In such contexts, blockchain can serve as a backbone for managing and sharing sensor data among utilities, operators, and regulatory bodies, eliminating the need for a central trusted authority.

Blockchain integration in IoT addresses trust, data integrity, and multi-party coordination challenges. As shown by Ayub et al. [2], blockchain addresses the core vulnerabilities of IoT, including insecure data transmission, poor access control, and lack of auditability, by providing a tamper-proof, decentralized ledger that enhances transparency and reliability in device interactions. In particular, blockchain fosters trust among mutually untrusted parties by leveraging smart contracts and permissioned ledgers to enforce access policies and automate transaction validation. This is especially relevant in industrial and infrastructure monitoring scenarios, where multiple stakeholders interact with heterogeneous IoT devices. Khan et al. [8] present a Hyperledger Sawtooth-based framework that combines chaincode-driven automation and re-encryption to ensure data confidentiality, trustworthiness, and traceability within Industrial IoT environments. Their architecture introduces both on-chain and off-chain communication channels, enabling secure and scalable transaction management even under constrained computational and network resources. Complementing these findings, Rizvi et al. [16] provide a broad overview of blockchain's role in IoT security, emphasizing its effectiveness in solving common threats such as spoofing, data tampering, and denial-of-service attacks through immutable logging and decentralized consensus.

3   Multi-tenant Water Distribution Network Monitoring Problem

We consider an environment where an operator is interested in monitoring the status of a water network collecting real-time data. We define the *WDN status* as the collection of all measurements in the network, such as water flow rates in pipes, pressures at nodes, and demand levels. Such data collection is usually performed using smart LPWAN sensors [6], such as those based on LoRaWAN, which can be distributed across the network to gather different measurements. We assume that the smart sensors deployed on the water network produce an accurate reading.

The problem that we investigate is how an operator can monitor the status of the full water network in a multi-tenant scenario, where multiple operators share responsibility for managing sections of the network. In an ideal scenario, the operator would be the sole entity responsible for the water network. In this case, all data collected from the sensors would be deemed trustworthy, with no concerns about potential alterations or tampering. The operator would have full control over the quality and reliability of the devices, ensuring that the information gathered is consistent and accurate. However, this configuration is often far from reality.

In scenarios where multiple operators are responsible for managing different sections of the water network, no single operator has access to all sensors across the entire infrastructure. As a result, individual operators cannot directly obtain measurements from all sources. This multi-operator setup makes impossible to directly obtain the full status of the entire water network. To address this, we have two main options, summarized in Fig. 2 and described in the remainder of this section: either use methods to estimate the status of a water network from a subsample of sensors, or collaborate between multiple stakeholders.

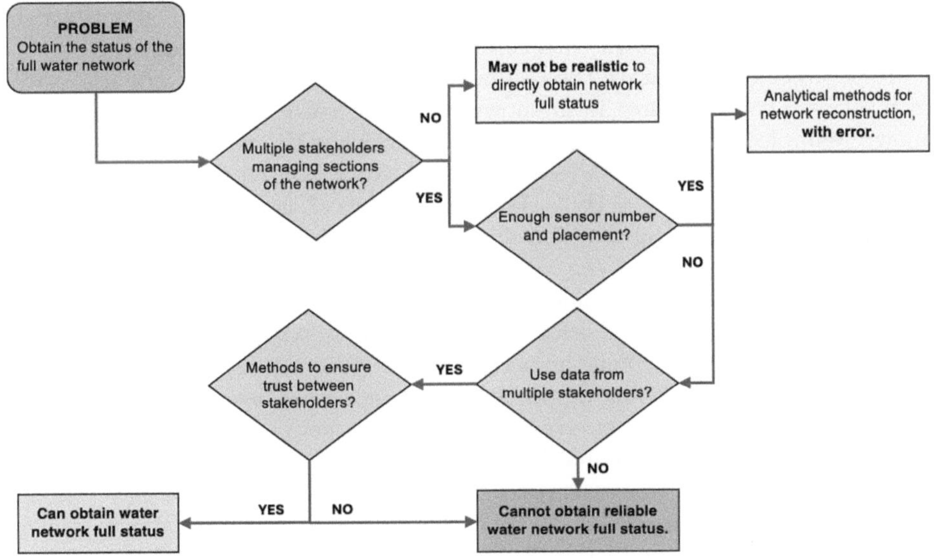

Fig. 2. Decision process diagram for reconstructing the status of a water network.

3.1 Analytical Methods for Network Reconstruction

One possible approach is to use reconstruction methods to obtain the status of the entire water network from a subset of available observations. In recent years, many data-driven methods have been developed to reconstruct flow or pressure fields , and to detect anomalies, by leveraging deep learning algorithms [19] or graph neural networks (GNNs), which are particularly suited for learning on graph-structured domains such as WDNs [22]. These approaches have the advantage of not requiring explicit mathematical modeling of the system dynamics. However, they typically require large amounts of training data, which is often unavailable in real-world water systems due to limited instrumentation, poor data quality, or missing measurements.

For this reason, model-based approaches remain widely used, with some crucial assumptions, such as the hypothesis that the underlying signals (e.g., pressure or flow) are band-limited or smooth over the network graph [5,20]. Other model-based techniques adopt more general assumptions to reconstruct partially observed networks. In this work, we show the application of a signal reconstruction method particularly well-suited for WDNs, which allows estimating flow values from a subset of sensor observations [4]. Although the subset of observed nodes can, in principle, be optimally chosen, here we focus on the case of random sampling, where sensor positions are randomly selected over the network.

We model the WDN as a graph $\mathcal{G} = (\mathcal{V}, \mathcal{E})$, where $\mathcal{V}$ represents the set of N vertices (corresponding to junctions, reservoirs and tanks), and $\mathcal{E}$ is the set of N_E edges (corresponding to pipes, valves, and pumps). The binary adjacency matrix $\mathbf{A} \in \mathbb{R}^{N \times N}$ has entries $a_{ij} = 1$ if there is a pipe connecting nodes i

and j, and $a_{ij} = 0$ otherwise. The incidence matrix $\mathbf{B} \in \mathbb{R}^{N \times N_E}$ describes the node-edge connectivity, with each column corresponding to an edge.

It is possible to separate the columns of $\mathbf{B}$ into two subsets: one associated with edges where the flow is unknown, and one corresponding to edges with known (sampled) flow values, obtaining respectively $\mathbf{B}^U$ and $\mathbf{B}^K$. This decomposition allows to formulate a reconstruction expression [4] to estimate the flow in unsampled links as $\mathbf{f}^U = \mathbf{B}^{U+} \cdot \mathbf{B}^K \cdot \mathbf{f}^K$, where $\cdot^+$ is the pseudo-inverse.

We applied this reconstruction algorithm to a real WDN, L-town, consisting of $N = 785$ nodes and $N_E = 909$ edges. The percentage of unknown flow values was varied using a random sampling strategy. As shown in Fig. 3, the reconstruction mean squared error (MSE), computed with respect to the ground truth, remains very low when the percentage of unknown samples is below 30%. However, as the percentage of missing data increases beyond this point, the reconstruction error grows by approximately an order of magnitude. This indicates that the reconstruction method is effective only when the fraction of unobserved links remains below a certain threshold, corresponding to have enough number of sampled flow values. Beyond this threshold, the reconstruction error becomes too large for the method to be considered reliable.

Taken together, the reconstruction methods (both analytical and data-driven) generally rely on having sufficient sensor coverage and strategically placed devices to provide meaningful data, otherwise the reconstruction error is too high. In other words, if the operator has an adequate number of sensors in critical locations, mathematical approaches can be applied to estimate the status of the entire network. However, if the sensor distribution is sparse or poorly positioned, this approach can lead to significant reconstruction errors.

(a) L-town WDN.

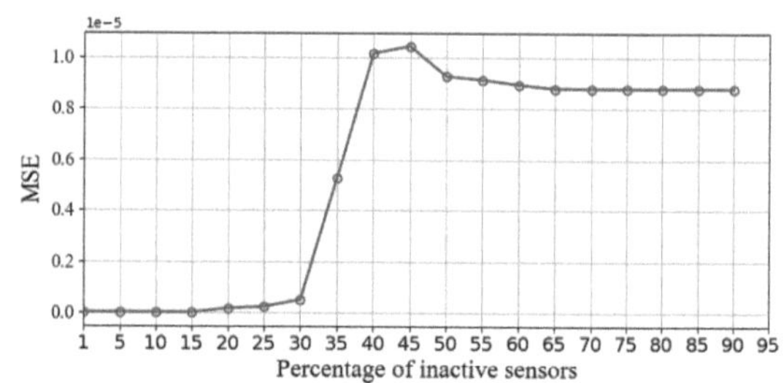

(b) Reconstruction error varying the percentage of inactive/missing sensors

Fig. 3. Water flow reconstruction in a real WDN.

3.2   The Need for Collaboration and Trust-Based Data Sharing

In the absence of sufficient sensor coverage, it is impossible to reliably reconstruct the state of a full WDN. In this situation, operators have enter into agreements with other tenants to access their sensor data. This requires a high level of trust between operators, as they must rely on data provided by others. The challenge here lies in ensuring that the data shared is reliable and its integrity is preserved, as the operator has no direct control over the sensors controlled by other entities.

There are several reasons why one operator might provide false data to another operator. For example, consider a sensor that monitors the water consumption of multiple users. An operator could manipulate the data from this sensor, leading to resource allocation or flow balancing decisions that do not reflect the true situation. This could be used strategically to undermine a competitor by artificially skewing the data. Another example is exploiting the presence of leaks in the network to intentionally alter the water flow to gain an advantage, perhaps for economic reasons, such as reducing operational costs or influencing pricing strategies. This type of manipulation could have a significant impact on the overall performance and fairness of the water network.

There is the need for strategies and mechanisms that ensure the trustworthiness of these agreements and collaborations. However, this is not an easy task. To address this, we propose DeLoRaN, a decentralized management system applied onto smart sensors in a water management environment. In the following sections, we will explore how this system ensures the trust of these agreements and collaborations.

4   A Solution for Secure Water Management

DeLoRaN [12], represented in a WDN context in Fig. 4, moves the network control from a centralized approach to a distributed and decentralized one, by removing the head Network Server and merge its duties with the gateways at the edge of the network, while still keeping full LoRaWAN compliance. Instead of running the network server as one organisation's service, it performs network control procedures as deterministic smart-contracts calls on a permissioned blockchain (Hyperledger Fabric [1] in the reference build). A block is recorded only after several independent stakeholders endorse it, so the ledger itself becomes the "network server of record". All other dashboards and REST APIs merely read from or write to that shared, append-only truth.

Placing the network-server logic on a jointly operated ledger removes subjective considerations in the control plane of the WDN. A join request, a LoRaWAN Adaptive Data Rate (ADR) message or a downlink command is valid only after several parties have signed the corresponding block. Once an uplink hash or gateway signature is sealed on-chain, altering or erasing it is effectively impossible, so questions about missing packets can be settled by simply inspecting the timeline. Session keys are derived inside chain-code, removing a critical point of compromise, while gateways, sensors and valves appear on-chain as asset tokens, which means custody, leasing or transfer happens as a ledger operation, not as paperwork. In practice this turns infrastructure governance from mutual goodwill into verifiable cryptography.

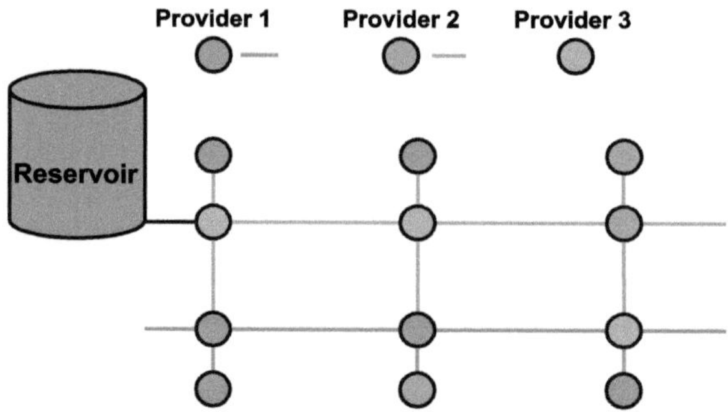

Fig. 4. The image illustrates the role of DeLoRaN in the context of Smart WDNs. Sensors are placed on physical assets within the water distribution system, sending their messages to the distributed control architecture powered by DeLoRaN. The blockchain ensures secure and transparent communication between the different stakeholders (A, B, and C), eliminating the need of trust for the management of a multi-tenant WDN in real-time.

When the same logic is applied to a water-distribution network, the advantages are clear. Maintenance contractors receive only the payloads they are entitled to read, yet everyone, including regulators, can prove that specified packets were forwarded or, conversely, that they went missing. Transparency mandates are easier to satisfy, because a regulator can audit hashed digests of every flow-meter reading without seeing proprietary consumption figures. The tokenisation of field assets even allows temporary emergency delegation: during a drought a civil-protection agency can take control of selected valves for a clearly bounded period, enforced entirely by chain-code.

In Fig. 5, we present two cases: the first illustrates the classic LoRaWAN network management with multiple operators, and the second case involves the use of DeLoRaN. In the first case, summarized in Fig. 5a, multiple stakeholders own their devices, each with its own LoRaWAN network server. These network servers send their data to their respective application servers. When stakeholders need to exchange data, they retrieve it from their application servers and transmit it. However, they have full control over the data being managed and transmitted, and they have the possibility to modify and tamper with the data. In the second case, summarized in Fig. 5b

By using DeLoRaN, and thus a distributed database, we eliminate the need for trust, as the stakeholders no longer need to communicate directly with each other. They can remain isolated, and there is no need for one stakeholder to report its device data to another stakeholder, as they all access the same database. Furthermore, by doing this, we are shifting the inter-stakeholder communication, performed by not trusted application servers, to DeLoRaN and its decentralized management system.

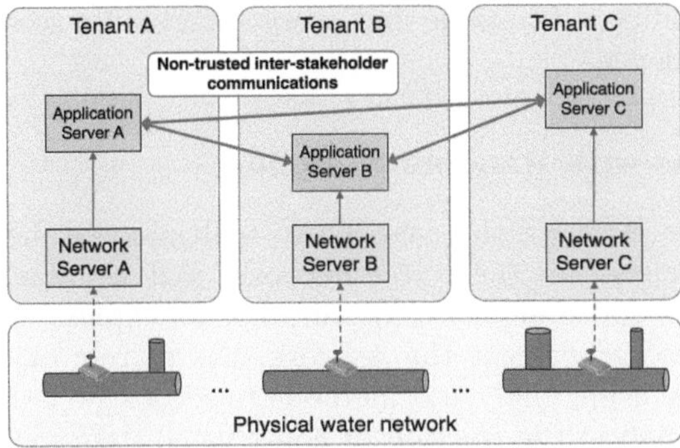

(a) LoRaWAN management where each tenant possesses its own Network Server.

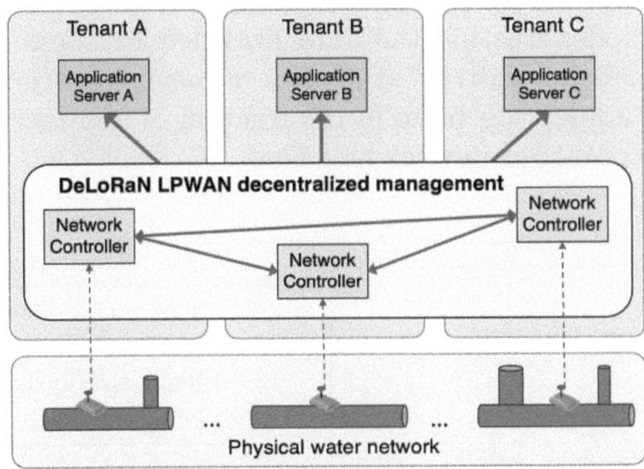

(b) LoRaWAN management through decentralized DeLoRaN architecture.

Fig. 5. LoRaWAN management in case of multiple tenant-owned Network Servers and decentralized DeLoRaN architecture. DeLoRaN eliminates the need for non-trusted communications happening between different tenants.

4.1   A Case Application of DeLoRaN on Water Distribution Networks

A practical consortium might begin with four main entities: the primary utility supplier, a wholesale supplier, the municipal IT office and an analytics provider. A jointly run certificate authority issues identities and allows new subcontractors to be enrolled without downtime. The ledger can be split into an open channel for device registries, join logs and QoS metrics; a second channel that stores hashed traffic events; and private collections that hold decrypted payloads only for parties that need them. Safety-critical actions can require endorsement from the city IT peer plus at least one supplier, while routine metric writes may rely on a lighter quorum. With this arrangement many operators share the same spectrum and gateway fleet, yet none is forced into blind trust: accountability is continuous, liability is traceable and every stakeholder sees exactly the same cryptographic evidence.

4.2 Evaluations with Random Sampling

In this section, we evaluate the case where multiple stakeholders collect data from the smart sensors in the water network, and we aim to determine the overall state of the entire network. Specifically, we explore the case in which a tenant, in order to reconstruct the network, has to rely on data provided by other stakeholders, using analytical methods to reconstruct the full WDN.

In Fig. 6, we analyze the fraction of non-trusted data measurements as the fraction of devices under control increases. Some devices may have a non-trusted behavior because a portion of them is controlled by a third-party stakeholder. In this scenario, each device produces a single measurement. If we rely on generic sub-sampling methods, trusting the data provided by these third-party stakeholders, we may include non-trusted devices in our reconstruction process. As a result, we observe a linear decrease in the fraction of non-trusted measurements as the number of controlled devices increases.

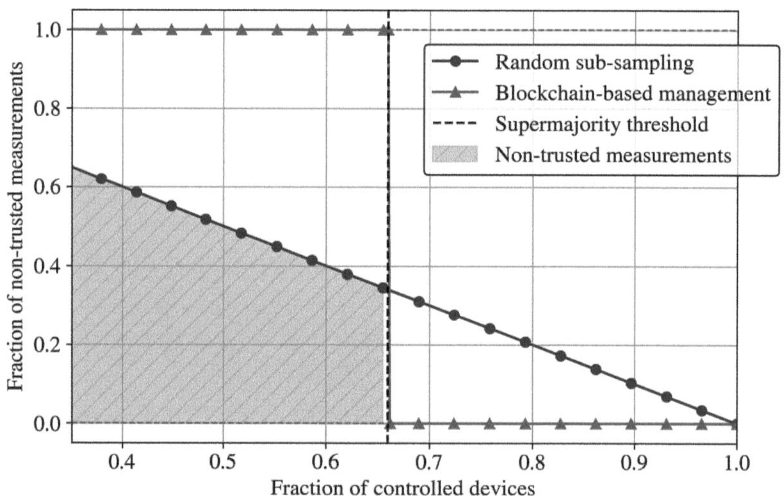

Fig. 6. Fraction of non-trusted measurements in relation with the fraction of non-trusted devices in the network.

However, if we use DeLoRaN to manage the IoT sensors, the devices from third-party stakeholders will provide untampered measurements. This is because the stakeholder cannot modify the data, as they do not control their own network server. This situation holds true when the Byzantine super-majority threshold of 66% + 1 node is reached. In DeLoRaN, when the number of potentially Byzantine devices exceeds the 33% + 1 threshold, the underlying blockchain is no longer considered trusted, and it could potentially fall under the control of byzantine devices, leading to a situation where up to 100% of the measurements could become non-trusted.

Thus, in other words, if the number of devices belonging to other stakeholders exceeds 33%, the best approach would be to include measurements from all devices using methods for network reconstruction in the calculations. In this case, one would risk to have a fraction of non-trusted measurements in the reconstruction, which depends linearly on the amount of controlled devices. If one tenant controls at least 66%+1 devices, the optimal approach would be to use DeLoRaN to manage the data traffic from these devices. In this case, one would not risk to have non-trusted measurements in their calculations.

5   Conclusions

In conclusion, this paper highlights the potential of a decentralized control for ensuring trust, data integrity, and transparency in multi-tenant WDNs. The fragmentation of WDNs, with multiple operators managing different sections, could lead to data inconsistencies and disputes, especially when relying on third-party sensors. DeLoRaN addresses this by decentralizing control and embedding data integrity through blockchain, anchoring sensor data at the point of reception to provide a tamper-proof, transparent, and verifiable record. This significantly reduces chances of disputes, particularly in financial and operational decision-making. While the paper presents a theoretical framework, future work will focus on real-world implementation to evaluate the feasibility of our approach. Case studies will be crucial for refining the system for large-scale deployment. The approach could also apply to other critical infrastructure sectors, such as smart electrical and gas grids, where similar trust issues exist [21] [3]. Insights from DeLoRaN for WDNs could benefit industries requiring secure, transparent data sharing. Implementing decentralized systems will require addressing regulatory, legal, and ethical challenges, especially regarding data privacy and ownership, so future work should also explore DeLoRaN's integration with existing regulatory frameworks. In summary, blockchain integration into multi-tenant WDNs addresses challenges of trust, data integrity, and transparency. By providing a decentralized, verifiable framework, DeLoRaN enhances cooperation between independent operators and improves efficiency, offering a path toward a more sustainable and transparent future.

Acknowledgments. This work was supported by the European Union - Next Generation EU under the Italian National Recovery and Resilience Plan (NRRP), Mission 4, Component 2, Investment 1.3, CUP B53C22004050001, partnership on "Telecommunications of the Future" (PE00000001 - program "RESTART").

Disclosure of Interests. Authors have no competing interests.

References

1. Androulaki, E., et al.: Hyperledger fabric: a distributed operating system for permissioned blockchains. In: Proceedings of the Thirteenth EuroSys Conference, EuroSys 2018, pp. 1–15. ACM (Apr 2018)
2. Ayub, A., Laghari, A.A., Shaikh, Z.A., Dacko-Pikiewicz, Z., Kot, S.: A survey on the integration of blockchain with iot to enhance performance and eliminate challenges. Sustainable Comput. Inform. Syst. **30**, 100512 (2021). https://doi.org/10.1016/j.suscom.2020.100512
3. Carvalho, R., Buzna, L., Bono, F., Gutierrez, E., Just, W., Arrowsmith, D.: Robustness of trans-european gas networks. Phys. Rev. E, Statist. Nonlinear Soft Matter Phys. **80**, 016106 (2009). https://doi.org/10.1103/PhysRevE.80.016106
4. Cattai, T., Colonnese, S., Garlisi, D., Pagano, A., Cuomo, F.: Graphsmart: a method for green and accurate iot water monitoring. ACM Trans. Sensor Netw. **20**(6), 1–32 (2024)
5. Cattai, T., Sardellitti, S., Colonnese, S., Cuomo, F., Barbarossa, S.: Physics-informed topological signal processing for water distribution network monitoring. arXiv preprint arXiv:2505.07560 (2025)
6. Garlisi, D., Restuccia, G., Tinnirello, I., Cuomo, F., Chatzigiannakis, I.: Real-time leakage zone detection in water distribution networks: a machine learning-based stream processing algorithm. In: International Symposium on Algorithmic Aspects of Cloud Computing, pp. 86–99. Springer (2023). https://doi.org/10.1007/978-3-031-49361-4_5
7. Insights, L.: Australian government in water ledger blockchain for trading water rights. Ledger Insights (2020). https://www.ledgerinsights.com/water-ledger-blockchain-australian-government-civic-trading-water-rights/
8. Khan, A.A., Laghari, A.A., Shaikh, Z.A., Dacko-Pikiewicz, Z., Kot, S.: Internet of things (iot) security with blockchain technology: a state-of-the-art review. IEEE Access **10**, 122679–122694 (2022). https://doi.org/10.1109/ACCESS.2022.3223370
9. Leonzio, D.U., Bestagini, P., Marcon, M., Quarta, G.P., Tubaro, S.: Water leak detection via domain adaptation. In: ICASSP 2024-2024 IEEE International Conference on Acoustics, Speech and Signal Processing (ICASSP), pp. 6365–6369. IEEE (2024)
10. Liu, J., et al.: Water scarcity assessments in the past, present, and future. Earth's Future **5**(6), 545–559 (2017)
11. Liu, Z., Kleiner, Y.: State of the art review of inspection technologies for condition assessment of water pipes. Measurement **46**(1), 1–15 (2013)
12. Locatelli, P., Cuomo, F.: Deloran: decentralize lorawan network server through blockchain. In: 2024 IEEE Wireless Communications and Networking Conference (WCNC), pp. 1–6 (2024)
13. NTT: Cile boosts water conservation with iot and lorawan (2024). https://services.global.ntt/en-us/about-us/case-studies/cile
14. Pagano, A., Garlisi, D., Giuliano, F., Cattai, T., Sapienza, F.C.: Swi-feed: smart water iot framework for evaluation of energy and data in massive scenarios. In: 2024 IFIP Networking Conference (IFIP Networking), pp. 583–585. IEEE (2024)
15. Pagano, A., et al.: A survey on massive iot for water distribution systems: challenges, simulation tools, and guidelines for large-scale deployment. Ad Hoc Netw. **168**, 103714 (2025)
16. Rizvi, S.A.A., et al.: Internet of things (iot) security with blockchain technology: a state-of-the-art review. J. Inform. Sec. Appli. **61**, 102925 (2021). https://doi.org/10.1016/j.jisa.2021.102925

17. Sarantakos, T., et al.: A tool to facilitate the design of smart contracts in smart water distribution networks. In: 2024 IFIP Networking Conference (IFIP Networking), pp. 708–713. IEEE (2024)
18. Sigalla, O.Z., Tumbo, M., Joseph, J.: Multi-stakeholder platform in water resources management: a critical analysis of stakeholders' participation for sustainable water resources. Sustainability **13**(16), 9260 (2021)
19. Tornyeviadzi, H.M., Seidu, R.: Leakage detection in water distribution networks via 1d cnn deep autoencoder for multivariate scada data. Eng. Appl. Artif. Intell. **122**, 106062 (2023)
20. Tsitsvero, M., Barbarossa, S., Di Lorenzo, P.: Signals on graphs: uncertainty principle and sampling. IEEE Trans. Signal Process. **64**(18), 4845–4860 (2016)
21. Union for the Coordination of Transmission of Electricity (UCTE): Annual report 2008: On the move. Tech. rep., UCTE (2008). https://eepublicdownloads.entsoe.eu/clean-documents/pre2015/publications/ce/report_2008.pdf, Accessed 3 July 2025
22. Vittori, G., Falkouskaya, Y., Jimenez-Gutierrez, D.M., Cattai, T., Chatzigiannakis, I.: Graph neural networks to model and optimize the operation of water distribution networks: a review. J. Indust. Inform. Integrat., 100880 (2025)
23. Wu, S., Zhao, P., Bai, M., Wang, J., Lan, Y.: A fine grained forecasting method for minute-level urban water demand. In: 2021 40th Chinese Control Conference (CCC), pp. 8298–8303. IEEE (2021)

A Comparative Study of Local Community Detection Algorithms in Static Graphs

Konstantinos Christopoulos$^{(\boxtimes)}$, Georgios Tsiamis, and Konstantinos Tsichlas

University of Patras, Rion, Greece
kchristopou@upnet.gr, {tsiamis,ktsichlas}@ceid.upatras.gr

Abstract. Local community detection is a specialized area within the broader field of community detection, focusing on the identification of communities centered around a set of initial seed nodes. Despite increasing research interest over the past two decades, a comprehensive assessment of the diverse existing methods and their performance under varying conditions remains challenging. In this paper, we conduct a focused comparative study of several well-known local community detection algorithms, applied specifically to static undirected graphs. We implement representative algorithms and evaluate their behavior, strengths, and limitations across standard benchmark datasets. Our aim is to provide clear empirical insights into the performance and trade-offs of these algorithms, thereby guiding researchers in selecting appropriate methods for their use cases. We also present implementation details and evaluation results to promote reproducibility and facilitate further investigation.

Keywords: local community detection · static graphs · comparative study

1 Introduction

Community detection seeks to identify groups of nodes that are densely interconnected within a network, helping to reveal the underlying patterns and relationships embedded in complex systems. Over the years, researchers have proposed numerous techniques to improve our understanding of network structures and to detect meaningful communities. Most traditional approaches concentrate on uncovering global community structures [1], and some extend to overlapping communities [2], where nodes can belong to multiple groups.

Global methods attempt to partition the entire network into distinct communities. However, with the exponential growth of real-world data, these techniques often fall short when applied to large-scale networks. In many practical scenarios, the goal shifts away from analyzing the full network and instead focuses on identifying local structures—smaller, relevant subgraphs centered around specific seed nodes. Such local structures is especially valuable in various domains: spotting

D. Garlisi and D. Chatzopoulos (Eds.): ALGOCLOUD 2025, LNCS 16349, pp. 122–137, 2026.
https://doi.org/10.1007/978-3-032-13744-9_9

suspicious activity in financial transaction networks, isolating functional protein modules in biological systems, or delivering personalized recommendations in e-commerce platforms. By extracting these localized communities, researchers and practitioners can efficiently analyze relevant substructures within vast and complex networks without processing the entire graph.

The key advantages of the local approach include its efficiency, as local community detection (LCD) methods are significantly more scalable compared to global approaches. This is because the analysis is limited to a small portion of the overall graph rather than the entire structure. Another important benefit is flexibility, since these methods allow for the selection of different evaluation criteria for community coherence, which can be adapted to the specific requirements of each application. Additionally, LCD supports targeted analysis of specific regions within a network, making it particularly useful in scenarios where a complete understanding of the network's global structure is unnecessary. Lastly, Local community detection typically starts from one or more predefined seed nodes and focuses on the surrounding network structure. These methods primarily utilize the local neighborhood of the seeds, often without fully considering the quality or influence of the selected nodes.

In this work, we focus on the practical analysis of existing local community detection algorithms applied to static graphs. Our contributions can be summarized as follows:

- Implementation of several well-established local community detection algorithms, enabling a unified and comparable framework for evaluation.
- Application and experimentation of these algorithms on a variety of real-world graphs to observe their behavior under different conditions.
- Comparative analysis, highlighting the strengths and weaknesses of each method based on performance metrics, community quality, and computational efficiency.

Our goal is to provide a clearer understanding of how local community detection algorithms behave in practice and to support informed decisions when selecting an appropriate method for a given problem. The remainder of this paper is organized as follows:

In Sect. 2, we provide a general categorization of local community detection methods, dividing them into two main categories. We then classify the specific algorithms we have implemented according to this framework. In Sect. 3, we detail the experimental setup and present a comparative analysis of the results. Finally, Sect. 4 summarizes our findings and outlines potential directions for future research.

2 Classification and Analysis of Local Community Detection Algorithms

This subsection presents the most important local community detection (LCD) algorithms that have been implemented and studied in the context of this work.

Each algorithm is categorized according to the general class it belongs to (Greedy or Non-Greedy), as defined in the relevant literature [4], and a summary of its core idea, operation, and main characteristics is provided. The classification and presentation of these algorithms aim to enhance the reader's understanding of the various approaches implemented, in preparation for the next section where these algorithms will be experimentally evaluated and compared in terms of their performance on selected networks.

Greedy Approaches. Greedy methods construct communities incrementally, based on step-by-step decisions that optimize a local objective function. These approaches are generally efficient and simple to implement but do not guarantee globally optimal solutions. The majority of local community detection algorithms fall into this category. Greedy approaches can be further divided into:

- **Seed-Centric Expansion:** These methods begin from one or more seed nodes and expand the community by adding neighboring nodes based on connectivity or similarity criteria.
- **Quality-Driven Expansion:** These algorithms add nodes that maximize a specific quality metric (e.g., local modularity, conductance) at each step.

Non-Greedy Approaches. Non-Greedy methods rely on more global or holistic strategies. They often take into account the overall network structure or the way information diffuses through the graph. While typically more computationally expensive, these methods can provide more robust and stable community detection outcomes [17]. They can be divided into:

- **Flow Propagation:** Algorithms in this class propagate information (e.g., labels) through the network. A representative example is the Label Propagation algorithm, where nodes adopt the most frequent label among their neighbors.
- **Random Walk-based:** These methods use the properties of random walks to identify community structure. Notable examples include:
  - *PageRank:* Estimates node importance based on the probability of visiting a node during a random walk.
  - *Heat Kernel:* Models the diffusion of heat (or information) from the seed node across the graph.
  - *Local Spectral:* Uses spectral properties (eigenvectors) derived from local graph structure around the seed node to uncover communities.

Greedy Algorithms

Local Community Detection based on Small Cliques. The algorithm by Hamann, Röhrs, and Wagner [3], "Local Community Detection based on Small Cliques," belongs to the category of local, seed-centric community detection methods. Instead of analyzing the entire network, it focuses on the "neighborhood" around a seed node, achieving high performance and linear complexity in large graphs.

- **Clique-Based Initialization:** Instead of starting from a single node, the algorithm identifies the maximal clique in the seed's (s) concentric neighborhood—that is, the set of nodes where every pair is connected. This ensures that the initial community is already a highly cohesive structure around the seed. Hamann et al. [3] emphasize that algorithms starting from a maximal clique (e.g., triangle) perform significantly better in terms of F1 score, especially in real-world networks with thousands of nodes.
- **Triangle-Based Community Expansion (TCE):** Community expansion is performed using triangles, evaluating each candidate edge using edge and node scores as well as a conductance test.

Iterative Local Community Detection with Seed Propagation. ILCDSP [5] (Iterative Local Community Detection with Seed Propagation) by S. Xia, R. Zhou, Y. Zhou, and M. Zhu is a local, iterative community detection algorithm that starts from one or more initial seed nodes and builds a subcommunity around them by successively adding the node with the highest Local Density Score, provided this addition decreases the group's conductance. At each step, it efficiently updates the number of "cut edges" and the community's volume to greedily decide which node to incorporate. The algorithm terminates when no new member further improves the quality function (conductance), thus detecting cohesive, locally isolated subcommunities without requiring full network traversal.

Local Community Detection Using Seeds Expansion. The algorithm by B. Xu, Z. Liang, Y. Jia, B. Zhou, and Y. Han [6] targets the identification of local communities around key nodes (leaders), based on egocentric theory and seed expansion. The main steps are:

1. **Leader Node Selection:** The graph is divided into k regions, and a leader is selected from each—typically, the k nodes with the highest degrees. These leaders serve as seed nodes for community expansion.
2. **Community Expansion from Each Leader:** Starting from a leader node, a community is formed initially containing only that node. Neighbors are examined and added if their similarity to the community exceeds a threshold.
3. **Similarity Threshold (σ):** Similarity is defined as the number of shared neighbors between the candidate node and nodes already in the community. A high threshold results in small, dense communities; a low one leads to larger but looser communities.

4. **Iterative Process:** Expansion continues until no node meets the similarity threshold, at which point the community is considered complete.
5. **Detection of Loosely Connected Nodes:** Nodes connected to the community but not meeting the threshold can be identified as peripheral or loosely connected.

The community size identified by the algorithm strongly depends on the similarity threshold σ.

A Seed-Insensitive Approach to Local Community Detection. The GMAC algorithm (Greedy Modularity Agglomerative Clustering) [7] by L. Ma et al. is a seed-centric algorithm for local community detection in networks, aiming to optimize the Compact Isolation metric—a local cost/quality function on graphs.
Starting from a seed node, it identifies the surrounding community without processing the entire graph. At each step, it adds the node that locally maximizes the Compact Isolation metric, which favors groups of nodes that are similar and minimally dissimilar. It uses a Louvain-like strategy at the local level and is suitable for large, dynamic graphs where full computation is infeasible.

Local Community Detection in Multilayer Networks. In [8], R. Interdonato et al. introduce ML-LCD (MultiLayer Local Community Detection), a greedy, seed-centric algorithm designed to find local communities by leveraging information from multiple layers (types of relationships) within the same network. The main idea is:

- Start from a seed node and begin forming the local community.
- For expansion, examine the neighbors across all layers and greedily select the node that best fits the community.
- If a candidate improves the community's cohesion, it is added; otherwise, it is rejected.
- The process terminates when no neighbor improves cohesion.
- Layer weights can be adjusted depending on the dataset and target communities.

Non-greedy Algorithms

LEMON Algorithm. LEMON (Local Expansion via Minimum One Norm) [9], developed by Y. Li et al., is a local spectral community detection algorithm for graphs. It constructs a local spectral subspace based on seed nodes and applies random walk techniques to generate features for nearby nodes. It employs a sparse membership vector (quality function) and minimizes the ℓ_1 norm to select nodes for inclusion. The final community comprises the nodes with the highest values in this vector.

Locally Biased Spectral Approximation for Community Detection. In [10], P. Shi et al. propose LBSA, a complete local spectral method that combines statistical physics with classical spectral computations for direct and accurate community detection.

Main steps include:

- **Local Sampling:** Techniques like random walk, personalized PageRank, or heat kernel diffusion are used to identify a subgraph around the seed nodes, greatly reducing the working graph size.
- **Locally Biased Spectral Approximation:** Starting from a normalized indicator vector for the seed nodes, a few iterations of Lanczos or power method are applied to the subgraph. This produces a local eigenvector of the transition matrix indicating each node's likelihood of community membership.
- **Community Delineation:** The eigenvector elements are sorted, and a local minimum of conductance is used to decide which nodes are community members.

Detecting Overlapping Communities from Local Spectral Subspaces. In [11], K. He et al. introduce LOSP, which assumes the local structure of a community lies near a seed node in a small subspace of the graph's spectral space.

The algorithm analyzes neighborhoods around seed nodes, avoiding full-network processing. After performing a few steps around each seed to form a limited subgraph, it conducts spectral analysis via iterative probability flows. The most cohesive subset is chosen based on local criteria (conductance), and nodes are added if connected via short paths to the seeds. The process repeats until optimal cohesion is achieved. It is ideal for large graphs due to its localized operation.

Multiple Local Community Detection. A. Hollocou et al. [12] propose Multicom, a non-greedy algorithm for detecting multiple, possibly overlapping communities around a node. This is based on the observation that, in real-world networks, nodes often belong to more than one community.

The core idea is:

- Apply a local detection algorithm to each seed node to find its associated community.
- Assign a vector value to each node reflecting its relationship with the initial communities.
- Use the DBSCAN algorithm to cluster these nodes, identifying overlapping communities.

This approach is effective for overlapping community detection but highly dependent on the chosen initial parameters.

Community Detection Using Boundary Nodes in Complex Networks. The method proposed by M. Tasgin and H. O. Bingol [13] uses label propagation focusing on boundary nodes—those connected to different communities—to identify community boundaries. This enables efficient and scalable analysis of large networks.

Initially, each node is assigned a community label. Then the algorithm checks boundary nodes for possible label changes. Each boundary node calculates a benefit score for each neighboring community based on shared neighbors and adopts the label of the community with the highest score. The process ends when all labels stabilize. This approach reduces computation since it avoids re-evaluating all nodes each iteration. However, its success depends on how clearly communities are separated.

Local Community Detection Based on Network Motifs. The LCD-Motif algorithm, introduced by Y. Zhang et al. [14], detects local communities in networks based on motif structures—small, recurring subgraphs such as triangles or quadrangles. Instead of relying solely on edges or node degrees, this approach incorporates higher-order structural features that better represent functional units in the network. Key steps include:

- **Motif-Based Similarity:** Define a similarity measure between nodes based on how often they co-occur in specific motifs (e.g., triangles).
- **Motif-Based Conductance:** Use a modified conductance measure that accounts for motifs rather than just edges.
- **Greedy Expansion:** Starting from a seed node or motif, the algorithm expands the community by including nodes that improve the motif-based conductance.

This approach is especially useful in networks where triangle or higher-order motifs are strong indicators of community structure, such as in biological or social networks.

3   Experiments

3.1   Datasets

Four datasets [15] were employed to assess the performance of the local community detection algorithms, with seed nodes selected randomly for each dataset. For the evaluation, we used the F1 Score, a widely adopted metric that balances precision and recall, providing a single measure of overall algorithm effectiveness. The key characteristics of each dataset and the evaluation metric are described below.

- **com-Youtube:** Representing the YouTube online social network, this dataset has 1,134,890 nodes and 2,987,624 edges. This smaller dataset, relative to others in the study, allows us to explore the algorithms' efficiency in sparse networks.

- **com-DBLP:** The DBLP collaboration network dataset consists of 317,080 nodes and 1,049,866 edges This graph represents a collaboration network where researchers are linked through co-authorship, making it ideal for testing triangle counting in academic and professional networks with a moderate community structure.
- **com-Amazon:** This dataset captures the Amazon product network, containing 334,863 nodes and 925,872 edges. Nodes represent products, and edges indicate co-purchase relationships, offering a scenario with a retail-based network structure.
- **Email-Eu-core:** Internal email network of a European research institute, containing 1,005 nodes and 25,571 edges. Nodes represent individuals, and edges exist if one person sent at least one email to another. Ground-truth communities correspond to 42 departments.

We assess our framework by comparing detected communities against ground-truth communities from each of our real datasets. Evaluation relies on precision, recall, and F1 score—the latter being the harmonic mean of precision and recall to penalize imbalanced results [16]. These are widely recognized as the most appropriate for classification and community detection problems in networks. Precision reflects the percentage of correctly identified nodes out of all nodes proposed by the algorithm, recall shows the percentage of true community members that were identified, and F1 provides an overall picture by combining the previous two metrics.

$$F_1 = 2 \cdot \frac{\text{Precision} \cdot \text{Recall}}{\text{Precision} + \text{Recall}}$$

3.2 Experimental Results on Email-Eu-Core

The evaluation of the algorithms on the Email-Eu-core dataset reveals significant differences in terms of individual metrics (F1, precision, recall) as well as the general behavior of different approaches: Greedy and Non-Greedy. The Email-Eu-core network features relatively clear, non-overlapping communities that reflect the structure of a university environment. LCD algorithms were tasked with successfully identifying these groups, starting from selected seed nodes and following their own expansion or optimization criteria.

The *Small Cliques* algorithm achieved the highest F1 score 0.482, clearly outperforming others. This is due to a strong combination of decent precision 0.425 and very high recall 0.810, indicating that it captures a large portion of the true community members, even if it includes some extraneous nodes. This is expected from algorithms based on clique expansion, leveraging strong internal connectivity.

In contrast, algorithms such as *Seed Expansion* and *LCD-Motif* showed very low F1 scores 0.090 and 0.091 respectively, despite exceptionally high precision 1.0 and 0.98. This indicates they return only a small,"safe" set of nodes, missing the majority of the actual community recall: 0.045 and 0.053. This conservative detection limits their practical utility when broader coverage is needed.

Algorithms like *ILCDSP* and *Multicom* had intermediate F1 values 0.290 and 0.443 respectively, showing more balanced detection with moderate recall, around 0.38–0.45 and precision 0.28–0.38.

Qualitative Assessment Greedy algorithms generally achieve higher precision but lower recall (except *Small Cliques*). *Small Cliques* effectively leverages the Email-Eu-core community structure due to strong internal connectivity, whereas methods based on local criteria comparisons do not perform as well. Non-Greedy methods have lower precision but better recall over 0.5, making them more suitable when capturing the full community is the goal, even at the cost of including external nodes (Table 1).

Table 1. Algorithm results on Email-Eu-core

Algorithm	F1	Precision	Recall
Multilayer	0.252	0.411	0.203
LCD-Motif	0.0909	0.980	0.0531
Small Cliques	0.4824	0.4253	0.8104
ILCDSP	0.290	0.379	0.378
Seed Expansion	0.090	1.000	0.045
GMAC	0.1446	0.7567	0.0943
Lemon	0.3519	0.2989	0.4677
LBSA	0.108	0.061	0.538
LOSP	0.1972	0.1471	0.5925
Multicom	0.4434	0.3721	0.5486
CDBN	0.0836	0.0445	0.9743

3.3 Experimental Results on Amazon Network

The evaluation on the Amazon Copurchasing Network—one of the most demanding and realistic datasets—reveals distinct behaviors of LCD algorithms. Unlike Email-Eu-core, Amazon features many nodes, overlapping community structures, and communities linked via user-product interactions.

General Observations. Algorithms perform significantly better on Amazon than on Email-Eu-core in terms of both F1 and the balance between precision and recall. This is due to Amazon's well-defined, dense product communities, in contrast to the more loosely structured university social groups.

Most algorithms show very high precision, 0.95-1.0, rarely confusing nodes from different communities. However, recall and consequently F1 varies substantially, revealing the differences in strategy among methods.

Multicom achieved the best overall result with an F1 of 0.9779, perfect recall 1.0, and very high precision (0.9568), effectively identifying all true community members with few false positives. Lemon also performed well with F1 equal to 0.8506, combining almost perfect recall 0.9971 with good precision 0.7540, making it suitable when maximum coverage is desired. Small Cliques and LOSP maintained high precision 0.997 and 0.9621, with improved recall compared to Email-Eu-core 0.688 and 0.6347, resulting in balanced F1 scores 0.752 and 0.7022.

CDBN and LBSA, both Non-Greedy, achieved moderate performance. CDBN showed perfect precision but lower recall 0.5341, while LBSA had the lowest F1 0.476, likely due to its simplistic community formation strategy. ILCDSP, Multilayer, and GMAC, all Greedy methods, had similar F1 scores, around 0.520.58, with excellent precision but modest recall 0.47. LCD-Motif and Seed Expansion again scored very low F1, 0.14 and 0.018, with perfect precision but extremely low recall, limiting their practical applicability (Table 2).

Table 2. Algorithm results on Amazon

Algorithm	F1	Precision	Recall
Multicom	0.9779	0.9568	1.000
Lemon	0.8506	0.7540	0.9971
Small Cliques	0.7520	0.9970	0.6880
LOSP	0.7022	0.9621	0.6347
CDBN	0.6242	1.0000	0.5341
Multilayer	0.5750	1.0000	0.4840
GMAC	0.5557	0.9950	0.4655
ILCDSP	0.5190	0.9190	0.4750
LBSA	0.4760	0.8000	0.3860
LCD-Motif	0.1400	1.0000	0.0757
Seed Expansion	0.0180	1.0000	0.0120

Comparison to Email-Eu-core. Amazon's complexity and size appear to favor most LCD algorithms. While coverage was a challenge in the smaller Email-Eu-core, in Amazon most methods achieved high F1 scores due to strong internal community cohesion. Algorithms that underperformed on Email-Eu-core (e.g., Seed Expansion, LCD-Motif) also struggled here, highlighting the importance of matching the method to the dataset structure.

Multicom and Lemon are the most reliable choices for Amazon-like networks. Although precision is high across the board, those achieving high recall truly leverage the strengths of LCD techniques.

3.4 Experimental Results on YouTube Social Network

The YouTube network constitutes one of the largest and most heterogeneous cases in the evaluation of local community detection (LCD) algorithms. In this dataset, communities are formed through users' free choice to join or manage groups, which leads to strong overlap, variable sizes, noise, and unclear boundaries between groups. YouTube is well-suited for stress-testing any LCD method, as it combines the challenges of large scale, diversity, and low cohesion.

Observations. A first look at the results reveals that no algorithm achieves particularly high F1 scores, which reflects the difficulty of the problem in the YouTube dataset. All metrics are lower compared to those of Amazon and Email-Eu-core. Notably, the highest F1 score (0.5865 for Multicom) is significantly lower than the top scores observed in the other datasets. The structure of YouTube, with large communities, multi-level overlap, and low density, appears to hinder both precision and recall for most algorithms.

Multicom achieves the highest F1 score here as well 0.5865, combining very high precision 0.946 with relatively low recall 0.425. This indicates that the algorithm can reliably identify community members but struggles to cover the full range of actual groups—a common challenge for LCD methods in networks with overlapping communities (Table 3).

Table 3. Algorithm results on YouTube

Algorithm	F1	Precision	Recall
Multicom	0.8110	0.8520	0.7740
Lemon	0.6830	0.8010	0.5950
Small Cliques	0.6270	0.6810	0.5830
GMAC	0.5810	0.8920	0.4370
Multilayer	0.5300	0.8260	0.3930
ILCDSP	0.5020	0.8310	0.3700
LOSP	0.4950	0.7540	0.3700
CDBN	0.4850	0.7220	0.3600
LBSA	0.3720	0.6700	0.2630
LCD-Motif	0.1240	0.9500	0.0680
Seed Expansion	0.0360	1.0000	0.0180

With an F1 of 0.5244, precision of 0.984, and recall of 0.4474, CDBN shows a conservative behavior: it returns almost exclusively undisputed members, omitting many peripheral community members. In contexts where avoiding false positives is a priority, CDBN's behavior is desirable, but it is restrictive in applications where coverage matters. The Small Cliques algorithm, with an F1 of 0.415, demonstrates one of the better balances between precision 0.385 and recall 0.578. Compared to other datasets, here recall remains relatively high but precision drops significantly, reflecting the noise and fluidity of communities in YouTube. Lemon differs significantly here: it has the highest recall 0.8176 among all, but very low precision 0.2812 and that gives the value of 0.3981 for F1. This means it tends to include a large number of nodes, including many incorrect ones, emphasizing coverage. In applications where it is important not to miss any member (e.g., discovery of rare interests), this behavior may be preferable.

The algorithms Multilayer, GMAC, and LOSP shows moderate or low scores in F1, 0.327, 0.3038 and 0.1895 respectively. Precision ranges from moderate to good (e.g., Multilayer 0.733, GMAC 0.5433), but recall remains below 0.3. This indicates an inability to detect the majority of members in communities with particular complexity. Seed Expansion, ILCDSP, LBSA and LCD-Motif algorithms have extremely low F1 scores, lower than 0.15. Especially Seed Expansion and LCD-Motif show perfect precision 1.00, but almost zero recall. This means they detect only the most certain nodes but miss almost the entire community. LBSA and ILCDSP also fail to capture the real nature of YouTube groups, mainly due to noise and heterogeneity.

Comparisons with Email-Eu-core and Amazon:
The picture in the Youtube dataset differs significantly. Where in Amazon and Email-Eu-core algorithms such as Multicom, Small Cliques, and CDBN performed much higher (F1 up to 0.97 in Amazon), here no algorithm exceeds 0.6. This difference highlights the role of graph structure: when communities are natural and well-defined (as in Amazon), our algorithms achieve better results. In Youtube, complexity, noise, and overlapping nature make detection difficult.

It is also interesting that algorithms that are "conservative" (Seed Expansion, LCD-Motif) maintain the same behavior, with minimal coverage but without false positives. Conversely, aggressive methods such as Lemon move to excessively high recall, sacrificing precision.

The analysis in Youtube reveals that LCD has limits when applied to networks with high heterogeneity, overlap, and complex dynamics. The user must choose the method based on whether clean communities (Multicom, CDBN) or completeness (Lemon, Small Cliques) are desired. However, most algorithms struggle to cope with this particular structure, confirming that there is no single method for all in local community detection.

3.5   Experimental Results on DBLP Collaboration Network

The DBLP dataset is one of the most representative networks of scientific collaboration, where nodes represent researchers and edges connect those who have co-authored at least one publication. Community detection in such networks often reveals research centers, thematic clusters, and collaborative teams with significant overlap. Due to its large size, rich overlapping structure, and complex scientific interconnections, DBLP constitutes a challenging domain for any LCD algorithm.

General overview and key observations: Unlike the challenging YouTube or the more"friendly" Amazon network, DBLP confronts LCD algorithms with a structure where scientific communities overlap, intersect, and evolve over time. Despite this complexity, some methods perform remarkably well: Multicom achieves an F1 score of 0.9291, the highest, combining nearly perfect recall 0.9951 and very high precision 0.8713. This shows its ability to fully detect the true members of research groups without introducing many false positives.

Overall, we observe a pattern:Non-Greedy methods perform exceptionally when the algorithm can leverage rich local information (e.g., Multicom, Lemon), whereas Greedy methods exhibit clearly lower F1 scores. This does not imply that Greedy methods lack value; rather, their conservative approach results in smaller, denser communities with fewer members (Table 4).

Table 4. Algorithm results on DBLP

Algorithm	F1	Precision	Recall
Multicom	0.9291	0.8713	0.9951
Multilayer	0.5310	0.7330	0.2490
Lemon	0.5232	0.8214	0.8176
CDBN	0.5040	0.9900	0.4474
Small Cliques	0.3360	0.7600	0.4010
LOSP	0.3340	0.7692	0.3187
LBSA	0.2860	0.9000	0.2600
ILCDSP	0.2680	0.5700	0.2660
GMAC	0.2674	0.8541	0.2327
LCD-Motif	0.1667	1.0000	0.0909
Seed Expansion	0.0930	1.0000	0.0530

Algorithm-Specific analysis:
With an F1 score of 0.9291, Multicom ranks first in this dataset, achieving recall 0.9951 and precision 0.8713. As seen also in Amazon, it can maximally exploit local links to identify full research communities. In DBLP, this is possible because researchers within the same thematic group tend to have very dense and stable connections. Multilayer scores 0.531 F1, Lemon scores 0.5232, and CDBN 0.504. Lemon achieves high recall 0.8214 but with relatively lower precision, indicating an aggressive strategy toward coverage. In contrast, CDBN adopts a more conservative strategy with high precision 0.990 but lower recall 0.4474.

Small Cliques and LOSP reach F1 scores of 0.336 and 0.334 respectively, with fairly balanced precision and recall (precision 0.76 − −0.77, recall 0.32 − −0.40). LBSA performs worse (F1 equal to 0.286), despite a good precision score 0.9, due to very low recall 0.26.

ILCDSP and GMAC algorithms show similar F1 scores, 0.268 and 0.2674 respectively, with good precision $(0.57 - -0.85)$, but low recall (< 0.27). This indicates a strategy that returns tightly-knit communities with high internal cohesion, but limited ground-truth coverage. As in previous networks, LCD-Motif and Seed Expansion algorithms yield the lowest F1 scores 0.1667 and 0.093, respectively), with perfect precision 1.0, but almost negligible recall, 0.0909 and 0.053. This suggests overly strict criteria for including new nodes, causing most true community members to be missed.

Comparative Discussion with Other Datasets: DBLP differs markedly from YouTube in terms of group cohesion, while exhibiting less overlapping complexity than Amazon. However, it retains clear scientific associations, which Multicom fully exploits. Most algorithms (excluding aggressive ones like Lemon) achieve better balance between precision and recall than in YouTube. It is also notable that algorithms like Seed Expansion, LCD-Motif, LBSA, and ILCDSP, which were already underperforming in other networks, fall even further behind here. Multilayer remains an effective Greedy option, especially for hierarchical or multi-level communities. Applying LCD algorithms to DBLP shows that the success of community detection depends primarily on how naturally and densely clustered the communities are, and on the algorithm's ability to exploit thematic correlations. Multicom is clearly the best choice in such networks, followed by Lemon, Multilayer, and CDBN for more specific requirements.

Multicom continues to lead, with an F1 score of 0.8110, precision at 0.8520, and recall at 0.7740. Its ability to maintain strong balance across metrics, even in more difficult environments, confirms its robustness. Lemon also performs strongly with an F1 of 0.6830, prioritizing high precision and achieving decent recall. Small Cliques, a Greedy approach, maintains respectable performance $(F1 = 0.6270)$, showing its adaptability even in looser community structures.bGMAC, Multilayer, and ILCDSP all achieve precision above 0.8 but fall short on recall $(below 0.45)$, suggesting they are conservative in expanding communities and may miss many actual members. LOSP and CDBN are slightly more balanced but still underperform compared to the leaders. LCD-Motif and Seed Expansion again show minimal coverage (recall $= 0.068$ and 0.018, respectively), which keeps their F1 scores at very low levels despite near-perfect precision

Overall, Non-Greedy methods outperform Greedy ones in the YouTube dataset, with Multicom and Lemon excelling thanks to their capacity to adapt to complex, overlapping structures. Conservative methods again struggle with recall. This reinforces the idea that community detection in real-world, loosely defined networks benefits from more flexible and expansive strategies.

4   Conclusion

This study conducted a systematic and in-depth comparative analysis of local community detection (LCD) methods on large, real-world networks. Through the implementation and experimental evaluation of eleven modern algorithms on four different datasets, the key factors influencing the performance and boundaries of LCD in practice were highlighted. One of the most important conclusions is that there is no universally superior algorithm. The effectiveness of each algorithm varies depending on the structure, size, degree of overlap, and clarity of the communities in each network. Algorithms that excel in clean or well-structured networks often exhibit moderate or low performance in noisier or more complex graphs.

However, there were algorithms that performed well across all four datasets. Specifically, Multicom proved to be consistent across all four datasets, showing high F1 scores in two of them, while in the YouTube and Email-Eu-core networks where it did not perform as well, it still achieved the highest scores compared to the other implementations. It was also found that Greedy methods are mostly characterized by high precision and lower recall. This translates into tight, clean communities that, however, do not achieve full coverage of the ground truth groups. On the other hand, Non-Greedy algorithms offer better completeness at the corresponding cost of precision.

As future work, we could consider incorporating additional types of algorithms for Local Community Detection, expanding the classification categories, and extending our study to dynamic networks.

Acknowledgment. "This research was supported by the Hellenic Foundation for Research and Innovation (H.F.R.I.) under the "2nd Call for H.F.R.I. Research Projects to support Faculty Members & Researchers" (Project Number: 3480). "

References

1. Li, J., et al.: A comprehensive review of community detection in graphs, Neurocomputing, pp. 128–169 Elsevier (2024)
2. Li, X., Peng, Q., Li, R., Ma, H.: Dual graph neural network for overlapping community detection. Supercomputing, vol. 80(2), pp. 2196–2222, 2024, Springer (2024)
3. Hamann, M., Röhrs, E., Wagner, D.: Local community detection based on small cliques. Algorithms, vol. 10(3), p. 90, year (2017) publisher MDPI
4. Community detection in graphs, Fortunato, Santo, Physics reports, vol. 486, number 3-5, pp. 75–174 (2010), publisher Elsevier
5. Xia, S., Zhou, R., Zhou, Y., Zhu, M.: An improved local community detection algorithm using selection probability. Math. Prob. Eng. **2014**(1), 406–485 (2014), publisher Wiley Online Library
6. Xu, B., Liang, Z., Jia, Y., Zhou, B., Han, Y.: Local community detection using seeds expansion. In: Second International Conference on Cloud and Green Computing, pp. 557–562 year (2012) IEEE
7. Ma, L., Huang, H., He, Q., Chiew, K., Wu, J., Che, Y.: GMAC: a seed-insensitive approach to local community detection. In: Bellatreche, L., Mohania, M.K. (eds.) DaWaK 2013. LNCS, vol. 8057, pp. 297–308. Springer, Heidelberg (2013). https://doi.org/10.1007/978-3-642-40131-2_26

8. Interdonato, R., Tagarelli, A., Ienco, D., Sallaberry, A., Poncelet, P.: Local community detection in multilayer networks. Data Mining Knowl. Discov. **31**, 1444–1479 (2017), publisher Springer
9. Li, Y., He, K., Bindel, D., Hopcroft, J.E.: Uncovering the small community structure in large networks: a local spectral approach. In: Proceedings of the 24th International Conference on World Wide Web, pp. 658–668, (2015)
10. Shi, P., He, K., Bindel, D., Hopcroft, J.E.: Locally-biased spectral approximation for community detection. Knowl.-Based Syst. **164**, 459–472 (2019), Elsevier
11. He, K., Sun, Y., Bindel, D., Hopcroft, J., Li, Y.: Detecting overlapping communities from local spectral subspaces. In: 2015 IEEE international conference on data mining, pp. 769–774 (2015), IEEE
12. Hollocou, A., Bonald, T. and Lelarge, M.: Multiple local community detection. In: ACM SIGMETRICS Performance Evaluation Review, pp. 76–83 (2018), publisher ACM New York
13. Tasgin, M., Bingol, H.O.: Community detection using boundary nodes in complex network. In: Physica A: Statistical Mechanics and its Applications, pp. 315–324 (2019), Elsevier
14. Zhang, Y., Wu, B., Liu, Y. and Lv, J.: Local community detection based on network motifs. Tsinghua Sci. Technol. **24**(6), 716–727 (2019), publisher TUP
15. Yang, J., Leskovec, J.: Defining and evaluating network communities based on ground-truth. In: Proceedings of the ACM SIGKDD workshop on mining data semantics, pp. 1–8 (2012)
16. Powers, D.M.: Evaluation: from precision, recall and F-measure to ROC, informedness, markedness and correlation, arXiv preprint arXiv:2010.16061 (2020)
17. Andersen, R., Chung, F., Lang, K.: Local graph partitioning using PageRank vectors. In: 47th Annual IEEE Symposium on Foundations of Computer Science (FOCS), pp. 475–486 (2006) IEEE

Renting Servers in the Cloud: Empirical Study on Real-World Data

Mahtab Masoori[(✉)], Lata Narayanan, and Denis Pankratov

Concordia University, Montreal, QC, Canada
mahtab.masoori@gmail.com, {lata.narayanan,denis.pankratov}@concordia.ca
https://www.concordia.ca

Abstract. We study the renting servers in the cloud problem (*RSiC*), inspired by job allocation in cloud computing environments. In this problem, jobs arrive sequentially in an online manner, and their sizes are revealed upon arrival. If a job's duration is also known at arrival, the scenario is classified as clairvoyant; otherwise, it is non-clairvoyant. Each job must be assigned to a server, with servers available on-demand and subject to a fixed capacity per unit of time. The number of servers that can be rented is unlimited, and the objective is to minimize the total rental time of all servers. In this paper, we evaluate the performance of nearly all existing clairvoyant and non-clairvoyant algorithms for the *RSiC* problem. Additionally, we introduce new algorithms, which were derived from combinations of existing algorithms. Some of the introduced algorithms outperform all previously known algorithms in our experimental evaluations. Unlike prior studies that exclusively utilized synthetic data, we use real-world Azure data from [4] in our experiments. This dataset captures large-scale virtual machine (VM) allocation across Azure's availability zones, offering a more practical perspective on the operational effectiveness of these algorithms.

Keywords: Renting servers in the cloud · scheduling · azure dataset · online algorithms · bin packing · dynamic bin packing · experimental evaluation

1 Introduction

Cloud computing has gained significant popularity in recent years, providing users with access to essential resources such as servers, storage, databases, and software via the internet. This model eliminates the need for substantial investments in physical hardware and software, reducing capital expenses and offering considerable cost savings. Users are billed only for the resources they consume, making it a cost-effective solution for businesses and individuals alike.

Cloud service providers deliver these resources over the internet, enabling users to submit jobs tailored to their specific requirements. Each job includes

Research is supported by NSERC, Canada.

D. Garlisi and D. Chatzopoulos (Eds.): ALGOCLOUD 2025, LNCS 16349, pp. 138–158, 2026.
https://doi.org/10.1007/978-3-032-13744-9_10

various parameters, such as submission time, required duration, and resource demands. Service providers must efficiently allocate these jobs to available servers, considering server capacity to optimize resource utilization. The total active time of physical servers directly impacts the provider's power consumption and operational costs. Inefficient placement decisions can lead to resource fragmentation and over-provisioning, both of which reduce overall efficiency.

The problem of renting servers in the cloud ($RSiC$), first introduced by Li et al. [7], models the scenario in cloud computing systems where jobs arrive sequentially, and the cloud provider must allocate them to available servers. In $RSiC$, jobs are presented in an online manner and must be assigned to servers with finite capacities immediately upon arrival. The algorithm's decisions are irrevocable, as we assume that transferring a job to another server mid-execution is prohibitively costly. The primary objective is to minimize the total cost of all rented servers, where the cost of a server is proportional to the duration of its utilization.

Over the past decade, $RSiC$ has received significant attention from researchers. This problem has been studied under two primary settings: the *clairvoyant* setting, where both the duration and size of each job are known at the time of submission, and the *non-clairvoyant* setting, where no information about a job's duration is available upon submission.

Most research in this area has focused on theoretical aspects, proposing algorithms and analyzing their theoretical performance measured by their *competitive ratio*, which is the worst-case ratio across all possible inputs, of the cost of the algorithm and the cost of an optimal offline algorithm that knows the entire input sequence in advance. Most papers used the assumption that each job requires only a single resource [1,5,7,8,10,11]. Recently, however, Murhekar et al. [9] extended the study of $RSiC$ to scenarios where jobs request multiple resources.

Experimental results using random data [5] demonstrated that the *MoveToFront* algorithm is the best non-clairvoyant algorithm for the one-dimensional setting. This finding was later corroborated by Murhekar et al. [9], who showed that *MoveToFront* empirically outperforms other algorithms even in the multi-dimensional (d-dimensional) setting. Later, Li et al. [6] introduced a new clairvoyant algorithm called *Greedy*. Their results showed that *Greedy* outperforms existing algorithms—both clairvoyant and non-clairvoyant—in most scenarios. Specifically, it surpasses *MoveToFront*, the previously best-performing algorithm in experiments, and $HA^{\oplus d}$, the algorithm with the best competitive ratio. However, all these findings are based on evaluations using randomly generated inputs.

While theoretical worst-case analysis is based on carefully constructed worst-case inputs that are unlikely to occur in practice, experiments on uniformly random data may also not yield meaningful insight about performance on inputs that actually occur in practice. For example, in the context of sorting algorithms, the realization that many input sequences are not random but are often nearly sorted, led to the development of *adaptive* sorting algorithms [3].

In this paper, we aim to assess the performance of nearly all existing algorithms for *RSiC* using a *real-world dataset*. Specifically, we leverage the Azure dataset from [4]. This dataset provides comprehensive insights into large-scale virtual machine (VM) allocation across Azure's availability zones, offering a practical and realistic perspective on the operational effectiveness of these algorithms. Since *RSiC* is an online problem, we adapt the classical competitive analysis framework to evaluate algorithm performance. We report the empirically derived competitive ratio for the specific inputs, using lower bounds on the optimal cost, which is computationally infeasible to determine exactly.

1.1 Our Contributions

- We introduce a new category of algorithms, which we call *weakly clairvoyant* algorithms. In this setting, the exact durations of jobs are not known at the time of their arrival. Instead, jobs are classified by users into two categories: long-duration and short-duration based on a pre-specified threshold. Thus, the category of a job is provided at the time of arrival of the job.
- To the best of our knowledge, this is the first study to evaluate the performance of clairvoyant, weakly clairvoyant, and non-clairvoyant algorithms for *RSiC* using real-world data. Our experiments confirm that clairvoyant algorithms generally outperform weakly clairvoyant algorithms, which in turn outperform non-clairvoyant algorithms.
- In the clairvoyant setting, we demonstrate that among previously considered algorithms *HA* [1] has the best empirical performance. *Greedy* [6] offers a simpler alternative, avoiding the complexity of *HA* while maintaining competitive performance. By combining *HA* and *Greedy* algorithms, we introduce the *Greedy-Hybrid* algorithm, which achieves the best empirically derived competitive ratio among all known algorithms, including *HA*. We introduce another algorithm called *Greedy-Greedy* that is conceptually simpler than both *HA* and *Greedy-Hybrid* and for a careful choice of parameters outperforms *HA*.
- We introduce several weakly clairvoyant algorithms; our experiments show that two of our new algorithms in this setting *FirstFit-FirstFit* and *FirstFit-BestFit* offer improvements over the empirically derived competitive ratios of *FirstFit* and *BestFit*.
- In the non-clairvoyant setting, *FirstFit* emerges as the strongest performer with real-world data. Although *MoveToFront* [5] performs well in experiments with synthetic random inputs, its performance with real-world datasets was weaker than that of *FirstFit*.

To sum up, based on this study, we can make the following recommendations. In the clairvoyant setting, we recommend using *Greedy-Hybrid* or *Greedy-Greedy*. In the weakly-clairvoyant setting, we recommend *FirstFit-FirstFit* as a safe and dependable choice (as opposed to *BestFit*-based algorithms, which have infinite worst-case competitive ratio). In the non-clairvoyant setting, we recommend using *MoveToFront* for datasets where there is small variation in job durations, and *FirstFit* for datasets with larger variation in job durations.

Organization. Sect. 2 introduces key definitions and notation. Section 3 gives a more detailed description of the related work. Sections 4 and 5 detail the dataset and present the experimental results. Proposed algorithms are discussed in Sect. 6. Section C examines server usage, providing insights into the problem and algorithm performance. Conclusions are in Sect. 7.

2   Preliminaries

The input to the d-dimensional *RSiC* problem is a sequence of n items $\sigma = (\sigma_1, \ldots, \sigma_n)$, where item i is a triple (a_i, f_i, s_i), denoting a job starting at time $a_i \in [0, \infty)$ and finishing at time $f_i > a_i$ where multi-dimensional resource demand $s_i \in [0, 1]^d$ such that s_i^j denotes the size of the job σ_i in the jth dimension for $j \in [d]$. We assume that an algorithm for *RSiC* has access to a supply of identical servers of capacity 1 in each dimension. Thus, for every time t the combined size of jobs assigned to a particular server at time t must not exceed 1 in every dimension. The *duration* of a job i is $f_i - a_i$. An important parameter of the input sequence is $\mu(\sigma) := \frac{\max_i(f_i - s_i)}{\min_i(f_i - s_i)}$, which is the ratio of the maximum duration of a job to the minimum duration of a job in the sequence. By scaling, we can assume that the duration of every job lies between 1 and μ, that is, $1 \leq f_i - a_i \leq \mu$ for every job σ_i.

We say that a job $\sigma_i = (a_i, f_i, s_i)$ is *active* or *alive* at time t if $t \in [a_i, f_i)$. Two jobs σ_i and σ_j are said to be *non-overlapping* if $[a_i, f_i) \cap [a_j, f_j) = \emptyset$, otherwise they are said to be *overlapping*. Note that representing active times of jobs by half-open intervals allows us to consider two jobs such that one starts at exactly the same time as the other one finishes as non-overlapping. Jobs are presented in an order that respects their starting times, i.e., $a_1 \leq a_2 \leq \cdots \leq a_n$. The *span* of the input sequence is the interval $[0, T)$ assuming that the first job arrives at time 0 and the last departure of a job is at time T.

Opening a server signifies the start of its rental period, typically marked by the assignment of the first job to it. A server is considered *active* or *alive* at time t if it currently hosts at least one scheduled job that remains active at t. A server is considered *closed* when it will no longer receive any future job assignments; it is important to note that this status is determined by the algorithm rather than an inherent characteristic of the server itself. Once a server is closed it is no longer open. Despite being closed, a server may continue to be active until all its assigned jobs are completed. Once all jobs are finished, the server is *released*. Additionally, we define the duration of each server B as the time interval from its opening until its last active job finishes.

For an arbitrary online algorithm ALG and $t \in [0, T)$, we use $\text{ALG}(\sigma, t)$ to denote the number of servers opened by ALG that are active at time t. We use $\text{ALG}(\sigma)$ to denote the total cost of ALG on input σ, i.e., the sum of the durations of servers opened by ALG. Similar notation is used for the offline optimal solution OPT, where $\text{OPT}(\sigma, t)$ refers to the number of active servers used by OPT at time t, and $\mathrm{OPT}(\sigma)$ represents the total cost of the optimal solution on input σ. Observe that

Proposition 1.

$$\mathrm{OPT}(\sigma) = \int_0^T \mathrm{OPT}(\sigma, t)dt, \ and$$

$$\mathrm{ALG}(\sigma) = \int_0^T \mathrm{ALG}(\sigma, t)dt.$$

We note the following general lower bound on $\mathrm{OPT}(\sigma)$, and reproduce its proof for completeness.

Lemma 1 (Murhekar et al. [9]). $\int_0^T \lceil \|s(\sigma, t)\|_\infty \rceil dt \le \mathrm{OPT}(\sigma)$

Proof. As the capacity of each server is 1 for every dimension $j \in [d]$; any algorithm needs at least $\lceil \|s(\sigma, t)\|_\infty \rceil$ servers to pack the total load at any time t. Therefore, $\mathrm{OPT}(\sigma, t) \ge \lceil \|s(\sigma, t)\|_\infty \rceil$. Using Proposition 1, we can conclude:

$$\int_0^T \lceil \|s(\sigma, t)\|_\infty \rceil dt \le \int_0^T \mathrm{OPT}(\sigma, t)dt = \mathrm{OPT}(\sigma).$$

The *competitive ratio of* ALG *on a sequence* σ is $\mathrm{ALG}(\sigma)/\mathrm{OPT}(\sigma)$. An online algorithm ALG is said to be (*asymptotically*) ρ-*competitive* if there exists a constant $c \ge 0$ such that for all input sequences σ:

$$\mathrm{ALG}(\sigma) \le \rho \cdot \mathrm{OPT}(\sigma) + c. \tag{1}$$

The infimum over all such ρ is denoted by $\rho(\mathrm{ALG})$ and is called the *competitive ratio* of ALG.

We implemented both clairvoyant and non-clairvoyant algorithms in order to evaluate their performance on the real-world data set. An important class of algorithms that we shall frequently reference is called *AnyFit*. *AnyFit* algorithms open a new server only when no existing server has sufficient capacity, ensuring a new server is opened only when absolutely necessary.

The following is a list of non-clairvoyant algorithms that we implemented[1]:

- **NextFit** [5]: keeps only one open server at each time. When a job arrives, if it does not fit in the existing open server, that server is closed and a new one is opened to accommodate the job. Note that it is *not* an *AnyFit* algorithm.
- **ModifiedNextFit** [5]: assigns jobs with sizes greater than a specific threshold separately from the other jobs using the *NextFit* algorithm.
- **FirstFit** [7]: an *AnyFit* algorithm which maintains the servers in the order they are opened and assigns a job to the first server with sufficient available space.

---

[1] Many of these algorithms have been introduced for the first time for the bin packing problem and later extended to the *RSiC* setting. The citations that we present here are the first mentions of these algorithms in the context of *RSiC*.

- **LastFit** [9]: an *AnyFit* algorithm that keeps the servers in the reverse order of their opening and assigns a job to the first server with sufficient available space.
- **ModifiedFirstFit** [7]: assigns jobs with sizes greater than a specific threshold separately from the other jobs using the *FirstFit* algorithm.
- **BestFit** [7]: an *AnyFit* algorithm that keeps the servers in the decreasing order of their remaining capacity and assigns a job to the first server with sufficient available space.
- **WorstFit** [6]: an *AnyFit* algorithm that keeps the servers in the increasing order of their remaining capacity and assigns a job to the first server with sufficient available space.
- **RandomFit** [6]: an *AnyFit* algorithm that assigns a job to a random server that can accommodate it if such servers are available, and otherwise opens a new server to accommodate the job.
- **MoveToFront** [5]: an *AnyFit* algorithm that orders servers in decreasing order of the last time a job was assigned to it.

The following is a list of clairvoyant algorithms that we implemented:

- **Departure Strategy** [11]: the span is split into intervals of length τ each, where $\tau > 0$ is a constant. Classifies jobs into categories according to their departure times. Each category contains all jobs that depart in a time interval of length τ.
- **Duration Strategy** [11]: classifies the jobs into categories such that the max/min job duration ratio for each category is a given constant α. Given a base job duration b, each category includes all the jobs with durations between $b\alpha^{i-1}$ and $b\alpha^i$ for an integer i.
- **Hybrid Algorithm (HA)** [1]: classifies jobs according to their length and their arrivals. All the jobs whose lengths are in range $[2^{i-1}, 2^i]$ for integer $1 \le i \le \lceil \log \mu \rceil + 1$ and whose arrival times are in time interval $[(c-1)2^i, c2^i)$ for an integer c are assigned to a separate category of servers.
- **Greedy** [6]: Order servers in decreasing order of their *finishing times*, that is, the maximum of the finishing times of jobs currently in the server. Assign the newly arrived job to the first server in the order that has sufficient capacity. If no such server exists, open a new server and assign the job to it.
- **New Hybrid ($HA^{\oplus d}$)** [6]: partitions input σ into $\sigma = \sigma^{(1)} \cup \cdots \cup \sigma^{(d)}$, where $\sigma^{(j)}$ is the subset of jobs whose maximum size is achieved in dimension j. The algorithm runs d independent copies of the HA algorithm – one for each $\sigma^{(j)}$.

3   Related Work

RSiC, also known as *MinUsageTime Dynamic Bin Packing*, was first introduced in 1-dimensional setting ($d = 1$) by Li et al. [7]. They proposed and studied *FirstFit, BestFit, AnyFit,* and *ModifiedFirstFit*. In particular, they showed the suprprising result that the *BestFit* algorithm does not have a bounded competitive ratio. Kamali and Lopez-Oritz [5] showed a lower bound of μ on competitiveness of any deterministic algorithm. In addition, Kamali and Lopez-Oritz [5] studied *NextFit* and introduced *MoveToFront*. They showed that both algorithms achieve $O(\mu)$-competitiveness. Ren et al. [12] proved that *FirstFit* packing achieves a competitive ratio of $\mu + 3$. The clairvoyant setting for $d = 1$ has been studied in [1,11]. Azar et al. [1] proposed *HA* which classifies jobs according to their length and their arrivals. They proved that *HA* achieves $O(\sqrt{\log \mu})$-competitiveness. In addition, Azar et al. showed that every clairvoyant deterministic algorithm has competitive ratio at least $\Omega(\sqrt{\log \mu})$.

In d-dimensional setting, Murhekar et al. [9] proved that *MoveToFront* has an upper bound $(2\mu+1)d+1$. They also generalized various upper and lower bounds of algorithms such as *FirstFit* and *NextFit* from dimension 1 to dimension d. In particular, they showed a lower bound of $d(\mu + 1)$ for *AnyFit* algorithms. In [6], Li et al. showed how to extend arbitrary one-dimensional algorithms to d dimensions using a general direct-sum property. They also introduced two new algorithms for the problem: *Greedy* and $HA^{\oplus d}$.

Some of the mentioned papers presented experimental results. However, all the experimental results in prior works were with respect to random inputs: each bin has an integer capacity E in each dimension; the size, arrival time, and duration of each input item are distributed uniformly. These experiments in $d = 1$ of Kamali and Lopez-Oritz [5] indicated that *MoveToFront* has best performance among all known non-clairvoyant algorithms. *BestFit* also had excellent performance in their experiments (in contrast with the worst-case performance discussed earlier). Murhekar et al. [9] extended the random experimental setting of [5] to multiple dimensions $d > 1$ and obtained similar results. Additional experiments in this random setting and multiple dimensions were performed by Li et al. [6], showing that *Greedy* algorithm ranks among the top performers.

In the offline setting, *RSiC* is clearly $\mathcal{NP}$-hard, as it generalizes Bin Packing. *RSiC* admits constant approximation algorithms: Ren et al. [11] presented the 5-approximation algorithm called *Duration Descending FirstFit* and the 4-approximation *Dual Coloring* algorithm. The best known approximation ratio for *RSiC* is ≈ 3.38 due to Buchbinder et al. [2].

4   Experimental Setup

We begin by describing the dataset, which captures a segment of Microsoft's Azure Compute workload consisting of a set of VM requests. Each VM request corresponds to a specific VM type, detailing requirements for CPU (core), memory (RAM), SSD (solid-state drive), NIC (network bandwidth), and HDD (hard drive), with resource values presented in fractional units. In addition, each VM request comes with a "machine id" which corresponds to a compute node used to process the request. Note that machine id corresponds to a huge collection of homogeneous servers, and not a single server (in spite of what the term *machine id* might suggest). Since the *RSiC* problem assumes that the servers are identical, we run our experiments on a set of requests sharing the same machine id (for a couple of different choices of machine id), as discussed in the experimental section. Collected over a 14-day period, the dataset includes all VMs that overlapped with this timeframe. Jobs continued to be observed for 76 d after the data collection period. Jobs with a start time prior to the observation period are assigned a negative start time. Jobs that did not conclude within 76 days of the observation period's end are given a null end time. VMs are classified by priority—high (0) and low (1)—where low-priority VMs may be evicted in favor of high-priority VMs. This comprehensive dataset provides a realistic basis for analyzing VM allocation strategies in cloud environments. Detailed analysis of the dataset appears in Sect. A in the appendix.

In our experiments, each virtual machine (VM) request is treated as a job request, representing the demand for computational resources within the Azure environment. The dataset includes 34 different machine ids, corresponding to compute nodes capable of accommodating a significant volume of jobs each, as discussed before. Our analysis is restricted to machines 0, 1, and 4. Each job comprises five resource dimensions: CPU, memory, SSD, NIC, and HDD. Due to the frequent presence of null values in the HDD dimension, we discarded it from our analysis and focused on the remaining four dimensions. To ensure accuracy, we excluded jobs with negative start times or null end times from our analysis. Recall that such jobs either started prior to the collection time window, or terminated after the observation window.

The original dataset expresses resource values as fractions. For consistency with earlier experiments involving synthetic data, we convert all resource values to integers. In the experiments, we assume that each server has capacity $E = 1000$ in each dimension. Thus, the size of each job is an element of $\{1, 2, \cdots, E\}^4$ after conversion.

Machine 1 has nearly $4,000,000$ job requests. However, due to computational limitations, we analyze only a subset of these jobs. To ensure a meaningful comparison, the sampled dataset for machine 1 is approximately the same size as the dataset available for machine 0. Additionally, we consider a sample of the dataset where jobs with a priority 1 are excluded from both machines 0 and 1, as the eviction policy makes their duration data unreliable. This exclusion is reasonable because, as shown in Table 1, 89.51% of the jobs for machine 0 have a priority of 0. In addition, we also consider a full dataset of priority 0 jobs for machine 4, which is similar in size to the dataset for machine 0. To sum up, in this study we consider the following sub-samples of the original dataset:

1. Machine 0 handling both priority 0 and priority 1 jobs.
2. Machine 0 restricted to handling only priority 0 jobs.
3. Machine 1 processing a randomly sampled sequence of jobs, uniformly selected from its priority 0 job requests. To ensure consistency, we generate two independent random samples for machine 1.
4. Machine 4 restricted to handling only priority 0 jobs.

Table 1 provides a detailed summary of the datasets, including the number of jobs and the corresponding μ ratio for each configuration.

Table 1. Number of jobs and the ratio μ for each dataset used in this study.

	Machine 0, Priority 0	Machine 0, Priority 0 and 1	Machine 1, Priority 0 - Sample 1	Machine 1, Priority 0 - Sample 2	Machine 4, Priority 0
Number of Jobs	112,552	125,784	112,299	112,546	94,361
μ	11,794,735	11,794,735	104,761,079	52,083,077	74,512,162

As discussed in Sect. 3, computing the value of the offline optimal solution is an intractable problem. Consequently, it is infeasible to compute exact competitive ratios attained by the algorithms on the given datasets. Following the previous literature on synthetic datasets, we use the bound from Lemma 1 in place of OPT in the computation of competitive ratios. Note that this does not affect relative ranking of performance of algorithms, and it makes absolute performance of the algorithms potentially even better in reality than the reported numbers. By a slight abuse of terminology we shall refer to the ratio computed in this manner as the competitive ratio. Note that competitive ratios reported for our experiments are with respect to particular input sequences σ, and do not refer to the worst-case bounds over all inputs.

All experiments were conducted on a personal laptop equipped with an Apple M1 chip, featuring an 8-core CPU and 16 GB of RAM. The laptop operated on macOS Sonoma 14.5, and the code was developed in C++ using Visual Studio Code version 1.93.1.

5 Experiments on the Full Dataset

A comprehensive summary of the experimental results across all datasets is presented in Table 2. Observe that relative order of performance of the algorithms is rather stable across all datasets, despite some differences in absolute values of competitive ratios. On one hand, *NextFit* and *MNF* are the worst and *FirstFit* and *MFF* are the best among all non-clairvoyant algorithms. On the other hand, for clairvoyant algorithms, *HA* is the best and *Departure Strategy* is the worst. This variation is due to the differing number of jobs and values of μ for each machine. In the case of machine 0, the competitive ratio follows the same pattern whether jobs have mixed priorities (0 and 1) or only priority 0. Therefore, given this consistent pattern, we focus the remainder of our analysis on machine 0 with priority 0.

Next, we observe that for all algorithms, the results derived from the real dataset are worse than those obtained from the randomly generated inputs in previous studies [5,6,9]. For clarity, we reproduce the table of results from [6] for randomly generated data for $d = 4$; see Table 3 below. This is not surprising, as the previous random input experiments were done for small values of μ (specifically, $\mu \in \{1, 2, 5, 10, 100\}$), whereas real-world datasets that we considered have much larger μ. As discussed in [6], the competitive ratios of all algorithms increase with μ, assuming other parameters remain constant.

We also observe that the differences in algorithm performance for real-world data are more pronounced compared to the random input data. For instance, the

Table 2. Competitive ratio results for the *RSiC* problem on real-world data. Algorithms are listed in decreasing order of competitive ratio for machine 0, priority 0.

Algorithms	Machine 0, Priority 0, $\mu = 11,794,735$	Machine 0, Priority 0 and 1, $\mu = 11,794,735$	Machine 1, Priority 0-Sample 1, $\mu = 104,761,079$	Machine 1, Priority 0-Sample 2, $\mu = 52,083,077$	Machine 4, Priority 0, $\mu = 74,512,162$
Non-clairvoyant					
NextFit	4.48	3.70	8.88	8.85	1.67
MNF	4.48	3.70	8.88	8.85	1.67
WorstFit	2.81	2.76	3.47	3.51	1.52
RandomFit	2.55	2.64	3.14	3.13	1.34
MoveToFront	2.48	2.14	3.15	3.16	1.32
LastFit	2.24	1.93	3.11	3.14	1.37
BestFit	2.21	1.99	2.99	2.85	1.30
FirstFit	2.00	1.76	2.71	2.69	1.30
MFF	2.00	1.76	2.71	2.69	1.30
Clairvoyant					
Departure Strategy	6.17	4.88	13.53	13.20	1.95
Duration Strategy	1.83	1.69	2.23	2.22	1.18
Greedy	1.64	1.54	1.85	1.78	1.22
New Hybrid	1.30	1.24	1.67	1.67	1.15
Hybrid Algorithm	1.29	1.21	1.36	1.35	1.15

Table 3. Average competitive ratio results for the *RSiC* problem when $d = 4$ on randomly generated data (shared by the authors of [6] via personal communication).

	T=1000					T=5000					T=10000				
	$\mu = 1$	$\mu = 2$	$\mu = 5$	$\mu = 10$	$\mu = 100$	$\mu = 1$	$\mu = 2$	$\mu = 5$	$\mu = 10$	$\mu = 100$	$\mu = 1$	$\mu = 2$	$\mu = 5$	$\mu = 10$	$\mu = 100$
Non-clairvoyant															
NextFit	1.48	1.57	1.69	1.75	1.88	1.12	1.20	1.38	1.52	1.80	**1.04**	1.08	1.20	1.36	1.75
MNF	1.50	1.58	1.69	1.75	1.88	1.13	1.20	1.38	1.52	1.81	1.05	1.09	1.20	1.36	1.75
WorstFit	1.47	1.51	1.55	1.56	1.53	1.11	**1.18**	**1.32**	1.43	1.55	**1.04**	**1.07**	1.18	1.30	1.54
FirstFit	1.49	1.52	1.56	1.57	1.54	1.12	1.19	1.33	1.43	1.55	**1.04**	1.08	1.18	1.30	1.54
MFF	1.49	1.52	1.55	1.57	1.54	1.12	1.19	1.33	1.43	1.55	**1.04**	**1.07**	1.18	1.31	1.54
BestFit	1.47	1.50	1.54	1.54	1.48	1.12	**1.18**	**1.32**	1.43	1.52	**1.04**	**1.07**	1.18	1.30	1.52
LastFit	1.43	1.48	1.52	1.53	1.48	1.11	**1.18**	**1.32**	1.42	1.52	**1.04**	**1.07**	**1.17**	1.30	1.52
Random Fit	1.47	1.50	1.54	1.55	1.50	1.12	**1.18**	**1.32**	1.43	1.53	**1.04**	**1.07**	1.18	1.30	1.53
MoveToFront	1.43	1.48	1.52	1.53	1.48	1.11	**1.18**	**1.32**	1.42	1.52	**1.04**	**1.07**	**1.17**	1.30	1.52
Clairvoyant															
Departure Strategy	1.49	1.52	1.55	1.57	1.52	1.12	1.19	1.33	1.43	1.56	**1.04**	1.08	1.18	1.31	1.55
Duration Strategy	1.49	1.52	1.55	1.57	1.54	1.12	1.19	1.33	1.43	1.56	**1.04**	1.08	1.18	1.31	1.55
Hybrid Algorithm	**1.38**	1.50	1.59	1.64	1.60	**1.10**	1.20	1.37	1.50	1.64	**1.04**	1.09	1.21	1.36	1.63
New Hybrid	1.53	1.62	1.73	1.79	1.88	1.15	1.24	1.42	1.57	1.83	1.06	1.11	1.24	1.40	1.79
Greedy	1.43	**1.47**	**1.51**	**1.52**	**1.46**	1.11	**1.18**	**1.32**	**1.41**	**1.50**	**1.04**	**1.07**	**1.17**	**1.29**	**1.51**

competitive ratio of *NextFit* on synthetic data with $d = 4, T = 1000$, and $\mu = 100$ is 1.88, while the ratio for *FirstFit* is 1.54. In contrast, on the Azure dataset, the ratio for *NextFit* is 4.48 on machine 0 with priority 0, whereas *FirstFit* has a ratio of 2.00, nearly half that of *NextFit*. This highlights the critical importance of selecting the appropriate algorithm for real datasets, as choosing an ineffective algorithm can lead to significant costs for server providers.

We find that the algorithms *NextFit* and *FirstFit* share the same competitive ratio as their modified counterparts, *MFF* and *MNF*. As noted in [6], while the modified versions exhibit improved worst-case performance, they did not yield favorable results in experiments involving random data. Our analysis of Azure's datasets indicates that these modified versions maintain the same competitive ratio as the original algorithms. We hypothesize that this is because the majority of jobs in the real dataset have sizes less than half of the server capacity, as the modified algorithms differentiate jobs based on whether their sizes exceed or fall below this threshold.

In investigating the hypothesis, for machine 0, we found that out of a total of $112,552$ jobs of priority 0, only 656 jobs (approximately 0.58%) had a core size request greater than 500. Similarly, the number of jobs with memory exceeding 500 was also 656, constituting about 0.58% of the total. For SSD, only 514 jobs (around 0.46%) exceeded a size of 500, while for NIC, 637 jobs (approximately 0.57%) surpassed this threshold. These low percentages support our hypothesis about why *FirstFit* and *MFF*, as well as *NextFit* and *MNF*, perform similarly.

Interestingly, among the non-clairvoyant algorithms, *FirstFit* exhibits the strongest performance. Although *MoveToFront* excelled in experiments with random input sequences, it shows significantly poorer results compared to *FirstFit* in experiments with real data. We suspect that the restrictions on the selection of μ in the random input may account for this discrepancy. To further investigate this hypothesis, we conduct additional tests in the following section.

The results also reveal that nearly all clairvoyant algorithms, with the exception of the *Departure Strategy*, perform exceptionally well. We suspect that the poor performance of the *Departure Strategy* is due to the large value of μ and the wide span, as it categorizes jobs based on their duration, which may not be effective under these conditions.

Although *Greedy* outperforms *HA* in experiments with random data, *HA* demonstrates an advantage when applied to real-world datasets. For example, in the random data experimental results (see Table 3) with $d = 4$ and $m = 1$, *HA* achieves a better average ratio of 1.38 compared to *Greedy*'s performance which is 1.43. Notably, this is the only case in the random data experiments where *HA* outperforms *Greedy*. For other values of μ, $\{2, 5, 10, 100\}$, *Greedy* consistently performs better.

However, on the Azure dataset, as shown in Table 2, *HA* consistently outperforms all other algorithms, including *Greedy*, the competitive ratio of *HA* is 1.29 while *Greedy* has ratio 1.64. This advantage can be attributed to *HA*'s strategy of grouping jobs with similar arrival and duration into the same servers. As discussed in [5,6], jobs arriving at the same time are more likely to have similar durations. *HA* capitalizes on this property by efficiently assigning jobs with identical arrival times and durations to the same server. Indeed, this property seems to become important when the value of μ is large.

In Sect. B in the appendix, we confirm this hypothesis by restricting the jobs to smaller μ values to evaluate the impact on performance of the algorithms.

In Sect. C, we provide additional insights into why different algorithms exhibit varying levels of performance by examining the distribution of durations of servers opened by the algorithm, as well as the distribution of wasted capacity per server.

6   New Combined Algorithms

From the experiments described in Sect. 5, we can conclude that for datasets with larger values of μ and a large span, *HA* is the optimal choice. For smaller values of μ, *Greedy* performs better in the clairvoyant case. In the non-clairvoyant case, when μ is large, *FirstFit* is the preferred algorithm, while *MTF* generally performs well in the other case. Based on these observation, an interesting idea arises: what if we design an algorithm that dynamically selects between two existing algorithms based on a threshold? For example, such an algorithm could combine two algorithms A and B, where A is used for short duration of jobs while B is used for the jobs with long duration. By carefully selecting an appropriate threshold, incoming jobs could be assigned to the most appropriate algorithm. This raises a compelling question: could this combined approach surpass the performance of current algorithms?

To answer this question, we propose several new algorithms designed to enhance the performance of the packing process, surpassing all existing approaches in both clairvoyant and non-clairvoyant scenarios. For each algorithm of this combined approach, we categorize servers into two distinct types:

1. Type A servers, which are used by algorithm A to pack jobs with durations less than a predefined threshold τ,
2. Type B servers, which are used by algorithm B to pack jobs with durations greater than or equal to the threshold τ.

6.1   Combined Clairvoyant Algorithms

As shown in Table 2, all the existing clairvoyant algorithms except the *Departure Strategy* perform well on the Azure dataset. However, in this section, we want to achieve a better performance by proposing new algorithms that combine the existing algorithms based on the parameter τ.

The clairvoyant algorithms that we propose are as the following:

- ***Greedy-Hybrid***: In this algorithm, the *Greedy* algorithm is applied to type A and *HA* is applied to type B servers.
- ***Greedy-Greedy***: In this algorithm, the *Greedy* algorithm is applied to both type A and type B servers.
- ***Greedy-Duration***: In this algorithm, the *Greedy* algorithm is applied to type A and *Duration Strategy* is applied to type B servers.

We also introduce a new clairvoyant algorithm that differs slightly from the previous approach but still utilizes the parameter τ to allocate each job. The new algorithm is defined as follows:

- ***New Greedy***: If assigning a new job to the best server chosen by the *Greedy* algorithm causes its finishing time to exceed τ, the *New Greedy* algorithm opens a new server for the job. Otherwise, the job is packed into the server in the same way as the standard *Greedy* algorithm.

The main challenge lies in identifying the optimal value of τ to maximize the performance of these new algorithms. To tackle this, we employ a grid search approach, testing values of τ ranging from the shortest to the longest job duration. Initially, we set the range for τ to be one of $[10^3, 10^4, 10^5, 10^6, 10^7, 10^8, 10^9, 10^{10}]$ to determine whether a threshold exists that improves performance compared to the existing algorithms. Figure 1 compares the performance of these algorithms across various threshold settings with that of the *HA* and *Greedy* algorithms.

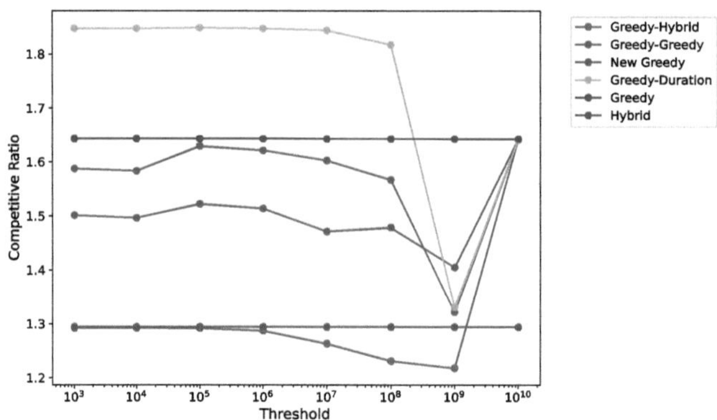

Fig. 1. Performance of the new combined clairvoyant algorithms for $\tau \in [10^3, 10^{10}]$, using data from machine 0 with priority 0.

As shown in Fig. 1, after $\tau = 10^6$, the *Greedy-Hybrid* algorithm achieves competitive ratios better than *HA*, with the best ratio occurring at $\tau = 10^9$, where it reaches 1.21. At this threshold, the competitive ratios of *Greedy-Greedy*, *New Hybrid*, and *Greedy-Duration* are also very close to that of *HA*.

Consequently, we focus on τ values around this interval to explore the potential for achieving even better ratios. As a result, we select τ to range from 10^8 to 10^{10}, with increments of 10^8. Therefore, we aim to evaluate a total of 100 points to observe any improvements, see Fig. 2.

Based on these experiments, we observe that the *Greedy-Hybrid* algorithm achieves a competitive ratio of 1.18 at a threshold of $\tau = 4 \times 10^8$, outperforming *HA*. Similarly, both the *Greedy-Greedy* and *Greedy-Duration* algorithms achieve a desirable competitive ratio of 1.28 at $\tau = 2, 5 \times 10^8$. Additionally, the *New Greedy* algorithm achieves a competitive ratio of 1.41 at $\tau = 1, 1 \times 10^8$. These results are particularly impressive, especially for *Greedy-Greedy*, as it is a very simple algorithm to implement and achieves a competitive ratio better than *HA*, which aligns with our objectives.

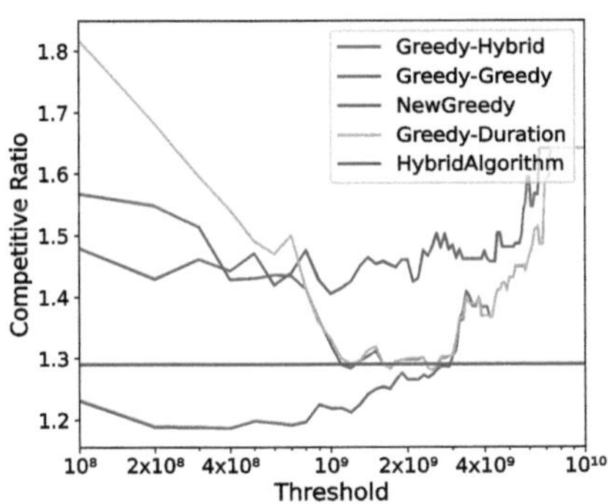

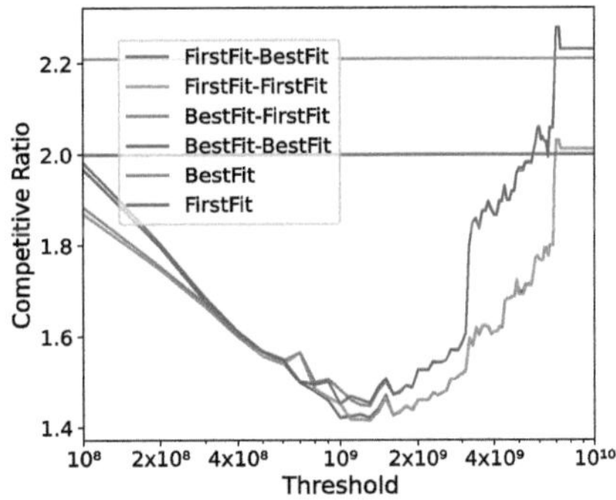

Fig. 2. Comparison between the competitive ratio of the new clairvoyant combined algorithms, on data from machine 0 with priority 0.

Fig. 3. The performance of the weakly clairvoyant combined algorithms over different values of τ, using data from machine 0 with priority 0.

6.2 Combined Weakly Clairvoyant Algorithms

As shown in Table 2, both *FirstFit* and *BestFit* consistently achieve the best competitive ratios in nearly all scenarios within the non-clairvoyant setting. Based on this observation, we propose new algorithms that combine *FirstFit* and *Best-Fit* using the parameter τ. In this setting, jobs are classified as long or short by the user, and the scheduler does not require knowledge of their actual durations at the time of arrival. Consequently, this setting is neither fully clairvoyant nor fully non-clairvoyant, and we refer to it as *weakly clairvoyant*. We introduce and evaluate the following weakly-clairvoyant algorithms:

- ***FirstFit-FirstFit***: the *FirstFit* algorithm is applied to type A and another independent copy of *FirstFit* algorithm is applied to type B servers.
- ***FirstFit-BestFit***: the *FirstFit* algorithm is applied to type A and *BestFit* is applied to type B servers.
- ***BestFit-BestFit***: the *BestFit* algorithm is applied to both type A and another independent copy of *BestFit* algorithm is applied to type B servers.
- ***BestFit-FirstFit***: the *BestFit* algorithm is applied to type A and *FirstFit* is applied to type B servers.

For these algorithms, we adopted the range of τ used in the experiments with clairvoyant algorithms, setting τ to vary between 10^8 and 10^{10}. Figure 3 presents the competitive ratios of the combined algorithms for various thresholds within this range. As shown in the figure, the performance of *FirstFit-BestFit* and *FirstFit-FirstFit* is nearly identical, as is that of *BestFit-FirstFit* and *BestFit-BestFit*. The results indicate an improvement over all existing non-clairvoyant algorithms. Notably, setting $\tau = 1, 3 \times 10^8$ allows *FirstFit-FirstFit* to achieve a competitive ratio of 1.41 and *FirstFit-BestFit* to reach 1.42, representing a significant improvement over the algorithms listed in Table 2. Similarly, *BestFit-BestFit* and *BestFit-FirstFit* achieve competitive ratios of 1.45 when τ is set to $1, 3 \times 10^8$ and 10^9, respectively.

7   Conclusions

In this paper, we evaluated the performance of existing clairvoyant and non-clairvoyant algorithms for the *RSiC* problem using real-world datasets. To the best of our knowledge, this is the first study to analyze the *RSiC* problem with real-world data. We also proposed a new class of algorithms, called weakly clairvoyant, as well as several specific new algorithms that demonstrate superior performance in experimental evaluations. Our analysis provides insights into the effectiveness of these algorithms and establishes a benchmark that may be useful for future research in this area.

Recall that in the clairvoyant setting job durations are known at the time of job arrivals; in the weakly clairvoyant setting, jobs are categorized as long or short at the time of arrival at the scheduler; and in non-clairvoyant setting nothing is known about the job durations at the time of arrivals. Our experiments with real-world data confirm that the clairvoyant algorithms tend to perform better than the weakly clairvoyant algorithms which in turn tend to perform better than non-clairvoyant algorithms.

In the clairvoyant setting, *HA* emerged as the most effective algorithm. However, *Greedy* stands out as a simpler alternative, avoiding the complexity of *HA*, which involves server categorization and extensive server usage. By combining the algorithms we were able to improve on the competitive ratio of *HA*. In particular, *Greedy-Hybrid* exhibits the best performance of all known algorithms including *HA* in terms of empirically derived competitive ratio. *Greedy-Greedy* which also beats *HA* offers a conceptually simpler solution.

In the weakly clairvoyant setting, *FirstFit-FirstFit* and *FirstFit-BestFit* have similar performance and improve upon the empirically derived competitive ratio of both *FirstFit* and *BestFit*. Since *BestFit* has infinite competitive ratio in the worst case, we recommend using *FirstFit-FirstFit* as a safer alternative.

In the non-clairvoyant setting, *FirstFit* exhibited the strongest performance overall. While *MoveToFront* excelled in experiments with random input sequences, its performance with real-world data was significantly weaker than that of *FirstFit*. Based on these findings, we recommend using *MoveToFront* for datasets with small variation in job durations and *FirstFit* for datasets with larger variation in job durations.

A   Analysis of the Dataset

Hadary et al. [4] provided valuable insights into the nature of VM workloads, highlighting their significant variability and non-uniform distribution. The analysis revealed that certain VM types dominate the workload, with some comprising nearly half of the total, while others occur much less frequently. A majority of VMs require relatively few cores, yet a subset of VM types exhibits significantly higher demands for computational resources, requiring a greater number of cores. Additionally, the authors observed substantial variation in VM durations, with many VMs running for only a few minutes, while others last for weeks or even months.

Another noteworthy finding was the diurnal patterns in VM requests. Peak demand typically occurs on Tuesdays, Wednesdays, and Thursdays, with request volumes dropping overnight but rising during the day, particularly with sharp spikes at 12:00 PM and 4:00 PM. This variability highlights the varying nature of workload demand, as observed in the study.

Figure 4 (left) illustrates the frequency of VM requests based on their core sizes. The patterns for memory, SSD, and NIC are similar and can be seen in Fig. 4 in the appendix. These figures reveal that for all these resource types, the majority of VM requests require only a small fraction of the total available capacity. Specifically, for core sizes, approximately 80% of VMs utilize less than 10% of the total core capacity, demonstrating the lightweight nature of most workloads. A similar trend is evident for memory, SSD, and NIC sizes, where the demand is predominantly concentrated within the lower ranges of the available resource capacity.

This consistent pattern across resource types highlights that while the large majority of VMs impose minimal demands, a small subset of resource-intensive VMs stand out as outliers, consuming a disproportionately large share of resources. These findings emphasize the importance of designing resource allocation strategies that are optimized to efficiently handle both the lightweight majority and the resource-hungry minority, ensuring balanced and effective utilization of computational infrastructure.

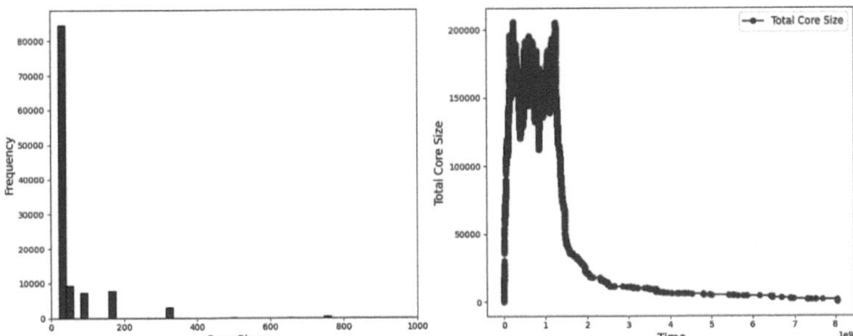

Fig. 4. The frequency of VM requests based on their core sizes for machine 0 (left). The total demand for computational resources in the core dimension at each time step for machine 0 (right). Note that all values are represented as integers. Other types of resources (memory, SSD, NIC) exhibit similar patterns.

In Fig. 4 (right), we present the total resource demand for core dimension over time. The other three dimensions exhibit similar patterns (omitted due to space constraints). At each time step, these figures show the cumulative demand for a particular type of resource over all jobs in the system. Recall that the collection period of new job arrivals spans 14 days, while monitoring of departing jobs spans for 76 additional days after the collection period. This explains the shape of these figures – initially the resource demand surges sharply when collection period begins, while the tail of the plot corresponds to the additional monitoring period when jobs are completing and leaving the system, but information about new arrivals is not collected during this time.

B   Experiments on μ-Filtered Data

We hypothesized that the difference in relative performance between algorithms on real data and synthetic data are caused by much higher values of μ in the Azure dataset. To evaluate the hypothesis we extracted a subset of jobs from Azure dataset to ensure smaller values of μ. We used the following procedure. For a given value of μ and a fixed value of d_{lower} – the shortest duration of a job, we process the dataset by keeping only those jobs whose duration falls in the interval $[d_{\text{lower}}, \mu \cdot d_{\text{lower}}]$, and removing the rest of the jobs. We refer to this process as μ-filtering. To create the final dataset for a given value of μ, we selected the value of d_{lower} to be the one that retained the largest number of jobs after μ-filtering. The results of this experiment for $\mu \in \{1, 2, 5, 20, 100\}$ and machine 0 priority 0 are presented in Table 4.

Table 4. Competitive ratio results for the *RSiC* problem on machine 0 for jobs with priority 0 after filtering the jobs based on μ.

Algorithms	Machine 0, Priority 0, $\mu = 1$	Machine 0, Priority 0, $\mu = 2$	Machine 0, Priority 0, $\mu = 5$	Machine 0, Priority 0, $\mu = 10$	Machine 0, Priority 0, $\mu = 100$
Number of jobs	13	28,051	49133	55,382	73,215
Non-clairvoyant					
NextFit	1	1.29	1.50	1.62	3.05
MNF	1	1.31	1.48	1.58	3.05
WorstFit	1	1.74	1.87	1.84	1.98
FirstFit	1	1.16	1.17	1.18	1.23
MFF	1	1.25	1.27	1.24	1.23
BestFit	1	1.21	1.22	1.23	1.31
LastFit	1	1.20	1.21	1.22	1.32
Random Fit	1	1.90	2.10	2.05	1.75
MoveToFront	1	1.16	1.20	1.22	1.40
Clairvoyant					
Departure Strategy	1	11.26	12.18	10.76	8.55
Duration Strategy	1	1.16	1.20	1.24	1.24
Hybrid Algorithm	1	1.59	1.90	1.82	1.39
New Hybrid	1	1.60	1.93	1.84	1.42
Greedy	1	1.13	1.15	1.14	1.12

As seen in Table 4, the ratios for various algorithms look similar to the results derived from the synthetic data, particularly for smaller values of μ. This trend suggests that imposing restrictions on μ can improve algorithm performance. However, certain algorithms, such as *NextFit*, *MNF*, and the *Departure Strategy*, still exhibit significant deviations from the synthetic data results.

C   Wasted-Space and Duration of Servers

In this section, we aim to gain additional insights into why different algorithms exhibit varying levels of performance. Our analysis will consider both clairvoyant and non-clairvoyant scenarios. Since the total cost of an algorithm for the *RSiC* problem is determined by the total cost of all servers utilized by the algorithm, it is evident that the cost depends on how efficiently jobs are packed into the servers. To estimate efficiency of the packing of a particular algorithm, we can examine the distribution of durations of servers opened by the algorithm, as well as the distribution of wasted capacity per server. In the rest of this section, we analyze how these factors influence algorithm performance.

Clairvoyant Algorithms

As shown in Table 2, among the clairvoyant algorithms, *HA* and *New Hybrid* demonstrate superior performance, while the *Departure Strategy* performs poorly, and *Greedy* shows moderate performance. To provide a clearer understanding and comparison of these algorithms, Table 5 and Fig. 5 present the number of servers utilized by each algorithm and the corresponding server durations. In Fig. 5, the servers are first sorted in ascending order by duration to create the plot. The x-axis represents the cumulative number of servers, while the y-axis displays the corresponding sorted duration values. This visualization helps us understand how frequently servers share the same duration, allowing us to assess how effectively the algorithm optimizes server allocation.

Table 5. Number of servers that clairvoyant algorithms used on jobs from machine 0 with priority 0.

Algorithms	*Greedy*	*HA*	*New Hybrid*	*Duration Strategy*	*Departure Strategy*
Number of Servers	1, 078	24, 322	16, 796	4, 953	76, 893

Table 6. Number of servers that each non-clairvoyant algorithm used data from machine 0 with priority 0.

Algorithms	*NextFit*	*MNF*	*WorstFit*	*FirstFit*	*MFF*	*BestFit*	*LastFit*	*Random Fit*	*MoveToFront*
Number of Servers	6, 549	6, 549	971	709	709	446	401	362	442

From Table 5 and Fig. 5, we observe that *Departure Strategy* employs the highest number of servers, nearly 76, 000 in total. Most of these servers have short durations, but there is a subset with significantly long durations, contributing to its poor performance. In contrast, *Greedy* utilizes far fewer servers— approximately 1, 000—which is significantly less than the number used by the *Departure Strategy*. On the other hand, the *HA* algorithm, which achieves the best performance among clairvoyant algorithms, uses around 24, 000 servers. Notably, only a small portion of these servers have long durations. This efficient balance of server usage and duration likely explains why *HA* outperforms the other algorithms.

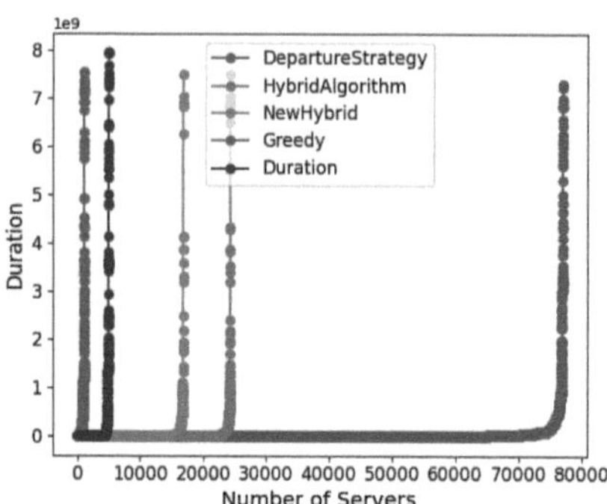

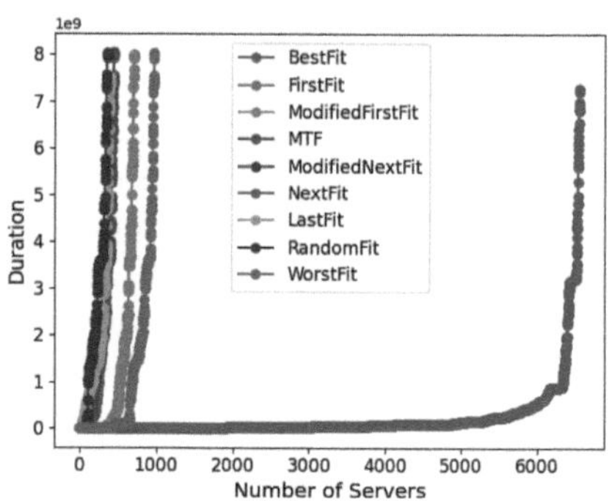

Fig. 5. Duration of servers for clairvoyant algorithms, using data from machine 0 with priority 0.

Fig. 6. Duration of servers for non-clairvoyant algorithms, using data from machine 0 with priority 0. Note that due to overlapping values, *MFF* hides *FirstFit*, and *NextFit* similarly hides *MNF*.

We observe that while *Greedy* uses fewer servers than *HA*, its performance is worse. Why is this the case? To answer this question, we conducted additional experiments to compare how tightly these algorithms pack jobs into each server.

In our database, each job is defined in four dimensions: core, memory, NIC, and SSD. In Fig. 7, we plot the cumulative distribution wasted space for the first dimension across the servers used by each algorithm. The x-axis represents the cumulative number of servers, while the y-axis displays the corresponding sorted wasted space values for each dimension. From these plots, we can see that the servers utilized by *HA* have significantly less wasted space across all dimensions. This indicates that *HA* achieves tighter packing of jobs, which contributes to its superior performance (Fig. 8).

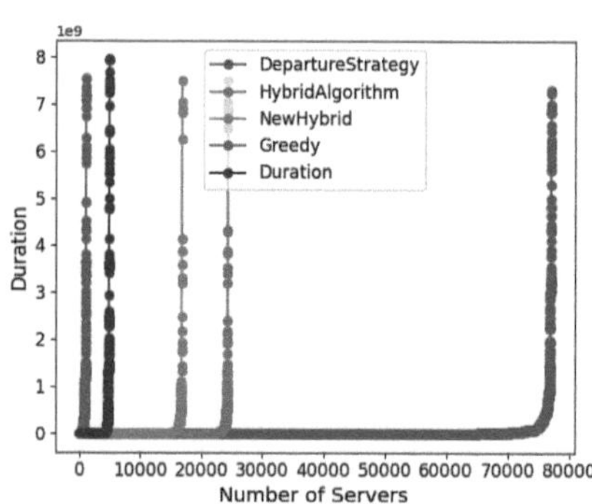

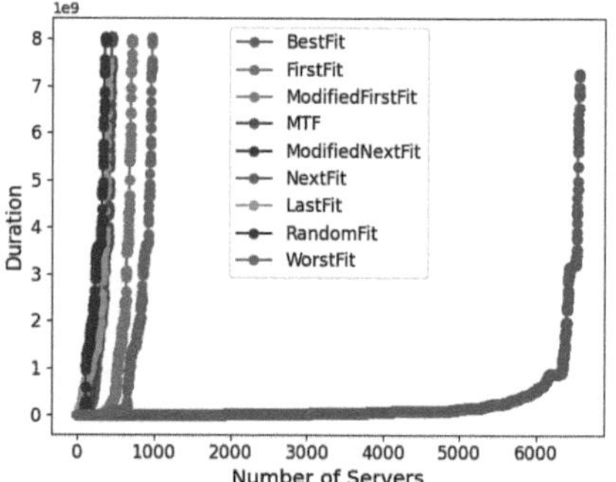

Fig. 7. Wasted-space of servers in the first dimension (number of cores) for clairvoyant algorithms using data from machine 0 with priority 0. Other dimensions exhibit a similar pattern.

Fig. 8. Wasted-space of servers in the first dimension (number of cores) for non-clairvoyant algorithms, using data from machine 0 with priority 0. Note that due to overlapping values, *MFF* hides *FirstFit*, and *NextFit* similarly hides *MNF*. Other dimensions exhibit a similar pattern.

While *HA* outperforms *Greedy*, *Greedy* performs better than *Departure Strategy*. This is because *Greedy* exhibits less wasted space in all dimensions—core, memory, NIC, and SSD—compared to *Departure Strategy*. The tighter packing of jobs in *Greedy* leads to improved performance relative to *Departure Strategy*, even though it still falls short of the efficiency achieved by *HA*. Finally, algorithms like *Departure Strategy* show significantly higher wasted space across all dimensions, resulting in poor utilization of server resources and the lowest overall performance.

Non-clairvoyant Algorithms

Next we analyze the performance of the non-clairvoyant algorithms. From Table 2, we observe that among all the non-clairvoyant algorithms, *FirstFit* demonstrates the best performance, while *NextFit* performs the worst. To investigate, we conducted the same experiments as we did for the clairvoyant algorithms, comparing the number of servers used and their durations across all non-clairvoyant algorithms. The results, summarized in Table 6 and illustrated in Fig. 6, highlight the differences in server utilization and duration across these algorithms. From this figure, we observe that *NextFit* utilizes nearly 6500 servers in total. While most of these servers have a short duration, there is a subset with very long durations, which negatively impacts its performance. In contrast, algorithms like *FirstFit* and *MFF* use significantly fewer servers (around 700 in total) compared to *NextFit*.

References

1. Azar, Y., Vainstein, D.: Tight bounds for clairvoyant dynamic bin packing. ACM Trans. Parall. Comput. (TOPC) **6**(3), 1–21 (2019)
2. Buchbinder, N., Fairstein, Y., Mellou, K., Menache, I., Naor, J.: Online virtual machine allocation with lifetime and load predictions. ACM SIGMETRICS Perform. Eval. Rev. **49**(1), 9–10 (2021)
3. Estivill-Castro, V., Wood, D.: A survey of adaptive sorting algorithms. ACM Comput. Surv. **24**(4), 441–476 (1992)
4. Hadary, O., et al.: Protean:{VM} allocation service at scale. In: 14th USENIX Symposium on Operating Systems Design and Implementation (OSDI 20), pp. 845–861 (2020)
5. Kamali, S., López-Ortiz, A.: Efficient online strategies for renting servers in the cloud. In: Italiano, G.F., Margaria-Steffen, T., Pokorný, J., Quisquater, J.-J., Wattenhofer, R. (eds.) SOFSEM 2015. LNCS, vol. 8939, pp. 277–288. Springer, Heidelberg (2015). https://doi.org/10.1007/978-3-662-46078-8_23
6. Li, Y., Masoori, M., Narayanan, L., Pankratov, D.: Renting servers for multi-parameter jobs in the cloud. In: Proceedings of the 26th International Conference on Distributed Computing and Networking, pp. 36–45 (2025)
7. Li, Y., Tang, X., Cai, W.: On dynamic bin packing for resource allocation in the cloud. In: Proceedings of the 26th ACM Symposium on Parallelism in Algorithms and Architectures (SPAA), pp. 2–11 (2014)
8. Li, Y., Tang, X., Cai, W.: Dynamic bin packing for on-demand cloud resource allocation. IEEE Trans. Parallel Distrib. Syst. **27**(1), 157–170 (2015)

9. Murhekar, A., Arbour, D., Mai, T., Rao, A.B.: Brief announcement: Dynamic vector bin packing for online resource allocation in the cloud. In: Proceedings of the 35th ACM Symposium on Parallelism in Algorithms and Architectures (SPAA), pp. 307–310 (2023)
10. Ren, R.: Combinatorial algorithms for scheduling jobs to minimize server usage time. Ph.D. thesis, Nanyang Technological University, Singapore (2018)
11. Ren, R., Tang, X.: Clairvoyant dynamic bin packing for job scheduling with minimum server usage time. In: Proceedings of the 28th ACM Symposium on Parallelism in Algorithms and Architectures (SPAA), pp. 227–237 (2016)
12. Ren, R., Tang, X., Li, Y., Cai, W.: Competitiveness of dynamic bin packing for online cloud server allocation. IEEE/ACM Trans. Network. **25**(3), 1324–1331 (2016)

Author Index

A
Arora, Sonika   31
Aslanidis, Theodoros   16, 58

B
Byabazaire, John   58

C
Cattai, Tiziana   108
Chatzopoulos, Dimitris   16, 58
Chouliaras, Andreas   58
Christopoulos, Konstantinos   122
Cuomo, Francesca   108

D
Del Mar Bosch-Belmar, Maria   1
Dimarca, Sergio   1
Doyle, Mark   16

G
Garlisi, Domenico   1

H
Hiremath, Gangadharayya   31

J
Josyula, Prashanth   31

K
Karathanasis, Konstantinos   73
Kontogiannis, Spyros   73
Kumar, Anant   31

L
Locatelli, Pierluigi   108

M
Mancuso, Francesco Paolo   1
Masoori, Mahtab   138
Mastorakis, Spyridon   58

N
Narayanan, Lata   138

P
Pankratov, Denis   138
Ping, Yani   94

S
Sakellariou, Rizos   94
Sarà, Gianluca   1
Schilleci, Silvia   1
Spadaccino, Pietro   108

T
Taormina, Vincenzo   1
Tinnirello, Ilenia   1
Tirana, Joana   58
Tsiamis, Georgios   122
Tsichlas, Konstantinos   122

W
Wiese, Lena   43

X
Xu, Mohan   43

Z
Zaroliagis, Christos   73

MIX
Papier aus verantwortungsvollen Quellen
Paper from responsible sources
FSC® C105338